22.50

COBBETT'S
CYCLOPEDIC SURVEY OF
CHAMBER MUSIC

VOLUME III

COBBETT'S CYCLOPEDIC SURVEY OF

CHAMBER MUSIC

Compiled and edited by

WALTER WILLSON COBBETT

With supplementary material
edited by
COLIN MASON

SECOND EDITION

VOLUME III

OXFORD NEW YORK
OXFORD UNIVERSITY PRESS

Oxford University Press, Walton Street, Oxford OX2 6DP

Oxford New York Toronto
Delhi Bombay Calcutta Madras Karachi
Retaling Jaya Singapore Hong Kong Tokyo
Nairobi Dar es Salaam Cape Town
Melbourne Auckland
and associated companies in
Beirut Berlin Ibadan Nicosia

Oxford is a trade mark of Oxford University Press

Published in the United States
by Oxford University Press, New York

© Oxford University Press 1963

ISBN 0 19 318305-6

First published 1963
Sixth impression 1986

Printed in Great Britain
by Antony Rowe Ltd, Chippenham

CONTENTS

VOLUME III

FOREWORD

THIRTY-THREE years after its original publication, *Cobbett's Cyclopedic Survey* is still the major work in its field, rivalled in scope and authority only by the collected works of Altmann. Since the last copies were sold in 1946, there have been frequent demands for a reprint or a new edition. The present re-issue is a compromise between the two. The two original volumes have been reproduced photographically exactly as they were, except for the insertion of symbols (explained on p. vii of Vol. I) in the margin which indicate a further reference in the new volume, either in the text or in the list of additional and corrected dates compiled by Nicolas Slonimsky, and a handful of small amendments (also compiled by Mr. Slonimsky) made in Cobbett's text. The new volume brings the survey up to date with an account of chamber music since 1929, but departs from Cobbett's editorial method, and is more selective in its coverage of the available material. For various reasons the use of a large team of contributors such as Cobbett called upon (140 of them) was impossible, and his lexicographic arrangement of the material was therefore impracticable. My compromise with the letter of Cobbett's title has therefore been, in making a one-man survey of the European contribution, to keep it within practicable limits by confining it to composers who have acquired some considerable international reputation, but within those limits to try to make the survey 'cyclopedic'. Except with a few composers who had, I felt, some claim to mention but not to a detailed account of their works (including some whose earlier works were described at length in C[1] but whose reputations have since stood still or declined), I have tried to give a complete list of each composer's output of chamber music, with dates (of composition except where I was unable to establish this), and a formal description of every important work.

Mr. Slonimsky and Mr. Martinov were left free to devise their own methods of covering their more unified territories. Mr. Martinov has also chosen to restrict the number of composers for inclusion, and to survey their work in detail, whereas Mr. Slonimsky has preferred to be more 'cyclopedic' in his coverage of composers, and more selective in his listing and description of their works.

Where Cobbett's method has been followed is in the restriction of the survey to published works, and in the acceptance of his definition of chamber music as 'extending from duos to nonets'—though there are occasional references to important works for larger ensemble and to unpublished works. And although the editorial and typographical methods of C have not been followed, the new volume is intended to serve much the same purpose as the original two volumes. It is, as far as it goes, a reference book, not a collection of essays nor a history—though the chapters are continuous, and are in a certain

---

[1] This symbol is used to refer to the first edition of the *Cyclopedia*.

sense a chronicle, country by country, of what has happened since 1929, the composers being dealt with (at least by Mr. Martinov and myself, though not so strictly by Mr. Slonimsky) in chronological order.

Nor is the new volume intended as a critical survey. With rare exceptions criticism and evaluation are expressed, if at all, only in the relative numbers of lines assigned to composers. Some of these evaluations, which have been concerned first with the 'size' of the composers and only second with the size of their chamber-music output, will, like the omissions, arouse objections. Some may think that I have been too generous to, say, Milhaud, Messiaen, and Janáček, and not generous enough to Martinů, Migot, and Skalkottas, but I feel that I can stand by these allocations with a fairly clear conscience—including the disproportion between the 75 lines for Messiaen's handful of works and 250 lines for Milhaud's vast output. British composers have been given more than their fair share in comparison with composers of comparable stature elsewhere, but this too I feel is justifiable, and probably inevitable, in an English book.

Finally, I must express my thanks to the numerous people to whom I am indebted in various degrees for help in making this volume more accurate and in bringing it to publication—in particular to Mr. John S. Weissmann, who read the proofs, and to Mr. Oliver Neighbour, who read the typescript. Both pointed out numerous omissions and suggested improvements. Mr. Weissmann also gave valuable help with the preparation of the bibliography. Mr. Leonard Duck of the Henry Watson Music Library, Manchester, and Mr. David Brown, formerly of the London University Music Library, must particularly be mentioned among the many others who have patiently borne my many inquiries and requests.

COLIN MASON

London, 1962

ACKNOWLEDGEMENTS

ACKNOWLEDGEMENTS are due to the following for permission to quote extracts from the works indicated:

Éditions Amphion, Paris: Pierre Boulez's Flute Sonatina. *Boelke-Bomart Inc., Hillsdale, N.Y.*: Schoenberg's String Trio. *Boosey & Hawkes Ltd.*: Bartók's Quartet No. 6 and Sonata for two pianos and percussion; Ernst Bloch's Quartet No. 2; Britten's Phantasy Quartet, op. 2, Quartet No. 1, op. 25, and Quartet No. 2, op. 36; Copland's Quartet for piano and strings; Janáček's Quartet No. 1, Quartet No. 2, and Violin Sonata (by courtesy of the original publisher, SHV, Prague); William Schuman's Quartet No. 2; and Stravinsky's Duo Concertant, In Memoriam Dylan Thomas, Septet, and Three Shakespeare Songs. *Boosey & Hawkes Ltd. (Anglo-Soviet Music Press Ltd.)*: Kabalevsky's Quartet No. 2; Myaskovsky's Quartet No. 1, Quartet No. 5, Quartet No. 8, and Quartet No. 13; Prokofiev's Quartet No. 2, op. 92; Shebalin's Quartet No. 6; and Shostakovich's Octet for strings, op. 11, Quartet No. 2, Quartet No. 6, and Trio, op. 67. *Bote & Bock*: Boris Blacher's Quartet No. 3. *J. & W. Chester Ltd.*: Lennox Berkeley's String Trio and F. Poulenc's Sonata for flute and piano. *Durand et Cie*: Messiaen's Quatuor pour la Fin du Temps; Milhaud's Quartet No. 3 and Sonatina for clarinet and piano; and Roussel's Quartet. *Heugel et Cie*: Milhaud's Quartet No. 14, Quartet No. 15, Quartet No. 16, and Quintet No. 3; and Poulenc's 'Cello Sonata. *Hinrichsen Edition Ltd. London (C. F. Peters)*: Schoenberg's Fantasy for violin and piano. *Hinrichsen Edition Ltd. London (Suvini Zerboni)*: Petrassi's Quartet and Serenata; Dallapiccola's Two Studies for violin and piano; and Matyas Seiber's Quartet No. 2. *Alphonse Leduc et Cie*: Messiaen's Theme and Variations for violin and piano. *Alfred Lengnick & Co. Ltd.*: Rubbra's String Quartet No. 2. *Novello & Co. Ltd.*: Bliss's Quartet No. 2. *Keith Prowse Music Publishing Co. Ltd.*: Gerhard's String Quartet. *Oxford University Press*: Rawsthorne's Quartet No. 1, Quartet No. 2, and Violin Sonata; Vaughan Williams's Quartet No. 2 and Violin Sonata; and Walton's Violin Sonata. *G. Ricordi & Co. (London) Ltd.*: Pizzetti's Quartet No. 2. *Éditions Salabert, Paris*: Honegger's Quartet No. 2, Quartet No. 3; Martinů's Violin Sonata; and Milhaud's Quartet No. 11. *G. Schirmer Inc., New York (Chappell & Co. Ltd., London)*: Schoenberg's Quartet No. 4, Samuel Barber's Quartet, op. 11; Bloch's Quartet No. 3; Harris's Piano Quintet, and William Schuman's Quartet No. 4. *Schott & Co. Ltd.*: Elliott Carter's Quartet No. 2; Fortner's Quartet No. 3 and Sonata for 'cello and piano; Peter Racine Fricker's 'Cello Sonata, Quartet No. 1, Quartet No. 2, and Octet; Iain Hamilton's Piano Trio; Hindemith's Quartet No. 5, Septet, Sonata for cor anglais and piano, and Sonata for violin and piano (1939); and Michael Tippett's Quartet No. 1, Quartet No. 2, and Quartet No. 3. *Martin Secker & Warburg Ltd.*: Thomas Mann's *Genesis of a Novel*. *Universal Edition (London) Ltd.*: Bartók's Quartet No. 2, Quartet No. 3, Quartet No. 4, Quartet No. 5, and Violin Sonata No. 1; Stockhausen's Zeitmasse; Berio's Circles; and Pierre Boulez's Le Marteau sans Maître. *Universal Edition (Alfred A. Kalmus Ltd.)*: A. Casella's 'Cello Sonata and Serenata; E. Krenek's Quartet No. 5 and Quartet No. 7; Gunther Schuller's Quartet No. 1; and Webern's Concerto for Nine Instruments, Quartet, op. 22, Quartet, op. 28, Songs, op. 18, no. 2, and String Trio, op. 20. *Joseph Williams Ltd.*: Alan Bush's Dialectic.

EUROPEAN CHAMBER MUSIC SINCE 1929

By COLIN MASON

AUSTRIA AND GERMANY

A N account of chamber music in Austria since 1929 is concerned mainly
with Schoenberg and Webern. Their successors are to be found in Germany, and farther afield, while Austria herself is producing no outstanding work, and remains prominently on the musical scene today chiefly by virtue of Schoenberg's and Webern's still increasing reputation, and as the home of Universal Edition, which is still the most adventurous publisher of the most revolutionary post-1945 scores. The active musical leadership is now German. Hindemith is still productive, and although he now lives abroad, musically he is identified mainly with Germany, and exerts a very strong influence there on the more conservative younger composers. In addition several other German composers have come into international prominence since 1945.

Among the older Austrian composers Schoenberg's very conservative contemporary Franz SCHMIDT (**C**, d. 1939) added to the String Quartet in A mentioned in **C** a second one in G (1929), a Piano Quintet in G (1926) and two quintets for clarinet, string trio, and piano, in B flat (1932) and A (1938). The piano part in the Quintet in G was written for the left hand alone, for Paul Wittgenstein, but is also published in a version for two hands (made by Friedrich Wührer).

The last work by SCHOENBERG described by Egon Wellesz in **C** is the String Quartet No. 3, written in 1927. His fourth and last quartet, commissioned by Mrs. Elizabeth Sprague Coolidge, followed in 1936. It is more expansively romantic in expression than any of the chamber works of the 1920's, and has become the best known of the four quartets, although more perhaps by the frequent quotation of its opening page, as a classic example of some of the possibilities of the twelve-note method, than by actual performances.

In it Schoenberg sticks fairly closely to traditional forms, and although he is said to have considered that he had abandoned sonata form in the first movement, the outlines of such a form, somewhat obscured by the processes of continuous development and telescoping of themes in the 'reprise', are discernible. The definition of themes is by the rhythmic as much as by the melodic shape, which as in any classical work varies more remotely in the development section than in the recapitulation, where recognition is usually fairly easy. The various turning-points in the form, the transitions from one main section of the score to another (from first to the second subject, for example), are also clearly marked in a fairly traditional way, by an almost complete thematic relaxation, emphasized some-times by a sustained ritardando, or some exceptional feature of dynamics or scoring. The music seems to switch off and free-wheel gently to a standstill, or sometimes to apply the brakes hard, as in Ex. 1, before restarting on the next section. A further illustration of the reduction of thematic density in cadential or transitional passages is provided by Exx. 2 and 3, showing respectively the principal melodic theme and a fragment of the more lyrical, expansive presenta-tion of it in the coda.

In the rather minuet-like second movement the extended and highly organized form is more complex. The ternary structure is that of a traditional minuet and trio, each of its parts being also in ternary form, but the unusual length of the movement, Schoenberg's continuous development of his material in recapitula-

tion, and his use in the middle sections both of the larger and of the smaller
ternary structures, of material from their principal sections, make it exceptionally
taxing and confusing to follow. Among the remarkable features of scoring in this
movement is the muting of one or more parts (sometimes only for one or two
phrases, and sometimes including the principal melody), while the other instruments continue unmuted. This is the method in most of the first section, though
in some of it all four parts are muted, as they are again in the final statement of
the main theme in the coda. The last two movements in contrast are very straightforward in form. The 'Largo' is a simple binary movement with an exposition in
three sections, and a varied reprise of almost identical dimensions, each half of
the movement opening with the often-quoted tune for the four instruments in
unison. Ex. 4 shows part of the equally important second main theme of the

Ex. 4

movement. This passionately expressive and declamatory movement is one of
the most readily grasped in all Schoenberg's later music, with its one powerfully
melodic line dominating a warm and rich harmonic texture that even when
elaborately figured is not thematically complex. The final movement is a sonata-
rondo with two extended episodes, the second a variant of the first, and exactly
half as long, beginning identically, then gradually diverging. The middle statement of the main theme is at a different pitch, and considerably varied, suggesting
almost a short development section.

In both of his last two chamber works Schoenberg used a single-movement
form. The String Trio, op. 45, was written in 1946 at the commission of the
Department of Music at Harvard University for a course on modern compositional techniques. It was probably for this reason that Schoenberg indicated in
the score the formal outlines of the work, rather as Bartók did in his third
quartet. There are five sections, of which the second and fourth are described as
first and second episodes. The formal divisions are not quite so strictly or symmetrically defined as these indications suggest, and the extreme elusiveness of the
note-series on which the work is based, or rather the variety of ways in which
it is segmented and distributed, creates some ambiguities of thematic definition
also. In Part 1, which is in ternary form with a codetta, the thematic emphasis, both melodic and harmonic, is on the interval of the minor second, as in
Exx. 5 and 6, from the first and third sections of Part 1. The central section of this
part contains the prominent complete twelve-note melodic statement of Ex. 7.
Two other, different twelve-note melodic sequences, in shorter note-values,
appear immediately before and after the central section, but although fragments
of these are thematically prominent, none of the three sequences is established as
the basic series of the work.

A similar formal construction is found in the First Episode, which is in an arch-like form (ABCBA) with a codetta. A is melodically fragmentary, B is a recitative-like preparation for the central section C, which has an extended melody on which the codetta is also founded. Part 2 begins with a development of the groups of semitones of Part 1, including a rhythmic variant of Ex. 7, leading to a cantabile section in 9/8 on new material developed from the changing-

Ex. 5

Ex. 6

Ex. 7

note figure, again followed by a codetta. Further new material is introduced in the Second Episode, remotely derived from the two preceding sections, and freely developed until a unison recalls the recitative of the First Episode, and leads to Part 3, which gives a condensed recapitulation of the first three sections, reducing their 179 bars to just under half that number. At first the original material is repeated almost exactly, and at the original pitch, but when the central section of the First Episode is reached the recapitulation begins to diverge widely from the exposition, both in the pitch and the general presentation of the material. The reprise of the cantabile section of Part 2 leads after two bars into the final codetta, in which a rhythmic figure from the Second Episode is prominent. In *The Genesis of a Novel* Thomas Mann has the following interesting paragraph on this work: 'We had Schoenberg to our house one evening, and this is the place to mention it. He told me about the new trio he had just completed, and about

the experiences he had secretly woven into the composition—experiences of
which the work was a kind of fruit. He had, he said, represented his illness and
medical treatment in the music, including even the male nurses and all the other
oddities of American hospitals. The work was extremely difficult to play, he said,
in fact almost impossible, or at best only for three players of virtuoso rank; but,
on the other hand, the music was very rewarding because of its extraordinary
tonal effects.'[1]

The Fantasy, op. 47, for violin and piano (1949), also in one movement, is
remarkable among other things for its specific description on the title-page as for
violin, with piano accompaniment—i.e. not a sonata-type duet in the now customary sense, in which the partners are equal. In form it resembles the Lisztian or
Bartókian rhapsody, with two main sections, the first mainly slow, florid, and
emotionally volatile, the second quick and gay. The first half consists of a succession of variation-like episodes with differing tempo- and character-indications
(grave, lento, grazioso, &c.). A return to the opening tempo brings a quasi-

Ex. 8A

Ex. 8B

recapitulation, followed by a cadenza leading to the quick second section, marked
'scherzando'. This is in the simplest ternary form, the reprise being a tone higher,
with a varied accompaniment-texture and a complete re-phrasing and transformation of the second theme of the exposition. Exx. 8 a and b show corresponding
bars in the two sections. A codetta based mainly on the middle section of the
scherzo leads to a brief recapitulation of some material from the slow section,
and a concluding cadenza.

<hr />

[1] This is quoted from the published English version of Mann's book *Die Entstehung des
Doktor Faustus*. The original German for the final two words is *Klangwirkungen*, which means
more strictly 'sound effects'.

In addition to these instrumental works, the *Ode to Napoleon Buonaparte*, op. 41 (1942) must be included in Schoenberg's output of chamber music, although the original piano quintet version of the accompaniment to the recitation of this may also be performed orchestrally. Unlike the instrumental part of *Pierrot Lunaire* it is merely an accompaniment, and although carefully planned and self-sufficient in form (the second of its three lengthy sections being a characteristically developed reprise of the first, and the third a coda), it is relatively simple in texture and content compared with his chamber music proper. Tonal associations are unusually strong. One of the most important thematic elements is the common chord with minor and major third sounding simultaneously, and there is much other triadic harmony. Counterpoint and melodic ornamentation throughout the work are also more harmonically inspired and conceived than in most of Schoenberg's works.

Chamber-music arrangements made by other hands of some of Schoenberg's works have been published, presumably with the composer's approval. There is a piano quintet version by Webern of the Chamber Symphony No. 1, a piano trio version of the Serenade, op. 24, made by Felix Greissle, who also arranged the Wind Quintet as a sonata for violin (or flute) and piano, and for clarinet and piano.

Of Schoenberg's two Austrian pupils, Berg and Webern, BERG wrote no chamber music between the 'Lyric Suite' for string quartet, the last work discussed in **C**, and his early death in 1935, except an arrangement (1935) of the second movement of the Chamber Concerto as a Trio for violin, clarinet, and piano. WEBERN, in contrast, applied himself mainly to chamber music, although rarely to the traditional media. The works up to and including op. 15, discussed by Edwin Evans in **C**, cover Webern's early 'atonal' period. At the time of Op. 15 he was already beginning, in common with Schoenberg and Berg, to experience the need for some fairly systematic method of organizing his musical material, to replace tonality. His first experiment was with canon. The last song of Op. 15 was a strict double canon in contrary motion, and in the Five Canons, op. 16, for soprano, clarinet, and bass clarinet (1924), he used strict canon as his structural method throughout. Nos. 1, 3, and 5 are in three parts, Nos. 2 and 4 in two, and contrary motion is used in Nos. 1, 2, and 5. In his next work, the Three Folk Texts, op. 17, for high voice, clarinet, bass clarinet, and violin (doubling viola), composed in the same year, he took up instead the twelve-note method newly formulated by Schoenberg, and to this he adhered in all his subsequent music. Op. 17 was his fifth consecutive set of songs with instrumental ensemble, and it was quickly followed by a sixth, the Three Songs, op. 18, for high voice, E flat clarinet, and guitar (1925). (The first set was the Four Songs, op. 13, not included in **C** as the accompaniment is for thirteen wind instruments.) These six sets, thirty-one songs in all, and barely as many minutes' music as that, were Webern's total output over a period of nearly twelve years (1914–25). They are an important part of his output, but for many years performances of them were even rarer than of his instrumental works, owing to the extreme difficulty of the vocal lines, and the rare call for such curious instrumental ensembles as are needed for them. But since 1945, as Webern's younger disciples have begun to turn their attention to similar combinations of solo voice with small and unusual instrumental ensembles, new kinds of chamber-music concert have arisen into which these works by Webern can be fitted more often. Ex. 9 is a characteristic fragment from Op. 18.

Ex. 9

Webern returned to purely instrumental chamber music in 1927, in the String Trio, op. 20—and also, like Schoenberg at the same period, to an approximately 'classical' formal organization, although his scale is much smaller and the sequence of his two movements not traditional. The first (Adagio) is rondo-like and the second a sonata-movement, in character and tempo more like a typical first movement, strictly classical in form, complete with double-bar repeat, and recapitulation of the second subject a fourth higher. The texture is generally simpler and more transparent than in the song-accompaniments, but the writing for the instruments is extremely elaborate. The first movement is muted throughout, and in both movements all three instruments are required to change almost from note to note from arco to pizzicato and back. There is frequent use of harmonics, and col legno is used in the second movement. Exx. 10 *a* and *b*, which are the corresponding bars in the exposition and recapitulation of the second subject of the second movement, show the nature of Webern's thematic treatment of the sonata form and of his instrumental writing.

In the Quartet, op. 22, for tenor saxophone, clarinet, violin, and piano (1930) Webern adopts again an almost purely canonic technique. The first of the two movements (Sehr mässig) is in a binary form nearer to that of the Scarlattian sonata than to the more modern sonata form, with double-bar repeat of both

halves, though with a clear 'development' section distinguished from the exposition and recapitulation by being *entirely* canonic. The exposition consists
of two statements of the note-series on the saxophone, accompanied by a
symmetrical double canonic duet on the other two instruments, each phrase
being answered immediately by its inversion. In the 'development' section the
entire material is presented in this canonic technique, but more densely, and in

Ex. 10A

Ex. 10B

the recapitulation the 'theme' of the exposition is presented by all three melody
instruments, with the piano alone providing the canonic accompaniment. The
same technique of symmetrical canonic inversion is employed a great deal also
in the more extended structure of the second movement (Sehr schwungvoll),
but the perpetual variation and avoidance of all recognizable recapitulation make
the form more difficult to follow and classify. Ex. 11 illustrates the canonic
technique in the first movement, and Ex. 12 the extremely spare texture of most
of the second movement, which is characteristic of all Webern's later music.

The Concerto, op. 24, for nine instruments (flute, oboe, clarinet, horn,
trumpet, trombone, violin, viola, and piano) was written in 1934 for the sixtieth
birthday of Schoenberg, as Berg's Chamber Concerto had been written for the
fiftieth. (The published full score contains a facsimile of a message by Schoenberg written in 1947.) This work might be summarily described as perpetual
canonic variations on the harmony of the simultaneous major-minor third. The
twelve-note series (see Ex. 13) consists of four variants of the same three-note
group, and the entire work consists of permutations of this sequence. In the first

movement (Etwas lebhaft) a variant of the canonic technique of the first movement of the Quartet, op. 22, is used throughout, each three-note phrase being answered immediately, as in the series itself, by its retrograde inversion. This is again in clear sonata form (this time without double bar), with a greatly varied

Ex. 11

Ex. 12

Ex. 13

recapitulation. The development (quoted in full in Ex. 14), occupying bars 26–34 of the total 69 bars, is distinguished from the rest by the exclusion of all instruments except piano, violin, and clarinet, and by the length of the phrases on the violin and clarinet. Except in two bars at the climax of the recapitulation these are the only phrases in the entire work, on any instrument other than the piano, of more than three consecutive notes. The development is also distinguished by the first appearance in the movement of grace-notes, apparently used to some extent to indicate the presence of serial puns, to add to the density and intensity of the musical and thematic content. A liberal use of these grace-notes throughout the recapitulation is one of the means of modification of the material of the exposition, and preserves something of the new intensity it has acquired in the

Ex. 14

development. A more rudimentary and concealed symmetry is also discernible in the last movement (Sehr rasch), in which, as in the middle movement (Sehr langsam), the technique of perpetual canon by retrograde inversion remains very prominent.

As the Concerto, op. 24, is perpetual variations on the major-minor third, the String Quartet, op. 28 (1938), dedicated to Elizabeth Sprague Coolidge, might be described as perpetual variations on the name or motive BACH. The note-series (see Ex. 15) consists of three transpositions of this motive—the middle one

Ex. 15

inverted. As the serial basis of the Concerto could almost be regarded as a three-note rather than a twelve-note series, so the Quartet might be analysed as being based on a four-note or even a two-note series—since the series falls into six pairs of notes each a semitone apart. Nearly the entire work is in double canon. Webern adopts a traditional form in the middle movement, a scherzo and trio (again with double bar), of moderate tempo (Gemächlich), fulfilling the function of both scherzo and slow movement rather in the manner of some of Brahms's middle movements. The first part, in steady 2/4 crotchets throughout, is in double canon at the major third, and the reprise differs only in that the order of the parts is reversed, so that the canon is at the minor sixth (i.e. the major third below). The trio section, also in strict double canon by inversion, is in a more flexible 3/8 rhythm. In the first movement (Mässig) a slight similarity of formal method can be observed. After the first fifteen bars the whole movement is in double canon—at the major sixth until bar 78, then again with the order of the parts reversed for the remainder of the movement, making a canon at the minor third. This section is clearly intended to function as a reprise, but no suggestion of sonata form can convincingly be read into the earlier part of the movement, which is best regarded as a set of canonic variations. The finale (Sehr fliessend) is similar in construction. It begins with a double canon at the tritone, passes through several sections of varying tempi and kinds of figuration, in canon at varying intervals, returning finally to the canon at the tritone, again with the order of the parts reversed.

A Piano Quintet by Webern, composed in 1907, immediately before Op. 1, and not included by the composer in his own catalogue of works, has been published since his death.

The various Austrian contemporaries of Webern and Berg whose reputation in the late 1920's stood similarly high, or seemed likely to do so, and whose early works are discussed in some detail in **C**, all went into emigration in the thirties, and have never fully recovered from the uprooting. Krenek, Toch, and Pisk went like Schoenberg to America, and Wellesz to England. The later chamber music of Toch and Pisk is described in the American section, and Wellesz's in the British. Only KRENEK, the youngest composer in this group, has to some extent resumed his position in European music.

He has continued to be prolific in chamber music as in other fields, though not all of his works are published. His fifth and sixth string quartets were composed before he left Europe in 1938. The earlier of them, composed in 1930, is in his neo-classical style of that period, conspicuously exemplified in the middle movement, a set of variations on the theme shown in Ex. 16. This is pure classical pastiche, very engaging and expressive. In the more serious outer movements, headed respectively 'Sonate' and 'Phantasie', there are strong and intentional echoes of Beethoven. The Phantasie, an extended slow movement, is an attempt at non-thematic musical construction on a large scale. The scale of the quartet as a whole is vast, and the duration given in the score is 45 minutes. Shortly after this work Krenek began to use twelve-note technique, and the sixth quartet (1936) is one of the first works of this new period. It is in five movements. Each of the first four movements uses one form of the note-series, and the finale is a fugue with four subjects (each taken from one of the preceding movements) in which all four forms of the series appear in all transpositions. In an article, 'Zu meinen Kammermusikwerken 1936–1950', published in the *Schweizerische Musikzeitung*, March 1953, concerned mainly with his serial methods in this and his later chamber works, Krenek described the sixth quartet as the extreme example of 'construction' in his work. Thereafter he was more concerned again

Ex. 16

with 'expression'. He considers the seventh quartet (1943–4) his best work of the period covered in the article. This too is in five thematically related movements, with another complex fugue, this time as the central climax of the work. There are three fugue-subjects, shown in Ex. 17 as they appear together at the beginning of the final section of the movement. A feature of the serial technique of the

Ex. 17

work, as of several others by Krenek at this period, is that the themes are made up of different three-note motives from the basic twelve-note series, which is not itself ever stated in full. The quartet is 'Dedicated in Gratitude to the Vivifying Spirit of my American Students'.

Other works mentioned by Krenek are the String Trio (1948); another work for the same ensemble, entitled *Parvula corona musicalis ad honorem J. S. Bach* (1950), which the composer describes as being written in 'classical' twelve-note technique, on a series in which the figure BACH is the central motive; the Sonatina for flute and clarinet (1942), described as a simple twelve-note study without experimental intention; the Sonata for violin and piano (1944–5), similar in serial method to the seventh quartet; and the Trio for clarinet, violin, and piano (1946) and Sonata for viola and piano (1948), which are not written wholly in twelve-note technique.

Contemporary with Krenek are Hans Erich Apostel (b. 1901) and Hanns Jelinek (b. 1901), who established themselves only after 1945. Both are rather academic followers of Schoenberg and Berg, whose pupils they were. APOSTEL has written two string quartets, the first of which was composed for Berg's fiftieth birthday. Its slow movement is a set of six variations on a six-bar theme from Act 2 of *Wozzeck*, and the scherzo is based on the initials of Berg and Apostel (ABHEA). His second quartet is a single movement in five sections symmetrically laid out and thematically related after the model of Bartok's fourth and fifth quartets. His other works include a Quartet for woodwind and horn, and Five Bagatelles for woodwind trio.

JELINEK has written several pieces for varying chamber ensembles as part of his series called *Zwölftonwerk*, op. 15, which is written 'for the use of performers, for the pleasure of listeners, for the stimulation of teachers, for the instruction of pupils' and dedicated to 'all friends and lovers of compositions in the twelve-tone system'. The chamber-music works are a String Trio, a Divertimento for three clarinets and basset-horn, a Sonatina for wind trio, and Four Canons for two flutes.

Gottfried von EINEM (b. 1918), an Austrian pupil of Blacher, has written a solitary and attractive Sonata for violin and piano, in a tonally free but simple, almost neo-classical style very much like Blacher's own, light and clear in texture and lively in rhythm. The first movement is in 7/8, sustained throughout with much ingenuity and variety.

In German chamber music since **C**, HINDEMITH is still the dominating figure, by reason not only of seniority and an individuality of style stronger than that of any of his successors, but also for sheer quantity of output. Fourteen important works were listed in **C**, published when he was in his early thirties, and he has since brought the number up to more than fifty.

Probably the most important and finest of his chamber works since **C** is the String Quartet No. 5 (1943), one of the most beautiful of all his works. It opens with a short fugue (Very quiet and expressive), followed by a sonata-movement (Lively and very energetic). The third movement (Quiet) is a set of variations, and the fourth (Broad and energetic) is a continuous sequence of tenuously linked sections which are then freely recapitulated, the material being combined in overlapping succession with the themes of the fugue and the variations, and the second and first subjects of the sonata-movement. The general tone of the work is very serene and lyrical, and more readily engaging to the ear than that of much of Hindemith's music, owing to a slightly greater indulgence than usual in ear-tickling harmonic effects, particularly in various kinds of major–minor false-relation, which are heard at the outset in the fugue-theme (see Ex. 18), and figure prominently both in the variations and in the finale.

Ex. 18

Something of this lyrical and engaging tone is preserved also in the String Quartet No. 6 (1945), but this is less perfect in form and less satisfying in content. The second and fourth movements, one a terse 'Scherzando' in rondo form, with two very brief trio episodes, the other an extended canon, elaborate in construction but in character similarly scherzo-like, are excellent pieces in Hindemith's wittiest vein, probably freer in fantasy and invention than anything in No. 5. But in attempting to make the lyrical first and third movements light enough in thematic and structural weight to balance these two, Hindemith has used a harmonically decorative rather than melodic kind of counterpoint, which is not characteristic of him and is thin rather than light in effect.

Besides the string quartets, Hindemith has written two quartets for more unusual combinations. That for four horns, called a Sonata (1952), is a fairly light-weight work in a simple style, the three movements of which may be played separately if desired, although there are distinct melodic similarities among them and the first two are clearly linked. The first is a short introductory fugato, the second a sonata-movement with the two subjects recapitulated in reverse order, and with a free-fantasia middle section based not on these subjects but on the theme of the fugato. The third movement is a set of variations on 'Ich schell mein Horn', one of which again, but this time more faintly, echoes the fugato theme. The other quartet, for clarinet, violin, 'cello, and piano (1938), is much more ambitious and weighty, one of the most complex in style and varied and interesting in texture of all Hindemith's work of its period. Its first movement is in sonata form, with three main subjects and a developed recapitulation in which the thematic emphases are changed. This is followed by an extremely florid slow movement in a ternary (ABA) form of elaborate organization, with much quasi-antiphonal writing between the piano and the trio of melodic instruments, and a greatly varied da capo. The finale is a rather episodic rondo with two main subjects. A work of somewhat similar calibre, in an earlier and tougher idiom, is the Trio, op. 47 (1929), for viola, heckelphone, and piano. The first movement, headed 'Solo, Arioso, Duett', begins with something like a three-part invention for piano solo, followed by a slow arioso for heckelphone and piano, derived from a phrase in the Solo, leading to the quick Duett, for the two

melodic instruments accompanied by the piano, which is constructed entirely
out of canonic and other elaborations of the themes already presented. The
second movement, called 'Potpourri', is in four thematically independent
sections, the first two of very strictly thematic counterpoint in perpetual canon
on several themes simultaneously, the other two freer and more toccata-like.

Owing to their unusual combinations of instruments, neither of these works
is likely to enjoy more than very infrequent performance, but in musical content
both are among Hindemith's most important chamber works. Equally important,
and perhaps likely to be heard slightly oftener, are the Septet for wind instruments (1948), and the Octet for wind and strings (1958), both in a fairly severe
vein and idiom and both in five movements. The Septet is the more attractive.
Its first movement is in an unusually compact sonata form, with a condensed and
developed recapitulation, built on three strong main thematic elements, all
unusually terse and incisive (Ex. 19 shows the first of them). A short, rhapsodic

Ex. 19

Intermezzo follows, leading without a pause into a lively and extended set of
variations on a rather square, simple tune, after which the Intermezzo recurs,
played in reverse. The finale, marked 'Alter Berner Marsch', is an elaborate
fugue on a variety of subjects and counter-subjects.

The Octet, written for the Berlin Philharmonic Octet, is for the same instruments as Schubert's Octet, except that there is a second viola part instead of a
second violin. It is not one of Hindemith's more inspired works, and the only
remarkable feature is the last movement, which like that of the Septet is fugal.
It is headed 'Fuge und drei altmodische Tänzer (Walzer, Polka, Galopp)',
and amusingly inverts the common formula of variations and fugue by starting
with the fugue, and then careering off into the three dances, based on variants of

the fugue-theme, which run through them passacaglia-fashion. The second movement is also a set of passacaglia-like variations.

The early Quintet for clarinet and strings (1923) is another important work that demands belated mention and attention after waiting over thirty years for publication. Its two outer movements, like the Intermezzi of the Septet, mirror each other. At the centre of the work is a scherzo-like quick Ländler, preceded by a mainly canonic slow movement in ternary song form (the recapitulation being condensed and broadened by means of the augmentation of the main theme), and followed by a short arioso, both leading without a break from and into the cancrizans outer movements.

Finally, among the bigger ensemble works, there is the String Trio No. 2, also relatively early (1933). This is uneven in quality, with a rather quiet and brief but musically weighty first movement, in an original kind of sonata form with the subjects shuffled about, followed by a scherzo-like sonata-rondo, slightly too long and repetitive but with some attractive material and one exciting passage of development. In the finale a very beautiful short slow section alternates with a quick section that is again unduly long, and of inferior thematic quality.

One other work for strings, composed a year later (1934) but not published for many years, is the Duet for viola and cello. This is in a single sonata-like movement, of energetic humour and rhythmic wit, with bars of two, three, and four beats in continuous irregular alternation. It has a three-part exposition in which the third part is an extension of the first. In the reprise the slightly contrasted theme which separates the related outer themes in the exposition is recapitulated before them.

Among Hindemith's large output of duet and solo sonatas the early works of opp. 11, 25, and 31, composed between 1918 and 1923, are discussed in C. Hindemith returned to this form only in 1935, and then within nine years wrote twenty-two new sonatas, including three for organ, three for piano, and one each for harp, piano duet, and two pianos. Of the remaining thirteen, ten were for wind instruments, one for viola, and two for violin, all with piano.

The first of them was the Sonata in E for violin and piano (1935), which immediately proclaimed the new and simpler style that was to characterize the later wind-instrument sonatas. It is in two rather short movements, of clear texture and form, the first (Ruhig bewegt), in 9/8 time, a sonata-movement with the subjects recapitulated in reverse order, the second one of the slow–fast–slow movements, in which the 6/8 rhythm of the fast section faintly echoes the 9/8 of the first movement. There is nothing in this work of the virtuoso writing of Hindemith's earlier sonatas for string instruments, and the violin part, in which there are only half a dozen double stoppings, could easily be played on a clarinet, or even an oboe, the more limited range of which is not very often exceeded. Much the same applies to the other Sonata for violin and piano (1939), though this is slightly more difficult and elaborate in style. Like its predecessor it also has a short first movement, this time almost monothematic, preludial in character, and more vigorous in tone. It is followed by a slow movement enclosing a very quick and rhythmically witty scherzo in 5/8 time, the animation of which is carried over into the recapitulation of the slow section in the form of a moto perpetuo of decorative semiquavers on the violin, at approximately the same speed as the quavers in the scherzo. The work ends with an enchanting fugue in rondo form, as deft and light in weight and tone as it is fugally complex. First there is a complete little four-part fugue on the main subject, followed by an extended and elaborate canonic episode on a new subject, then a reappearance of the fugue theme in combination with the canon theme, a second episode consisting of another four-part fugue on a third subject, and a final recurrence of the original fugue theme, now combined with both the other themes simultaneously. Ex. 20, showing the final combination of all the themes, before the coda, gives an idea of the character and charm of the movement and of the work as a whole.

Ex. 20

In the Sonata for viola and piano composed in the same year, Hindemith temporarily abandons this simplicity of form and lightness of tone. All four movements in this work are complex in style, and both extended and difficult to classify in form. The sonata form of the first movement is distinguished by the augmentation and extension of the themes in the recapitulation, the reversal of their order, and the rather remote thematic relationship of the fugue that serves instead of development. The same principle of reversing the order of the themes in the reprise is applied in the sonata-scherzo second movement. A Fantasy follows, based almost entirely on one motive, and forming an extended introduction to the finale, which like that of Hindemith's earlier Sonata for viola and piano (op. 11, no. 4) contains two variations bafflingly concealed within a rondo, where, as in the first movement, the main theme is augmented at its final appearance.

The Sonata for 'cello and piano (1948) displays the same weight and complexity of style, and its forms, although more straightforward, are of a similar breadth. It opens with a movement designated 'Pastorale', which consists of the exposition and condensed recapitulation of three themes, and is much bigger and more severe in harmony than is normally expected of a pastoral piece. The second movement is a rather march-like scherzo with a slow middle section and a re-capitulation decorated with a running accompaniment of semiquavers in the piano part, and the third a massive passacaglia. This work throughout is much more harmonic in conception than is customary with Hindemith, and also very uncharacteristic of his later harmonic idiom. In the scherzo, for instance, the unison piano-writing that is such a common feature of his sonatas is distorted by the flattening of the lower line by a tone for long stretches. This device, and the general strong dissonance of the harmony, recall some of the most daring of Hindemith's early works.

The only other sonata for a string instrument with piano is that for double bass (1949), a terse, light, and engaging work in which the piano inevitably has the lion's share of the thematic argument, and is given mainly light florid writing to compensate for its partner's tonal weight and limited flexibility. It opens with an 'Allegretto' in something like rondo form, followed by a short scherzo, and ends with a set of variations in which the decoration of the relatively simple theme becomes increasingly florid until the variations are suddenly interrupted by a free recitative, which leads to a final variation marked 'Lied', an ingeniously ambiguous piece based on a theme closely derived from the main theme, exhibiting characteristics of both strophic song form and so-called Lied form.

The wind-instrument sonatas form a compact group, and although their composition was distributed over eight years they might all belong to a single opus, like the early string sonatas, op. 11. Those for oboe and bassoon (both 1938) have a two-movement form similar to that of the Sonata in E for violin (see above), though with considerable differences in the internal organization. The second movement of the Sonata for oboe is exceptional in that the alternating slow and fast sections are based on transformations of the same theme. In the Sonata for bassoon the first movement is a short expressive pastoral piece marked 'Leicht bewegt', the second begins 'Langsam', leading fairly soon into a march, with trio, which in turn leads to a coda, marked 'Beschluss, pastorale', deceptively recalling, at a rather slower tempo, the rhythms and general mood of the opening, but with only the slightest and vaguest thematic affinity, hardly definable as a real relationship. The Sonata for cor anglais and piano (1941) is a single extended movement consisting of six sections (Langsam, Allegro pesante, Moderato, Schnell (scherzo), Moderato, Allegro pesante) which are in effect alternating variations on two themes, a formal conception remotely similar to that of Haydn's F minor piano variations. Exx. 21 and 22 show the two themes

as they first appear. Both the remaining woodwind sonatas are in four movements
of clear, more or less traditional, design, simple, melodious, and light in style
and tone, the one for clarinet (1939) rather more energetic and emphatic in its
moods. It may also be played on the viola. The Sonata for flute (1936) ends with
a brief march that recalls the first movement in the same faintly allusive manner

Ex. 21

Ex. 22

as the coda to the Sonata for bassoon, though rather more directly. A much
more direct thematic relationship links the first and last movements of the
Sonata for trombone (1941), both rather heavy, fanfare-like movements, between
which there come first a light 'Allegretto grazioso' mainly for piano, and a scherzo-
like movement called 'Lied des Raufbolds' (Swashbuckler's Song). Of the other
sonatas for brass instruments, the one for trumpet (1938) often recalls the style
of the weightiest of the woodwind sonatas, that for clarinet. (In a note in the
score the composer suggests that the trumpet sonata might be played on an oboe,
clarinet, violin, or viola, though he does not recommend concert performances
of it on these instruments.) It is in three movements, of which both the second
and third use different (but not absolutely contrasted) tempi in alternation. In
the second a moderato section in triple time alternates with a gavotte-like quick
section, while the third is a funeral march, with a long trio-like middle section
marked 'Ruhig bewegt', a varied reprise of the march, and a coda in which the

trumpet plays a chorale melody, 'Alle Menschen müssen sterben'—an effect from which Honegger may have borrowed the idea for the end of his Symphony No. 2.

In the Sonata for tuba and piano (1943), as in the one for double bass, Hindemith compensates for the weight of the instrument by giving the piano an animated part of unusual harmonic wit and interest, in which he surprisingly toys with a twelve-note idea. The three-movement form too is similar to that of the double-bass sonata. The first movement, marked 'Allegro pesante', is a freely developing fantasy-like piece, with a very brief, selective and varied recapitulation of earlier themes in the coda. Next comes a scherzo-like movement in simple ternary form, with a miniature passacaglia as a trio. The last movement, in which the twelve-note idea appears, is headed 'Variations', but is in a similar ternary form. The theme is a twelve-note tune announced at the beginning by the tuba, and immediately repeated by the piano. In the succeeding two variations the twelve-note idea goes underground, but is recalled to the surface in the codetta that ends the 'exposition'. This is followed by a development-like middle section consisting of, first, a variation marked 'Scherzando' for piano (with a single brief interruption from the tuba), then a recitative-like cadenza for tuba, with accompanying chord-progressions on the piano containing all twelve notes, culminating in two complete twelve-note chords. The entire 'exposition' is then repeated a minor third lower, with an added decorative part for the right hand of the piano.

In the two sonatas for horn and piano (1939 and 1943), the greater flexibility and more varied expressive possibilities of the horn permit a closer fusion of the two instruments. This is especially so in the first of them, which is the most lyrical and intimate of the sonatas for brass instruments, and avoids conspicuous ingenuities of form or texture in its three large-scale movements. The second horn sonata, which is also intended for alto horn or saxophone, is in a less extended four-movement form, similar to that of a Handel violin sonata, with two quick movements each preceded by a short slow one. The first is a lyrical prelude, the second a sonata movement with a fairly elaborate development section and an entirely new accompaniment in the recapitulation, kept up throughout both subjects. The third movement, which rises to a considerable harmonic climax within its fourteen bars, functions as a slow introduction to the finale, which has at its head the following text:

The Posthorn (Dialogue)
   Horn Player:
     Is not the sounding of a horn to our busy souls
     (even as the scent of blossoms wilted long ago,
     or the discoloured folds of musty tapestry,
     or crumbling leaves of ancient yellowed tomes)
     like a sonorous visit from those ages
     which counted speed by straining horses' gallop,
     and not by lightning prisoned up in cables:
     and when to live and learn they ranged the countryside,

not just the closely printed pages?
The cornucopia's gift calls forth in us
a pallid yearning, melancholy longing.
Pianist:
The old is good not just because it's past,
nor is the new supreme because we live with it,
and never yet a man felt greater joy
than he could bear or truly comprehend.
Your task it is, amid confusion, rush, and noise
to grasp the lasting, calm, and meaningful,
and finding it anew, to hold and treasure it.

The idea of this text is translated into music in a movement in three sections—
a scurrying piano solo, then a more leisurely, dance-like tune for the horn (with
accompaniment), and finally a recapitulation of these two sections simultaneously.

Apart from Hindemith's there have been few outstanding contributions to
German chamber music since 1930. Of his seniors PFITZNER (C, d. 1949) added
two string quartets (op. 36 and op. 50), and a Sextet, op. 55, for clarinet, violin,
viola, 'cello, double bass and piano (1945) to his list of chamber works given in C.
JARNACH (C), who although not a German is most closely associated with that
country, has added a work for string quartet under the title *Musik zum Gedächtnis der Einsamen* (1952), and Heinrich KAMINSKI (C, d. 1946) a *Hauskonzert* for
violin and piano (1941), *Musik* for two violins and harpsichord (or piano) (1931),
and some minor works.

Hindemith's approximate contemporaries Carl ORFF (b. 1895) and Werner
EGK (b. 1901) have contributed nothing to chamber music, nor has it strongly
attracted Karl Amadeus HARTMANN (b. 1905), whose two string quartets are not
among his most important works. The first is an early work, the published score
of which bears the title 'Carillon' (the name of a competition at Geneva in 1936
in which it won first prize). It was published only in 1953, after the String Quartet
No. 2, which was written in 1948. Both quartets have the romantic eloquence
typical of Hartmann, No. 1 showing the strong influence of Bartók's fourth
quartet, and No. 2 some influence also of Hindemith.

Boris Blacher (b. 1903) and Wolfgang Fortner (b. 1907) have paid more attention to chamber music. BLACHER's output includes four works for string quartet
(opp. 9, 16, 32, and the *Epitaph*, op. 41), sonatas for violin solo (op. 40), violin
and piano (op. 18), and flute and piano (op. 15), and two divertimenti for wind
ensembles (opp. 29 and 38). Most of these works are in an attractive neo-classical
manner, very clear in texture and form, and terse and simple in content. The
most extended, weightiest, and harmonically the richest of them is the String
Quartet No. 3, op. 32, which has a slightly unusual sequence of four movements,
ending with a 'Larghetto'. Ex. 23 shows the opening of the first movement.

In the later works, the Divertimento, op. 38, for flute, oboe, clarinet, and
bassoon, in two movements, and the Sonata, op. 40, for unaccompanied violin,

in three movements, Blacher makes use of elaborate schemes of variable metres, the only element of innovation in his music, and one of relatively slight intrinsic interest. Formally the most remarkable of his chamber works is the *Epitaph*, op. 41, for string quartet. This short piece (duration 7 minutes), composed in 1951 and entitled *Zum Gedächtnis von Franz Kafka*, is a rondo-like single

Ex. 23

movement consisting of six sections, of which the third and fourth are varied inversions of the first and second, the fifth is a recapitulation of the first, and the sixth a pizzicato coda opening with a double mirror-canon and gradually disintegrating. The second and fourth sections (i.e. the 'episodes') are cadenzas for unaccompanied 'cello and violin respectively.

FORTNER's chamber music includes three string quartets, a String Trio, a Serenade for flute, oboe, and bassoon, sonatas for violin, 'cello, and flute, each with piano, and a Suite for unaccompanied 'cello. This Suite, published in 1933, is the earliest of Fortner's works now available in print. It is in a plain diatonic style, and is characteristic of the composer's mature work mainly in the third movement, 'Canzone', which is subtitled 'Variazioni sopra una melodia antica del Trovatore francese'. Fortner is fond of such sets of variations on old melodies. The third movement of his Sonata for 'cello and piano is a 'Ballata: Variations sur un thème de Guillaume de Machaut', and the fourth movement of the Serenade for wind trio is a 'Partita zu einem Abschiedslied aus d. 16. Jahrh.' This is a witty and delightful work of rather Hindemithian neo-classical character, in six short movements, the last of which is a fugue on a subject derived from the song-melody of the fourth movement. The influence of Hindemith shows also in the idiom of the Sonata for flute and piano (1947), which is light and charming, and very simple and straightforward in tonality and form except for a Hindemithian formal curiosity in the last movement, a rondo in which the second 'episode' is an almost self-contained movement consisting of a theme, four variations, and coda. Another unusual form, also probably inspired by Hindemith's examples in the Clarinet Quintet and the Wind Septet (although other precedents exist), is found in the String Trio, which is an almost exact

palindrome. There are five movements. A brief opening 'Andante con moto', in
sonata form, is followed by a fantastically scored 'Allegro molto' of capricious
character, which keeps increasing in speed. The central movement, 'Andante
tranquillo', is a canon, from the middle of which the whole work returns in
retrograde motion to the beginning, with only one or two very slight changes.
This is one of Fortner's later works (1953), written after he had turned to twelve-
note technique and had begun to write in an idiom markedly different from that
of his earlier period. The first of his twelve-note works was the String Quartet
No. 3 (1948). (Scores of Nos. 1 and 2, written in 1929 and 1938, are no longer
available from the publishers.) In formal conception No. 3 is traditional, and in
tone more romantic than the earlier works, with a richly lyrical opening movement in sonata form, a da capo scherzo with a short trio in which witty use is
made of glissando effects, a contrapuntal slow movement in sonata form, and for
the finale, as in the Serenade and the Sonata for flute and piano, a fugue on an
extended, decorative, rapid theme worked out here within sonata form. Ex. 24
shows the fugue subject and countersubject.

Ex. 24

The Sonata for 'cello and piano, from the same period (published 1949), is
formally more experimental. The first movement has a two-part design in which
a complete sonata, with a contrasting middle section and a recapitulation of the
subjects in reverse order, is followed by a new scherzo-like episode, a further
development of the middle section of the sonata, and a final restatement of the
opening theme. The middle movement is again a da capo scherzo and trio,
and the last movement is the set of variations on a theme by Machaut referred
to earlier, in which there are harmonic allusions to the earlier movements. The
satisfying resolution of the harmonic intensity of the first two movements,
where ostinato-like dissonant progressions are almost obsessively used, in the
austere neo-classical counterpoint of the variations, is a remarkable imaginative
stroke. Ex. 25 shows the beginning of the first variation.

Behind these internationally established composers a second line of more
conservative and academic German composers has maintained a steady output
of chamber music of admirable anonymous competence, most of it heavily

influenced by Hindemith. The most notable among them are Max BUTTING (**C**), Johann Nepomuk DAVID (b. 1895), Fidelio FINKE (**C**), Harald GENZMER (b. 1909), and Kurt HESSENBERG (b. 1908), most of whom have been fairly prolific in this field.

Ex. 25

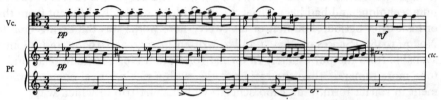

Among the younger German composers the outstanding figures are Hans Werner Henze (b. 1926), Karlheinz Stockhausen (b. 1928), and Giselher Klebe (b. 1925). HENZE's most important instrumental chamber work is the String Quartet (1952), in three movements, of florid and elaborate serial texture, owing something both to Schoenberg and to Webern. The exposition of the first movement is recapitulated in retrograde motion. In the last two movements, in which Henze makes systematic use of variable metres as found in Blacher, the formal outline is more elusive. The Wind Quintet (1952) and the Sonatina for flute and piano (1947) are lighter in character, though also rich in compositional interest. In the finale of the latter the tune of 'The Miller of Dee' is introduced with amusing effect. There is also an early Sonata for violin and piano (1946) in a surprisingly conservative romantic style, as well as an attractive Serenade for unaccompanied 'cello, composed in 1949.

In addition Henze has written two major works for voice with chamber ensemble, the first of which, *Apollo et Hyazinthus* (1949) he once named as his best chamber-music work. It is described on the title-page as 'Improvisations for harpsichord, alto voice and eight solo instruments' (flute, clarinet, bassoon, horn, and string quartet). The harpsichord has a prominent, almost concerto-like part, and the voice enters only at the end to sing a stanza by Georg Trakl, set to an expansive melodic statement of the twelve-note series on which the work is based, while the instrumental ensemble recapitulates various phrases from the 'improvisations' on it.

In *Kammermusik 1958*, commissioned by Norddeutscher Rundfunk, Hamburg, and dedicated to Benjamin Britten, Henze adapts the formal ideas both of Britten's Serenade and of his Canticle No. 3, to a setting of Hölderlin's *In lieblicher Bläue*, for tenor, guitar (or harp), and eight instruments—clarinet, horn, bassoon, and string quintet (or string orchestra). The twelve movements are arranged in three each of four different kinds: for the total ensemble; for the instrumental group without guitar or voice; for voice and guitar; and for guitar alone. Of the six instrumental movements the three for ensemble are headed Preface (1), Sonata (7), and Cadenza (9), but each of the three guitar solos

(Nos. 3, 5, and 11, marked Interludes I, II, and III), bears the title of a poem. The alternation of movements with and without voice is the simplest of several overlapping patterns in the difficult and complex formal scheme, in which the instrumental movements cover the same wide emotional range as the vocal ones, but take a different course, and are arranged to provide contrasts rather than transitions between them.

STOCKHAUSEN's best-known and most accessible chamber work is the *Zeitmasse* (1956), for flute, oboe, cor anglais, clarinet, and bassoon. This is notable as, among other things, an early and cautious example of post-serial 'indeter-

Ex. 26

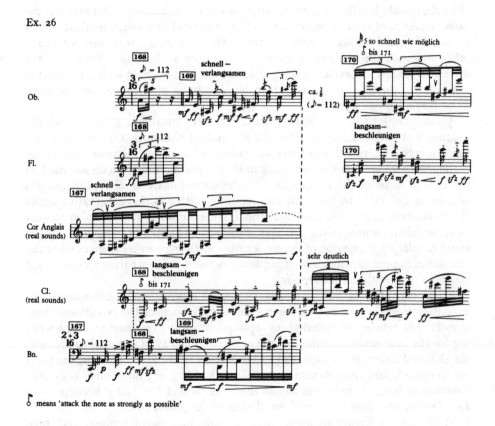

ƃ means 'attack the note as strongly as possible'

minacy', though this element in it is confined to a more frequent use of the device introduced some years earlier by Boulez in *Le Marteau sans Maître*, where the singer is directed to perform certain phrases 'as slowly as possible without taking breath'. He also adopts Boulez's idea, and develops his method, in the same work, of writing an almost continuous controlled rubato into the score. Ex. 26 is a fairly complex and characteristic page of *Zeitmasse*, showing in 'bars' 167–9 the oboe and cor anglais directed to begin quickly and decelerate, while the clarinet and horn begin slowly and accelerate. No more precise tempo markings are given for these passages, but the notation indicates their approximate relationship to each other, and to the brief phrases marked 'quaver 112' on oboe, flute, and clarinet, by means of the spacing of the note-heads, which are in such passages placed closer together as their duration decreases, and vice versa. But the score is not intended as an exact diagram of the sequence of notes to be heard (even supposing that it were possible to achieve this exact sequence in performance), nor as an ideal for the performers to aim at. The same sequence of pitches could hardly be reproduced in any two 'realizations', and still less the same sequence of relative durations. In 'bar' 170 an oboe passage marked 'as fast as possible', and an accelerando on the flute, must be co-ordinated with each other and with the clarinet accelerando beginning at 'bar' 168. Elsewhere the directions 'as fast [or 'as slow'] as possible' are sometimes given with a metronome indication of the slowest or fastest permissible tempo, or of the number of 'bars' to be played in one breath.

About one-third of the work consists of these overlapping and metrically independent cadenza-like rubatos. In the rest of the work the five parts are uniformly barred, and all simultaneously observe the many fluctuations of tempo —though there are some divergences in their dynamic lines, which are marked throughout in as much detail as Ex. 26. The texture of these metrically uniform sections is also more traditionally contrapuntal, with a fairly conservative use of the methods of post-Webernian melodic 'fragmentation'. There are also numerous chordal and homophonic passages of essentially harmonic conception, which stand in relation to the rest of the work rather as Stravinsky's cadences do to the rest in the Septet, as a moment of euphonious rest for the ear from the sustained stretches of complex counterpoint.

A less conspicuous but extremely successful innovation in *Zeitmasse* is the substitution of the cor anglais for the customary horn of the traditional wind quintet. The whole instrumental conception—including the mastery of the writing for the individual instruments, the colour and clarity of the total sound, and the skill and imagination with which, particularly in the free cadenzas, the parts are so spaced, and their dynamics so balanced, that every note tells—is as brilliant and striking a feature as any in the work, and it has justly become, with *Le Marteau sans Maître*, one of the classics of its generation.

Stockhausen's *Kreuzspiel* for six players (oboe, bass clarinet, piano, and three percussion players), composed in 1951 and published in a revised version in 1960, is an early example of 'pointillism' and of his concern with 'music in space'. He carefully specifies the grouping of the instruments and the relative heights at which the players should stand or sit—the wind players one on each side of the pianist (whose back is to the audience), and the three percussion players, who are occupied mostly with a series of tom-toms and small drums, around the piano behind them. Other works of Stockhausen include *Kontra-Punkte*, for ten instruments, an early quartet for piano and timpani, and *Refrain*, for three players (piano, celesta, and percussion).

KLEBE has written an interesting String Quartet, op. 9 (1950), romantic in expression and not problematic in idiom, in six short movements, thematically very closely linked. His Sonata for violin and piano, op. 14 (1952), and 'Elegia Appassionata', op. 22 (1955), for piano trio are more Webern-like and rarefied in idiom, full-textured but harmonically very fastidious, and delicate in sound. He has also written two sonatas (opp. 8 and 20) for unaccompanied violin.

Also highly talented, though somewhat more conservative, is Bernd Alois ZIMMERMANN (b. 1918), who has written excellent and effective sonatas for violin and piano, violin solo, and viola solo.

FRANCE

Since the string quartets of Debussy and Ravel, French chamber music has thrown up no important works of similar popularity. Those that come nearest to it are probably the several later works of ROUSSEL, which belong rather, with Debussy's late sonatas or Ravel's Trio and Violin Sonata, to the category of works highly esteemed but infrequently heard. Roussel wrote three major chamber works after the Serenade, op. 30, which was the last work discussed by M. D. Calvocoressi in **C**. These were the Trio, op. 40, for flute, violin, and 'cello, written in 1929 for Mrs. Elizabeth Sprague Coolidge, the String Quartet in D, op. 45 (1932), and the String Trio, op. 58 (1937). There are also a short Duo for bassoon and double bass (or 'cello), written in 1925 for Koussevitzky when he was made a Chevalier of the Légion d'Honneur, an 'Andante and Scherzo', op. 51, for flute and piano (1934), and an uncompleted Trio for oboe, clarinet, and bassoon on which he was working at his death. The Sonata for 'cello and piano listed in **C** does not appear to exist.

The most important of these is the String Quartet, the first chamber work in which Roussel had used an ensemble of strings only. On the title-page Roussel specifically states the key of the work (in contrast to his usual practice) as if to emphasize it. The emphasis is strengthened by the prominent appearance, in the principal themes of all the movements except the second, of a root-position arpeggio of the tonic triad, either major or minor. Exx. 27 and 28 show it in the first and third movements, Exx. 29a and 29b in the fourth. This is the only thematic connexion between the movements, except in the very remarkable fourth movement, which consists of an extended fugue followed by a still more extended rondo-like ternary section, which in scope and effect is really a separate movement, linked to the first half of the movement only by the reappearance of the fugue-theme towards the end. Ex. 29a is from the fugue-theme, 29b from the main theme of the finale. The formal complexity of this movement is greater than is normally found in Roussel, though he gave much attention to matters of form and development, as may be seen in the other three movements of the quartet. The mainly lyrical first movement is in a straightforward sonata form, the regularity and simplicity of which are slightly disguised by the anticipation of the second subject in the middle of the first. In the second movement (Adagio), also in sonata form, the recapitulation is varied and enriched, and the main melody of the first subject reappears in the bass instead of the treble. The third movement is an ingenious combination of rondo with scherzo-and-trio. The first three appearances of the ten-bar opening theme (see Ex. 28), the last of which is modified and transposed, are separated by two longer 'episodes', the second of which is a variant of the first. Then comes a short 'trio' section (meno vivo), followed by a tonally varied recapitulation of the main theme, and a coda containing allusions to the material of the 'episodes'.

Ex. 27

Ex. 28

Ex. 29A

Ex. 29B

The two trios are on a smaller scale, both in three movements of simple design. In op. 40 something survives of the sonorous quality of the Serenade (see **C**), despite the leaner texture. Roussel was still indulging his fondness for the flute, and scored the work with obvious pleasure in this particular, delicate blend of diverse instrumental tone. Throughout the work the different tone quality of the flute tends to make it to some extent a soloist, but in general the melodic interest is fairly evenly divided among the three instruments. In the opening movement (Allegro grazioso) the predominantly lyrical and almost pastoral tone is lightly and wittily intruded upon by a fanfare-like figure which becomes one of the main motives of the long development section. The second movement (Andante) is one of very polished and finely planned form. It is a ternary movement with varied reprise, in which the middle section reproduces in miniature the form of the whole. The first part is a contrapuntal duet for flute and viola over a rocking quaver bass. In the reprise the bass is slightly developed, and the flute and viola change parts. The middle section similarly begins with a duet, for the two string instruments, which is also recapitulated in varied form, on the flute and viola, after its own sixteen-bar middle section, dominated by a 'cello melody. The last movement is a brisk sonata-rondo with many changes of tempo, texture, and scoring.

Op. 58 is of similar neo-classical proportions and general style, but slightly different in character. The opening movement (Allegro moderato), in sonata form (with the order of the subjects reversed in the reprise), is crisper, the slow movement (also in sonata form, with a quasi-fugal first subject) is more weighty, and the finale (a simple rondo with a hint of a sonata-like second subject) is more boisterously gay, in a 6/8 metre more like that of a real dancing-jig than of a stylized one.

Only one movement of the unfinished Trio for woodwind has been published, in the special Roussel number of *La Revue musicale* (November 1937), with the following note:

Cette page, la dernière qu'ait écrite Albert Roussel, ne sera jamais mise dans le commerce et ne doit pas être exécutée publiquement, selon la volonté expresse de son Auteur relative aux manuscrits qu'il a laissés inachevés. Écrit pour le Trio d'Anches de Paris (MM. Morel, Lefebvre et Oubradous), cet Andante [the actual marking is Adagio] a été exécuté, par ces artistes, pour les amis d'Albert Roussel, à l'une des Auditions du mardi de la Revue Musicale, le 30 novembre 1937.

Of the other senior composers, SCHMITT (d. 1958), KOECHLIN (d. 1950), and D'INDY (d. 1931) continued to produce much chamber music, of which not all is published, and very little is ever heard outside France. Much the same applies to their hardly less prolific junior MIGOT (**C**). Migot's is the generation of 'Les Six', three of whose members have written chamber works that hold some place in the international repertory. Precedence must go to MILHAUD, for the sheer quantity of his output, which includes eighteen string quartets and an enormous number of other works. He is like a French counterpart of Hindemith, and his chamber music shares with Hindemith's the unusual distinction of being much more accessible to players of moderate ability than most chamber music by modern composers of comparable importance.

In his original article in **C** Edwin Evans dealt with the first seven quartets, written between 1912 and 1925, omitting No. 3, which was not then published. It was written in memory of Milhaud's close friend the poet Léo Latil, who had been killed in the war in 1915. The composer's original intention was that it should not be published until after his own death, but in 1956, forty years after its composition, he released it for publication. The score is dated 'Mars–Août 1916, en souvenir du Printemps 1914'. It consists of two movements, both marked 'très lent', the second a setting of a page from Latil's own diary, which he had left to Milhaud, on the subject of death, to be sung by a dramatic soprano (an idea possibly suggested by Schoenberg's Quartet No. 2). The music of both movements clings persistently round a few sorrowful harmonies. In the first movement the composer's favourite parallel thirds are very prominent. Ex. 30 shows the first entry of the voice in the second movement.

The later quartets show a greater consistency of style, and need not be discussed individually in such detail. There was a seven-year gap between Nos. 7

and 8 (1932), by which time the transition from the sharp neo-classical style of
the works of the twenties to a more benign, flowing lyrical style, already hinted
at in Nos. 6 and 7, was well on the way to completion—though Milhaud has
never altogether abandoned the neo-classical style, to which he more than
occasionally returns, with excellent results, in movements generally marked

Ex. 30

'très animé', 'décidé', or 'rude'. These markings occur more often in finales than
in first movements, which tend to be less vigorous, and are more often marked
with a 'modéré' or some other indication of a gentler animation. This was already
true of the earlier quartets. The first movement of No. 5, despite the sharp
harmonic clashes, is marked 'chantant', and that of No. 6 'souple et animé'.
Similarly, that of No. 8 is 'vif et souple', and of No. 16 'tendre'.

After the seven-year gap, No. 8 marks the beginning of Milhaud's connexion
with the United States of America. Although written in France, it is dedicated
to the famous American patroness of chamber music, Mrs. Elizabeth Sprague
Coolidge. So are No. 9 (1935), also written in France, and No. 10, begun on
board ship in the Atlantic when Milhaud emigrated to America in 1940, and
completed in New York for Mrs. Coolidge's annual birthday concert in Washington. All three quartets show the same mixture of neo-classical detachment and

wit with expressive lyrical sweetness, demonstrated at its simplest in No. 9, in which Milhaud indulges his delight in thirds and sixths almost throughout. The same style persists in the first and third movements of No. 11 (1942) too, written in California for the twentieth anniversary of the League of Composers, and dedicated to the Budapest Quartet, but the second and last movements move more decisively away from it, the one a brilliant muted scherzo in 5/8 time (see Ex. 31), the other dominated in character by an almost ritornello-like recurring harmonic progression of harsh tonic-dominant clashes.

Ex. 31

No. 12 (1945) is rather richer and more complex in style, perhaps as a tribute to the subtlety of the art of Fauré, to whose memory it is dedicated 'à l'occasion du centenaire de sa naissance 1845–1945'. The first movement is unusual in that the main 'animé' section is preceded and followed by a short introduction and coda (modéré), which cast a certain influence over the central section, where Milhaud strikes a most successful balance of animation and lyricism. There is a slow movement harmonically more severe and less ingratiating than many, with a good deal of approximately parallel movement of two parts, in which the distance separating them fluctuates between consonant and dissonant intervals. The work concludes with a brisk movement of somewhat simpler harmonic character.

No. 13 (1946) is one of the few in the series in which the first movement is of the vigorous rhythmic type, bearing the marking 'très décidé'. Its slow movement is a flowing Barcarolle in 7/8 time, and its finale, marked 'Mexicana' (the work was written partly in Mexico), is similar in rhythmic character to the first movement, though less percussively dynamic. In Nos. 14 and 15 (1948–9), dedicated to Milhaud's friend and advocate Paul Collaer 'avec trente ans d'amitié', the composer has performed the tour de force of writing two thematically independent works capable of being played either separately or together as an Octet (in which form the score is published). The idea was suggested, according to Georges Beck, when Milhaud received one day a batch of 84 pages of music paper with the staves grouped in eights. So he wrote a double quartet, as it might more properly be called than Octet, to fill the 84 pages exactly. The most remarkable feat is the first movement, marked 'animé', where he consistently combines his smooth flowing style, in No. 14, with his vigorous detached style in No. 15 (see Ex. 32). There is a greater consistency of texture in the extended slow movement,

Ex. 32

parts of which give the effect of having been conceived as a unified octet, though there are also extended passages where the two quartets, while playing to the same time-signature and observing the same bar-lines, have completely different speeds of real rhythmic movement, based on different principal note-values. The welding together of the two quartets into a seemingly indivisible octet is achieved in the last movement, where although they are still thematically distinct, they now have the same vigorous rhythmic character, and their texture is bound together by melodic and rhythmic figurations echoed and answered from one to another, giving an effect of complete thematic unity.

Milhaud's remaining three quartets, Nos. 16 (1950), 17 (1950), and 18 (1950–1), appear to form a group, and are presumably intended to be his final contributions to this form. At the head of the score of No. 18 there appears the following inscription: ' "Je veux écrire dix-huit Quatuors"—D. M. *Le Coq* Juin 1920.' And at the end of the score is written: 'Fin des dix-huit quatuors à cordes 1912–1951.' To each of these last three quartets, written in quick succession within a year, Milhaud gave a family dedication. No. 16 is inscribed 'à Madeleine, pour le 25ᵉ anniversaire de notre mariage, 4 Mai 1925–4 Mai 1950'; No. 17 'à Daniel [the composer's son] pour ses vingt-et-un ans'; and No. 18 'à la douce mémoire de mes Parents'. These dedications explain the particularly personal character of much in the three works. In No. 16 the first movement, marked 'tendre', is in Milhaud's most intimate and affectionate singing style, which is also found again in the slow third movement, where he makes much use of his favourite parallel thirds (see Ex. 33). This tenderness is the prevailing charac-

Ex. 33

teristic of the quartet, despite the animation, gaiety, and energy of the other two movements (see Ex. 34). In No. 17 the emphasis is reversed. Here the slow

Ex. 34

movement is marked 'tendre', but merely provides a contrast to the prevailing strong vitality of the work. The first movement bears the marking 'rude', one that Milhaud had used for some of his most powerful and exciting music of the twenties, the aggressive dissonant harmonic energy of which is also recalled here, as though in writing for his son's attainment of maturity the composer had tried to recapture the style of his own bold early maturity (see Ex. 35). A similar tone is sustained in the last movement, marked 'robuste'. The scherzo, marked 'léger et cinglant', is a brilliant, highly rhythmical piece with constantly changing bar-lengths and irregular accents, in a crisp neo-classical style, containing a witty and masterly fugue (à quatre contresujets).

Ex. 35

Milhaud's final quartet is very different in form and general character from any of the others. The dedication postulates a work of a particularly intimate kind, and the quartet is clearly intended to be in the nature of an epilogue to the series. The two extended outer movements are both marked 'lent et doux', and form a frame to the two faster movements, entitled 'premier hymne' and 'deuxième hymne', both quick and gay, the one sharp and lively in rhythm, the other a swift but smooth 6/8 movement marked 'alerte'.

Having fulfilled his early ambition to write eighteen quartets, Milhaud has not returned to this form since 1951. In a series of interviews with him published under the title *Entretiens avec Claude Rostand* (Julliard, Paris, 1952), the questioner asks the composer if there was not some humour intended in his statement that he would like to write eighteen string quartets—'one more than Beethoven'. Milhaud does not deny it, but suggests that there was more to it than that.

But in my mind, it was a way of taking up the defence of chamber music at a period when it was being sacrificed to the esthetic of mass-produced music, to the esthetic of the music-hall and the circus. Obviously, however, for this declaration, I was upholding the sometimes rather aggressive tone that was expected in *Le Coq*.

Elsewhere in the same book he says:

I took part in too much chamber music in my youth—sonatas, trios, quartets—played with my father at home or with the quartet of my dear old Bruguier [Milhaud's first violin teacher], not to have retained the taste for it. And besides, it is a form, the quartet above all, that conduces to meditation, to the expression of what is deepest in oneself —and with means limited to four bows. It is perhaps not the most directly appealing genre, but it is very satisfying for its austerity, for its character as essentially a vehicle of pure music, and also for the economy of means to which one must adapt oneself. It is at once an intellectual discipline and the crucible of the most intense emotion.

The remainder of Milhaud's chamber music shows a greater diversity of style than the quartets, and a much greater diversity of aim. Since completing the eighteen quartets he had embarked on a series of quintets, each for a different combination. No. 1, for piano and strings (1951), was written for the centenary of Mills College (1951). It is a fairly short work, in which the four movements are marked 'Avec Vivacité', 'Avec Mystère', 'Avec Douceur', 'Avec Emporte-ment'. No. 2 (1952), for string quartet and double bass, in four movements, is one of a number of works commissioned by the University of Michigan from various composers for the Stanley Quartet. It is a work of great charm, fairly light and simple in style and transparent in texture to allow for the weight of tone in the ensemble of the double bass, the particular character of which has stimulated the composer's imagination to some witty and delightful, but not frivolous, harmonic and melodic invention. In No. 3 (1953), dedicated to the Griller Quartet, a second viola is added to the string quartet. This is a work of weightier content, in which two terse but substantial and vigorous movements of considerable harmonic severity enclose an extended and very expressive slow

Ex. 36

movement (in 5/8 time throughout) in Milhaud's lushest harmonic vein—the lushness slightly disguised, however, by the complexity of the texture (see Ex. 36). No. 4, with two 'cellos, was written in 1956, in memory of Honegger. Each of the four movements has a subtitle, as follows: 'Très modéré (Déplora-tion sur la mort d'un ami)'; 'Animé (Souvenirs de jeunesse)'; 'Assez lent (La douceur d'une longue amitié)'; 'Animé (Hymne de louanges)'.

Mention should be made here of two other quintets principally for strings: the Concert Suite in D (1926) from *La Création du monde*, for string quartet and piano, which is simply a transcription of the original jazzy ballet score; and the work called *Jacob's Dreams* (1949), for oboe, violin, viola, 'cello, and double bass. This also, according to the catalogue compiled by Georges Beck, was originally a 'suite chorégraphique' (danced by Ted Shawm), in which each of the five movements bore a descriptive title. In the published miniature score, however, no such indications appear, and the work is presumably meant to be listened to as a concert work without any detailed programme. Its choreographic nature is not at all evident, and the composer could equally well have dropped even the title and called it simply a quintet for oboe and strings, as which it makes a coherent and self-sufficient suite of varied and attractive movements such as might appear in any of his other quartets or quintets. Among his later works is a Sextet for strings (published 1959).

For smaller ensembles of strings there are the String Trio (1947), marked No. 1 but not yet followed by a second, several sonatinas—one each for string trio (1940), two violins (1940), violin and viola (1941), and violin and 'cello (1953) —and the Duo for two violins (1945). These are all attractive works of rather lighter calibre. The String Trio No. 1 is in five short movements—a pretty, strumming 'Serenade' in the centre, with an expressive slow movement on each side, and lively outer movements. Its general character is witty, slightly similar to that of the quartets Nos. 6 and 7, with a strong contrapuntal emphasis in the last two movements, the one headed 'Canon' and the other 'Jeu fugué'.

Of sonatas in the more traditional sense, for one instrument with piano, Milhaud has not added many to the early violin sonatas mentioned in **C**. The only other original one for this instrument is that with harpsichord accompaniment (1945), which is dedicated to Alexandre Schneider and Ralph Kirkpatrick and is published with Kirkpatrick's suggested registration. The keyboard part may, however, also be played on the piano. The general harmonic style of this serious and engaging work is crisp and sharp, with little hint of archaism except in a certain florid abundance of ornamentation in the writing. Where Milhaud has made an essay in the archaic style is in his free transcription (unpublished) for violin and piano of the '10ᵉ Sonate de Baptiste Anet' (originally composed 1729), and in the Viola Sonata No. 1 (1944), composed 'sur des thèmes inédits et anonymes du XVIIIᵉ Siècle', a work of similar character to Stravinsky's *Suite Italienne*. This was apparently a period of keen interest on Milhaud's part in the viola. Shortly before this Sonata, dedicated to Germain Prévost, he had written for the same player the *Quatre Visages* (1943) for viola and piano (representing the contrasting youthful faces of La Californienne, La Wisconsinian, La Bruxelloise, and La Parisienne), and a few months later he wrote a Sonata No. 2 (1944) for viola and piano, dedicated 'à la mémoire d'Alphonse Onnou'. A pastoral first movement is followed by a funeral march marked 'dramatique' and a vigorous finale marked 'rude', the strongest movement in one of Milhaud's less inspired works.

Like many modern composers, Milhaud has been attracted by the possibilities of the use of wind instruments in chamber music. These works are generally lighter, more divertimento-like in character, than those for strings, but there is a notable exception in the Sonatina for clarinet and piano (1927), one of his most exciting and harmonically fierce works of the late 1920's, terse and crisp, in the same mood as the Concerto for percussion and small orchestra from the same period, especially in its two outer movements, which, unusually in Milhaud, are thematically related, giving the Sonatina the effect of one extended movement with a slow middle section. Exx. 37 and 38 from the first and last movements

Ex. 37

Ex. 38

III   D

show this relationship, and the general style of the work. More recently (1956) Milhaud has written a short 'Duo Concertant' in one movement, for clarinet and piano.

The Sonatina for oboe and piano (1954) is more like the early one for flute in mood and character, light but substantial, gay, all 'charme et vivacité', as the first movement is marked. All three of these wind-instrument sonatinas are attractive works not only to play but also to hear, although they are inevitably restricted by their nature mainly to domestic use. Another work of a similar kind is the Suite (1936) for violin, clarinet, and piano, taken from the incidental music to Anouilh's *Le Voyageur sans bagages*, which makes an attractive modern companion for this particular ensemble to Bartók's *Contrasts* and Stravinsky's suite from *The Soldier's Tale*. The various works for wind instruments without piano are mainly of a similar calibre. The most important of them is *La Cheminée du Roi René* (1939), a suite of seven pieces for wind quintet, descriptive of aspects of Milhaud's native and beloved Aix-en-Provence in the fifteenth century. Similarly attractive but slighter is the Suite (d'après Corrette) for wind trio (1937), taken from the incidental music for a production of *Romeo and Juliet*, consisting of eight little movements in eighteenth-century style, based on themes by Michel Corrette. The Four Sketches (1941) for wind quintet (also arranged for clarinet and piano) are arrangements of pieces originally composed for orchestra. Among his more recent compositions is listed a 'Divertissement en trois parties' for wind quintet (1958).

Besides all these works for more or less traditional chamber-ensembles, Milhaud has written many others for larger or more unusual groups of instruments (sometimes with voice or voices), including numerous works originally written as, or derived from, incidental music. Most of these are unpublished, and therefore do not fall within the scope of this volume, but mention should perhaps be made of the score for *Le Château des Papes* (1932) for vocal quartet, ondes martenot, trumpet, and two pianos. From this the composer has arranged a fragment under the title 'Adages', for vocal quartet and eight instruments, which is published, and has also made a three-movement suite (Choral-Sérénade, Impromptu-Étude, and Élégie), for ondes martenot and piano (unpublished). There are also a '4th musical version' of *Protée*, for flute, bassoon, violin, and 'cello (1955), and a nonet, *The Joys of Life* (1958). Most of the bigger works are only on the fringe of chamber music, and properly require a conductor. The same applies to most of the vocal chamber music, from which, however, the *Quatre Poèmes de Catulle* (1923) for medium voice and violin may be singled out as a set of delightful terse songs in which, like Vaughan Williams in his song-cycle *Along the Field* and Holst in his Four Songs for voice and violin, Milhaud makes most effective and attractive use of an odd medium. Mention should also be made of the *Cantate de l'enfant et de la mère* (1938), for reciter, string quintet, and piano, written for the twenty-fifth anniversary of the concerts of the Pro Arte Quartet, and intended to bring them together with Paul Collaer as pianist and the composer's wife as reciter, in celebration of their long friendship. It is a serious and beautiful setting of poems by Maurice Carême, in Milhaud's most intimate personal style.

Equal in importance, though much smaller in quantity, is the chamber music of HONEGGER (**C**, d. 1955), whose most important later works in this field were his String Quartets Nos. 2 and 3, completed in 1936 and 1937 respectively. (The second quartet listed in **C** did not exist at that time, and was not begun until 1934.) In addition to these works Honegger wrote a Sonatina for violin and 'cello (1932) and a Sonata for violin unaccompanied.

Both the later quartets adhere to the three-movement form of the first quartet, and the emotional character and relationship of the movements in both are similar to those observed by M. Godet in his account of No. 1 in **C**. A high expressive intensity is combined with close thematic and formal concentration. A broad ternary structure, generally sonata-like, is found in nearly every movement, and the subjects are often combined in the reprise. The slow movement of No. 2 is the most conspicuous example, in which the opening theme, shown in Ex. 39, is accompanied in the recapitulation by the agitated rhythmic motive of the middle section (𝄽). Similarly, in the slow movement of No. 3 the recapitulation brings back simultaneously elements originally presented separ-

Ex. 39

(Two violins continue *ostinato*, cello tacet)

ately, as introduction and first theme respectively. Both of these movements have something of the character of a cavatina or aria, though in thematic development and complexity of texture they go beyond the normal range of either. In the two first movements there is again some resemblance of form. The main thematic material in both is recapitulated roughly in reverse, though in No. 3 it continues to undergo development as well throughout this section. Exx. 40 and 41, the opening bars of the two movements, illustrate the strong rhythmic definition of Honegger's themes, and Ex. 42, from No. 3, shows another no less sharply defined theme in a later section of the exposition. Nearly all Honegger's themes in these works have equal rhythmic distinction, and reveal an outstanding inventiveness in the creation of contrasting rhythms within the same metre. He seeks unity by the combination of themes rather than in any motivic relation-ship between them, and when they are combined each retains its original rhyth-mic and melodic identity. In the working out of the material there is often some

Ex. 40

Ex. 41

Ex. 42

use of formal counterpoint, usually canon, which is very prominent in the String Quartet No. 3, both in the first movement and in the last. The last movements in both quartets are formally complex. In No. 2 the principal elements are a gigue-like 12/8 rhythm, which is kept up almost throughout, and an assertive, contrasting rhythm ( ) which is set against it as a second theme early in the exposition. The lengthy development includes a restatement of the opening theme, giving a suggestion of rondo form, and also introduces, in the gigue rhythm, the opening violin melody of the first movement. This seems to be intended as a passing witticism rather than as a significant 'cyclic' connexion. The last movement of No. 3, which is closely similar in form, is an exuberant contrapuntal piece, the main themes of which are shown in Exx. 43 and 44, both from the final section. In Ex. 44 the opening theme, originally announced

Ex. 43

Ex. 44

in crotchets, appears in augmentation and in canon, with contrapuntal imitations at different speeds in the two inner parts. Ex. 43 combines the second and third themes of the movement, both in quasi-canonic imitation. Earlier in the movement they have been heard separately, the second theme (on the first violin in the fragment quoted) in canon there also, and both against a quaver-ostinato derived from the opening theme.

The Sonatina for violin and 'cello is a lighter work, nearer to the character of the earlier Sonatina for two violins (1920), with an urbane, neo-classical opening 'Allegro' and a boisterous last movement with a lively theme that is almost perpetually present. The middle movement is designed on the same formal principle as the middle movements of the two quartets, ingeniously varied. It is a ternary form, in which the first section is a lyrical 'Andante', the second (doppio movimento) a 'Scherzando', and the third a variation on and recapitulation of the two sections simultaneously, at the 'Andante' tempo, with the rhythmic units of the 'Scherzando' halved to preserve the original speed of movement.

In addition to these works Honegger wrote *Trois Contrepoints* (1922), comprising a 'Prélude à 2 voix' (oboe and 'cello), 'Choral à 3 voix' (cor anglais, violin, and 'cello), and 'Canon sur basse obstinée à 4 voix' (piccolo, cor anglais, violin, 'cello); and a 'Petite Suite pour 2 instruments et piano' (1934).

The third important member of the original 'Les Six', POULENC (d. 1963), in his last thirty years, and more particularly after 1939, wrote several chamber works of rather more weight than any of the early works described by Edwin Evans in C. These included a Sextet for flute, oboe, clarinet, horn, bassoon, and piano (1932–9), sonatas for violin (1942–3), 'cello (1948), and flute (1957), all with piano, and an Elegy for horn and piano (1957) composed in memory of Dennis Brain. Most of these works are in Poulenc's more serious style, though to non-French ears the extreme sweetness of the harmony (sometimes straight out of Franck) and melody may seem incongruous. This is particularly so in the Violin Sonata, which was written 'à la mémoire de Federico Garcia Lorca 1899–1936'. This was composed in 1942–3 and revised in 1949, when a new version of the last movement was made. There are three movements, of which the first is marked 'Allegro con fuoco' and the last 'Presto tragico'. Between them comes an Intermezzo with the superscription 'La guitare fait pleurer les songes' (a quotation from Lorca, and an allusion to his own accompaniment of himself on the guitar in Spanish folk-songs). This is the most successful of the three. In the outer movements the 'fuoco' and the 'tragico' of the markings can hardly be reconciled with the very lyrical style and content of the music. A point of interest is the rather free and unsymmetrical form of all three movements.

A work of similar intention and character is the Elegy for horn and piano in memory of Dennis Brain, which appears to have been influenced, both technically and emotionally, by Britten's Canticle No. 3 (see p. 98). It begins with a twelve-note melody (Très calme) for the horn unaccompanied, followed by a questioning theme (Agitato molto) characterized by a hammering figure of repeated semiquavers. After a repetition of these two short sections in slightly varied form, a serenely flowing elegiac melodic line, distantly derived from the opening twelve-note theme, begins to take shape, and is sustained to the end, with one brief allusion to the repeated-note figure, and a cadence consisting of a final twelve-note statement on the horn over a unison C on the piano, resolving, or rather not resolving, on to a chord of C major with the minor seventh added. The general mood and style of the piece are very close to those of Poulenc's opera *The Carmelites*, and despite the sweetness of the music it is affecting in the same way.

A third 'memorial' work, the Sonata for flute and piano, written in memory of Mrs. Elizabeth Sprague Coolidge, is emotionally less ambitious, and is more in the nature of an 'hommage' than of an elegy. It is more neo-classical in character and generally light and witty in content and manner, despite the marking of the first movement 'Allegro malincolico'. Ex. 45 shows the opening theme. This movement is formally remarkable in that such development as there is happens within the exposition of the first subject. The first appearance of the second subject is followed immediately by a very condensed recapitulation of both subjects. The second movement is an attractively sentimental 'Cantilena', the piano part of which is characteristically marked 'doucement baigné de pédale', and the last movement a 'Presto giocoso' which contains allusions to both subjects of the first movement. The Sonata for 'cello and piano is more expansive, in four movements on a large scale, very sweet and lyrical in tone, and more romantic

Ex. 45

than the Flute Sonata, without the 'tragic' passion of the Violin Sonata. It was sketched in 1940, completed in 1948, and the published score is marked 'New corrected edition 1953'. The four movements are 'Allegro—tempo di marcia'; 'Cavatine'; 'Ballabile—très animé et gai' ('Ballabile' means, in effect, 'dance-like'); and 'Largo', leading to 'Presto'. Ex. 46 shows the beginning of the main tune in the middle section of the third movement.

Ex. 46

The Sextet is nearer in style, as in date, to his more frivolous early works, with a vein of sentimentality. There are three movements, of which the middle one, headed 'Divertissement', is in simple ternary form, with a faster middle section. Its first phrase of melody echoes the opening phrase of Mozart's C major Piano Sonata K. 545. The outer movements are characteristically free in form, though there is a gesture of recapitulation in the first, and certain melodic and rhythmic shapes, freely varied, recur throughout the work.

Of the lesser members of 'Les Six', AURIC has written a Sonata for violin and piano and a Trio for oboe, clarinet, and bassoon.

Contemporary with 'Les Six' was Jacques Ibert (**C**, d. 1962), who had much in common with them—as did also the slightly younger Henri Sauguet (b. 1901). IBERT's most important chamber work is a String Quartet, which is marked on the title-page 'MCMXLIV', and on the last page 'Rome–Antibes (1937–1942)'. It is an attractive work with a characteristically French mixture of wit and sentiment, and a satisfying weight of content and depth of interest. The first movement has exercise-like C major neo-classical figurations, an easy tune, and an inventive development; the second is a lush and richly harmonized 'Andante' in ternary song form, the third a scherzo (presto), pizzicato throughout, and the fourth a fugal sonata-rondo of rather grittier substance than the rest. In addition to this quartet Ibert has written numerous works for various wind ensembles.

A String Quartet (No. 2) is SAUGUET's most important chamber work also (No. 1 appears to be discarded or unpublished). Written in 1947–8, and dedicated 'A la mémoire chérie de ma mère', it is a pleasing work, of unpretentious charm and sweetness, with a more deeply expressive slow movement that within the innocent idiom of the work as a whole is harmonically arresting. There is also an attractive Trio for oboe, clarinet, and bassoon (1946), of lighter character.

In the generation following 'Les Six', a group of four young composers— Olivier Messiaen (b. 1908), André Jolivet (b. 1905), Yves Baudrier (b. 1906), and Daniel-Lesur (b. 1908)—decided to form a school, known as 'La Jeune France', the ideals of which were opposed to those of 'Les Six'. Rejecting the ideals of detachment and neo-classicism, they wanted to restore emotional expressiveness and intensity to French music. Like 'Les Six', the group did not long retain its unity, nor did its members all keep pace. MESSIAEN rapidly emerged as the most important. He has written relatively few chamber works: *La Mort du Nombre*, for soprano, tenor, violin, and piano (1930), Theme and Variations for violin and piano (1932), Fantasy for violin and piano (1933), the *Quatuor pour la Fin du Temps* (1941), and *Le Merle Noir* for flute and piano (1952). The most important of these is the quartet, scored for violin, clarinet, 'cello, and piano, written while the composer was a war-prisoner, and first performed, with himself playing the piano, in Stalag VIII, on 15 January 1941. The published score contains a long preface by the composer, beginning with a condensed quotation of the first six verses from Chapter X of the Revelation of St. John ('And I saw another mighty angel come down from heaven', &c.), which was the direct inspiration of the work. This is followed by some general observations on the plan of the work, a commentary on each of its eight movements, a brief exposition of the theory of Messiaen's musical language, and some general instructions for the performers. The commentary, which is too long to quote, is in effect an outline of the religious 'programme' of the work, and is essential to a proper understanding and appreciation of it. For this the reader must be referred to the published score. The following comments are offered by way of a supplementary and more formal description.

First movement: 'Liturgie de Cristal.' Clarinet and violin both play florid lines 'comme un oiseau' over an ostinato progression of 29 chords, repeated five times, on the piano, and a five-note ostinato (on a whole-tone scale) in harmonics on the 'cello (see Ex. 47). At the fourth rotation of the chord-sequence the third chord is omitted, and a final sixth rotation is cut short after the first 23 chords.

Ex. 47

Second movement: 'Vocalise, pour l'Ange qui annonce la fin du Temps.' A ternary movement, the outer parts representing the might and grandeur of the Angel, the middle part the 'impalpable harmonies of the heavens', with a plainsong-like melody on the two string instruments, in unison and muted, accompanied by pianissimo cascades of chords representing drops of water in a rainbow (see Ex. 48). The brief third part recapitulates only the coda to the first part, inverted.

Third movement: 'Abîme des Oiseaux.' A ternary movement for solo clarinet, in which the outer sections are a slow melody, marked 'désolée', and the middle section is another bird-song episode, marked 'gai, capricieux'. The movement ends with a very brief variant of the coda to the middle section.

Ex. 48

Fourth movement: 'Intermède.' A scherzo, without piano, in a rondo-like arch form, described by the composer as 'de caractère plus extérieur que les autres mouvements, mais rattaché à eux, cependant, par quelques "rappels" mélodiques'. This movement was the first to be composed, and was originally performed in the prison camp as a separate piece. The rest of the work was built round it when Messiaen was asked by his fellow prisoners to write more.

Fifth movement: 'Louange à l'Éternité de Jésus.' 'Cello and piano alone. A ternary melody for the 'cello, with varied and condensed reprise, accompanied by very slow, sweet chords on the piano.

Sixth movement: 'Danse de la fureur, pour les sept trompettes.' A movement

Ex. 49

of elaborate formal and metrical construction, for all four instruments in unison throughout, to suggest the sound of gongs and trumpets. Ex. 49 shows the opening theme, with its curious metrical divisions.

Seventh movement: 'Fouillis d'arcs-en-ciel, pour l'Ange qui annonce la fin du

'Temps.' A still more elaborate arch-like form, with thematic references to the first, second, and sixth movements.

Eighth movement: 'Louange à l'Immortalité de Jésus.' Violin and piano alone. This is closely similar in character to the fifth movement. A binary movement with a very sweet melody on the violin, marked 'expressif, paradisiaque', accompanied by equally sweet chords on the piano. The movement is in two 'stanzas', which begin identically and diverge half-way through.

A violin melody of similar character appears as an obbligato to a soprano aria in the final section of the very early cantata *La Mort du Nombre*, accompanied by harmonies already characteristic of the later Messiaen. The soprano aria is preceded by a tenor recitative, with two brief interruptions by the soprano and two unaccompanied phrases contributed by the violin.

There is much also in the Theme and Variations for violin and piano that is characteristic of his mature music. Its not quite square 28-bar melody, constructed on the AABA[1] pattern, in four 'lines' of 7, 7, 6, and 8 bars respectively, and the fairly close adherence to the shape of the theme in the five variations, mark it as still to some degree a student work, though a highly accomplished and effective one, and an unusual contribution to the violin and piano repertory. Exx. 50*a* and *b* show 'lines' A and B of the theme. The Fantasy of the following year for the same combination remains unpublished.

Ex. 50A

Ex. 50B

Le Merle Noir (i.e. The Blackbird), for flute and piano, is a test-piece written for the Concours du Conservatoire National de Musique. Its form is somewhat enigmatic. An exposition in four short sections is immediately recapitulated, with the last two sections transposed, sonata fashion. Then follows an extended coda consisting of bird-like cadenzas for the flute, with an elaborate accompaniment consisting of a twelve-note series and its simultaneous retrograde inversion, repeated four times, rising in pitch by a semitone each time, followed by a repetition of the whole process with the twelve-note counterpoint inverted. The pianist is directed to keep the sustaining pedal down throughout this section.

The other three members of the 'Jeune France' group have not achieved Messiaen's international recognition. Their early ideals are well exemplified in André JOLIVET's String Quartet, written in 1934, two years before the group was formed. It is a very emotional work, of complex, eclectic atonal harmony. Some idea of its harmonic style is given in this quotation from the English fore-word to the published score:

André Jolivet's Quartet thus unfolds the stages of a veritable tournament, musically depicted by the struggle between an essentially rational, sound and strong interval, the perfect fifth, and its rival, the augmented fifth, radiating a magic power—a rival which is derived from the former, and yet in utter contrast as to its character, as if there were no kinship between the two. The fight is not anarchical, but rationally organized.

The central slow movement, according to the same note, 'consists of two chorals, which are respectively focussed on each of the two antagonistic chords'. In the last movement there is some clarification of harmony and texture, and also of form, the outlines of a rondo being more clearly discernible here than the formal principle of the first movement, which is obscured by the continuous thematic variation.

Jolivet's other chamber music includes a Serenade for wind quintet (1945), which is unusual in that the oboe is treated as a soloist (the work is also published in a version for oboe and piano). This is in a lighter and simpler style, as is suggested by the titles of its four movements (Cantilène, Caprice, Intermède, Marche Burlesque). In addition Jolivet has written a suite of *Pastorales de Noël*, for flute, bassoon, and harp, and a *Suite Liturgique*, for voice, cor anglais (doubling oboe), 'cello, and harp.

Of the same generation as the 'Jeune France' group is Jean FRANÇAIX (b. 1912), who writes light neo-classical music belonging to the same tradition as Sauguet's, Ibert's, and the early music of 'Les Six'. Among his chamber works are a String Quartet, String Trio, Wind Quintet, various works for other wind ensembles, a Quintet for flute, harp, and strings, and sonatinas for violin and for trumpet, both with piano.

The most prominent of the younger French composers, Pierre BOULEZ (b. 1925), has published no instrumental chamber music except an early Sonata for flute and piano (1946). His extended work for string quartet, the *Livre pour Quatuor*, is still in progress, and is not yet published. The Flute Sonata is percussively vehement and complex in style, in a single-movement form with faint traces of traditional outlines. The exposition consists of a slow introduction, a short quick theme, a slow 'second subject' with sustained trills almost through-out, another quick section marked 'Scherzando, avec humeur', and a coda alluding to the second subject and the introduction. A long development at the 'Scherzando' tempo follows, interrupted half-way through by references to the earlier material of the exposition. There is a short coda which recapitulates a few bars from the beginning and end of the exposition. The note-series on which the work is based contains several short thematic motives of similar shape, which help to give coherence to the perpetually varied and fragmentary texture. So also do the long trills in the 'second subject', which is an almost traditional musical conception. Ex. 51 shows a fragment from this section, and also one of the main serial melodic motives of the work.

Ex. 51

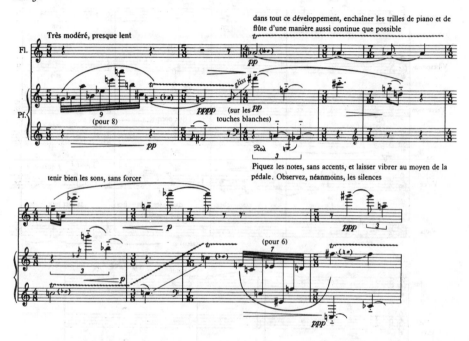

In Boulez's later work the nearest he comes to chamber music is in the three cantatas (*Le Marteau sans Maître* and the two *Improvisations sur Mallarmé*—'Le vierge, le vivace et le bel aujourd'hui' and 'Une dentelle s'abolit') with accompaniments for differing small and unusual instrumental ensembles, each including an elaborate percussion group.

Among the remarkable features of these works, which have aroused something of the same intense interest and controversy as were aroused forty years earlier by Schoenberg's *Pierrot Lunaire*, is their very distinctive tone quality. The sound comparatively rarely goes below the tenor range, and the general pitch level is unusually high. This applies particularly to *Le Marteau sans Maître* (1954), for contralto, flute in G, xylorimba, vibraphone, guitar, viola, and a large percussion section for a single player. The characteristic sound quality of this work has been described by Stravinsky as 'like ice cubes clicking together in a glass'. The slight monotony of tone-colour resulting from the limitation of pitch-range, and from the sparing use of sustained sounds, is largely offset by the great variety of detail

in the scoring. Each of the nine movements is scored for a different combination
of instruments, and the full ensemble comes into play only in the sixth movement (where the percussion player, however, uses only the maracas) and the last
movement, where more of the percussion instruments are used, including the

Ex. 52

deep gongs, which have been silent throughout all the preceding movements.
Purely as sound, this last movement, with its sonorous, crisp concerted chords
and deep notes of the gong, is a wonderfully effective and exciting tonal conclusion.
Ex. 52 shows the beginning of this movement.

There are four vocal movements (the third, fifth, sixth and ninth movements), of which the first and third are 'The Raging Artisan' ('L'artisanat furieux') and 'Executioners of Solitude' ('Bourreaux de Solitude'), and the second and fourth different settings of the same poem, 'Fine Building and Foreboding' ('Bel édifice et les pressentiments'). These four movements stand out clearly as real songs, with an angularly florid but singable and dominating vocal line. The third of them, a sustained slow movement which seems to be the emotional climax of the work, is the most immediately communicative and compelling of the nine movements.

The remaining five movements are all related, at least by title, to these songs. The first and seventh are headed respectively 'Before' and 'After "The Raging Artisan"', and the second, fourth, and eighth are all called 'Commentary on "Executioners of Solitude"'. The thematic and formal relationships that these titles seem to indicate are to say the least elusive, and the enigmatic poems by René Char, which might be described as examples of 'socialist surrealism', provide few clues to extra-musical relationships that might helpfully be followed up.

Although the importance and originality of the work have been widely acknowledged, no commentator has yet come forward with a detailed study or elucidation of its musical content or structure. Among its admirers is Stravinsky, who in an interview with Robert Craft, published in 1957, said: 'It will be a considerable time before the value of Le Marteau sans Maître is recognised. Meanwhile I shall not explain my admiration for it but adapt Gertrude Stein's answer when asked why she liked Picasso's paintings: "I like to look at them"—I like to listen to Boulez.' Among the features of the work that particularly attracted Stravinsky's attention was the continuous fluctuation of tempo in certain sections, 'where you are never in a tempo but always going to one'. Stravinsky considered this 'an important innovation . . . able to effect a new and wonderfully supple kind of music'. Similar rhythmic devices occur in 'Une dentelle s'abolit', where the composer has devised an improved notation for them. In this work there are also certain passages where the tempo is determined by the length of breath of the singer, who is directed to sing prescribed phrases 'aussi lent que possible sans respirer'.

ITALY

Chamber music in Italy has lost rather than gained ground since C was published. The notable works written by Pizzetti, G. F. Malipiero, and Casella (d. 1947) in the 1920's have had few successors from them, and fewer still from the two outstanding younger composers, Dallapiccola and Petrassi (both b. 1904). Malipiero has carried the flag, not very high, with his seven string quartets and a number of other works, nearly all of which have been dedicated to Mrs. Elizabeth Sprague Coolidge—possibly out of gratitude for the award of the Coolidge Prize to his first quartet Rispetti e Strambotti (not to his second, as stated in C), which established his reputation in this field. Most of the Italian chamber music composed by those of his generation owes its existence to the inspiration or encouragement of Mrs. Coolidge rather than to any native interest in the medium. Pizzetti's Piano Trio (1925), briefly referred to in **C**, and his String Quartet No. 2 (1932–3), his only subsequent chamber work, were both written at her request, as was Casella's Sonata in C major for 'cello and piano (1927). Casella's Serenade (1927) was written for a competition run by the Musical Fund Society of Philadelphia (in which it shared the first prize with Bartók's Third Quartet), and his Sinfonia, op. 53 (1932), at the request of the League of· Composers of New York for the tenth anniversary of the League. Only his 'Sonata a tre' (1938) was written to an Italian commission, for the Venice Festival. Of the younger composers Dallapiccola has written only two works for violin and piano, apart from numerous sets of songs with mixed instrumental accompaniment, and Petrassi attempted no major work of chamber music proper until his String Quartet in 1958 (although he had written two earlier concertante works for solo instruments and chamber orchestra). Since the Quartet he has written a Serenade for five players and a String Trio, also both to foreign commissions.

The senior of these composers, PIZZETTI, whose most important work has been operatic and vocal, has written no chamber music since 1932. The only additions to the list of his works in **C** are the *Tre Canti* for 'cello and piano (1924), which has also been transcribed for violin and piano, and the String Quartet in D (1932–3). The Piano Trio, then quite recent and referred to there only in a footnote, is expansively lyrical in character, sensitively written, and finely shaped. There is a curious and effective rhythmic feature in the last movement (headed 'Rapsodia di Settembre'), where at the beginning the parts of the two string instruments are barred in 3/2 and marked 'calmo e contemplativo', while the piano part has the time-signature 3/4 × 3 and is marked 'Vivace (non presto)'. As the movement progresses the rhythmic differences gradually become blurred, though the distinctive opening quaver motive in the piano part remains almost exclusive to the pianist. A beautiful coda (larghissimo) restores the rhythmic contrast again in new terms.

The String Quartet No. 2 is not so purely lyrical in conception. Although the actual musical material remains basically lyrical, there is a certain deliberate, almost 'academic', severity in the mainly contrapuntal working out of it, which, despite the extended scale of the work, is consistently 'thematic', with very little. rhapsodic digression in the traditional and straightforward forms of the four movements. A 'classical' inclination is also evident in the prominent use of the BACH motive, which opens the first movement (see Ex. 53) and becomes the predominant thematic element of the last movement. Ex. 54 shows a de-chromaticized appearance of it (against an accompaniment thick with allusions to the original chromatic motive) towards the end of the last movement, before the final resolution into the broad D major chorale-like coda. Among the other conspicuous features of the work, which is described on the title-page as 'in D', is the modal flexibility. The key-signature is as often D minor (or D Aeolian) as D major, and in the coda to the last movement the Mixolydian C natural is prominent, and is persisted in by the 'cello almost to the last bar. In the 'Adagio', which is in sonata form without a development section, the first and second subjects appear in the unfriendly keys of F sharp major and its enharmonic relative minor.

Ex. 53

Ex. 54

MALIPIERO's seven string quartets are unusual in formal conception. Most of them, and of his other chamber works, are in one-movement form, and many of them have slightly enigmatic titles. Those of the first two quartets (**C**), *Rispetti e Strambotti* and *Stornelli e Ballate*, refer to poetic forms. In the preface to No. 2 the composer wrote that this work was the continuation of the *Rispetti e Strambotti*, and the same might easily be said of all the later ones. No. 3 (1931) is called *Cantari alla Madrigalesca*, and No. 6 (1947) bears the title *L'Arca di Noé* (Noah's Ark) without further elucidation. The title of No. 5, *Dei Capricci*, is explained by its consisting of sections intended for string quartet in the original (and abandoned) chamber-orchestral version of Malipiero's comic opera *I Capricci di Callot*, which was written in 1942. Presumably it is because the

III   E

material was composed then that the quartet version is numbered the fifth in the series, although the score bears the date 1950—i.e. three years later than No. 6. The only two quartets without titles are No. 4 (1934) and No. 7 (1950). Although not divided into so many separate short sections as the first two quartets, the later ones follow a similar formal principle. They are episodic and rhapsodic, with little recurrence or development of the material. In No. 4 a rhythmic transformation of the opening theme provides the subject of a short fugato near the end, followed by a coda which gives a thematic résumé of the work. In No. 5 the opening 26 bars are repeated exactly at the end, and in No. 6 each of the three main sections ends with the same 6 bars, at a different pitch each time.

Similar formal methods are found in Malipiero's other chamber works, which include a quartet entitled *Epodi e Giambi* (again poetic forms) for violin, oboe, viola, and bassoon (1932), a 'Sonata a cinque' (1934) for flute (or violin), violin, viola, 'cello, and harp (or piano), *Dialogo No. 4* for wind quintet (1956), 'Sonata a quattro' (1954) for flute, oboe, clarinet, and bassoon, 'Sonata a tre' (1928) for piano trio, and the Sonata for 'cello and piano (1942), in which a hazy ternary outline is perceptible. The 'Sonata a tre' is unusual in that the first movement is for 'cello and piano alone, the second for violin and piano alone, and only the third for all three instruments. All three movements are subdivided into several sections at different tempi, and there is some recapitulation in the third movement of material from the other two. On the fringe of chamber music there are the *Ricercari* (1925) and its sequel the *Ritrovari* (1926), both for eleven instruments, and each in five movements.

Despite the initial success of *Rispetti e Strambotti*, neither this work nor any of its successors in Malipiero's output has won a place in the repertory. Technically they are easy by modern standards, and musically unproblematic except in their elusiveness of form, but the lack of melodic or other idiomatic distinction in their easy-going flow of counterpoint so heavily outweighs these advantages that they have not commended themselves either to professional or to amateur players.

CASELLA's later chamber works, though fewer in number, are more varied and more stimulating. They comprise the Sonata in C major for piano and 'cello (the instruments are given in that order on the title-page), composed in 1927 and listed in C without comment, the Serenade for five instruments, composed in the same year, the Sinfonia, op. 53, for four instruments (1932), and the 'Sonata a tre' for piano trio (1938). A 'Barcarolle and Scherzo' for flute and piano (1904) should also be added to the list. In the 'Cello Sonata he returns to the seventeenth-century conception of the form, with four movements in two, each half consisting of a slow section followed by a fast. The opening 'Preludio' (Largo molto e sostenuto) leads straight into a lively 'Bourrée', and the slow movement (Largo) similarly into the final 'Rondo quasi "giga" '. It is one of the purest and most successful examples of the neo-classical style, very simple and clearly defined in tonality but with many overlappings of the diatonic harmonies. The idiom and style of the work are somewhere between those of Stravinsky's *Suite Italienne* and 'Duo Concertant'. The formal outlines are traditional, but as usual in Casella are blurred by the sketchiness and freedom of the recapitulations. The 'Bourrée' is a rather elaborate sonata-rondo in which after the second statement of the theme and second episode the three sections of the exposition are recapitulated in reverse order. Ex. 55 shows the entry of the 'cello in the third movement.

Ex. 55

The Serenade is lighter in character. When the jury awarded it the prize in the Philadelphia competition they praised it as 'an authentic model of purely Italian style in fŏrm and spirit, and in its characteristically continuous melodic flow'. It is scored for clarinet, bassoon, trumpet, violin, and 'cello, and is in six movements (March, Minuet, Nocturne, Gavotte, Cavatina, and Finale 'alla napoletana'). In the 'Gavotte' only the wind instruments play and in the 'Cava-

Ex. 56

tina' only the strings. The predominant tone of the work is gay and humorous. Ex. 56 from the first movements illustrates the style.

The Sinfonia is a curiously designed work in two linked movements (Largo solenne–Allegro molto vivace) which seem more like the last two movements of a sonata than a self-sufficient 'introduction and allegro'. In the first movement a slow, weighty contrapuntal theme for the full ensemble alternates quasi-antiphonally with more decorative passages on the piano. The quick movement is a short, light rondo.

The 'Sonata a tre' is similar in character and idiom to the Sonata for 'cello and piano, and ends, like that work, with a movement in 'Tempo di Giga'. In his autobiography *Music in My Time*, Casella says that he had been putting off the composition of a work in this medium for twenty years. He solves the difficult problem of reconciling the piano and strings 'by giving an almost exclusively lyric function to the strings, and leaving to the piano an almost purely rhythmic and harmonic assignment. The form continues and develops that of the last works, essentially constructive and architectonic, always based on the interior logic of the musical discourse.' There are three fairly extended movements, the second of which opens with a canonic twelve-note idea, abandoned after a few bars.

Goffredo PETRASSI did not write any chamber music proper until he was past fifty, although he has three earlier works which are near to it—the 'Introduction and Allegro' for violin and eleven instruments (1933), the 'Sonata da Camera' for harpsichord and ten instruments (1948), and the short *Dialogo Angelico* for two flutes (1948). His String Quartet (1958) is in an extended single movement (23 minutes) in four main sections, of elusive form. It opens with a short melodic phrase for all four instruments in unison (Ex. 57), which is a quasi-serial melodic

Ex. 57

source for much of the work. The first three notes, inverted in the following three, and the first four notes, of which the last four are a slightly rearranged retrograde inversion, are the most prominent motives. In the first section the whole theme appears twice, in extreme augmentation and divided among the instruments, as a solo melody in a decorative chromatic texture. In this form it is the principal theme of a kind of sonata-structure, the smaller motives playing an important part in the development section. This is followed by two short sections in which new material is presented and the opening theme is abandoned —first an 'allegretto' dominated by the interval of the minor sixth, then an agitated and rhythmically dramatic 'presto', which leads into a new section marked 'vigoroso'. Here the basic motives of Ex. 57 come to the surface again in the thematic material, expounded in a free fugue. Finally, the tempo subsides to 'adagio', and the harmony and melody clear to a near-diatonic simplicity. Ex. 58 (which contains all twelve notes) is treated serially in an intricate canon which uses all four forms of the series, and the quartet ends with a strong suggestion of a perfect cadence in D flat major.

The Serenade for flute, viola, double bass, harpsichord, and percussion (1958), commissioned by the Basle section of the ISCM for their thirtieth anniversary, is also in one movement, and similar in structure, though on a smaller scale (14 minutes). It opens with a cadenza-like exposition for flute, and as in the String Quartet the first six notes, consisting here too of a three-note motive

Ex. 58

followed by its near-inversion (see Ex. 59), are thematically important throughout. After a middle section in which new material is presented, the viola, double bass, and harpsichord each have a cadenza in turn before the coda. Instrumental colour and effects, including flutter-tonguing and col legno, play an important

Ex. 59

part in the work. The flute is also directed in several places to play a sustained note with precisely marked undulating dynamics (see Ex. 60). There are faint

Ex. 60

neo-classical associations not only in the employment of the harpsichord (the piano is not suggested in the score as an alternative) but also in the figuration for it and to some extent in the general texture. The percussion instruments used are small cymbal, small tom-tom, temple block, triangle, and crotales.

Similar formal and technical methods characterize the String Trio (1959), commissioned by the Elizabeth Sprague Coolidge Foundation, in which the opening four-note motive again pervades the work. In this case it is a strictly diatonic one, EDGA, though a chromatically compressed variant of it, in the form of the BACH motive and its permutations, also conspicuously appears. As in the Serenata there are cadenzas (though here concerted ones) for the three players, and the scoring abounds in 'effects'. Like both of Petrassi's other chamber works it is in a single movement, though the various central episodes are fairly clearly differentiated into what might have been called scherzo, chorale, and recitative.

DALLAPICCOLA has written only two instrumental chamber works, both for violin and piano—the Two Studies (1946–7), which like Petrassi's Serenade was commissioned for a concert of the Basle section of the I.S.C.M., and the *Tartiniana Seconda* (1956). The Two Studies also exist in a modified and expanded version as Two Pieces for Orchestra, and the *Tartiniana Seconda* is also arranged, to conform with his earlier *Tartiniana* (1951), for violin and chamber orchestra.

The first of the Two Studies is a Sarabande in simple ternary form, based on a twelve-note series announced at the beginning by the violin unaccompanied (Ex. 61). Throughout the exposition, which adheres strictly to the classical

Ex. 61

sarabande rhythm, the violin melody is confined to increasingly florid but simple variants of the series. In the middle section a different melodic series is introduced (see Ex. 62) and the rhythm is varied. Two brief canonic allusions are

Ex. 62

made to the original theme. In the reprise the material of the exposition is condensed and the order of events reversed. The second study is headed 'Fanfara e Fuga', and is based on the same series as the middle part of the Sarabande (Ex. 63). The fugal working is close and intensive, but straightforward and clear. In the last five bars the main theme of the Sarabande is emphatically restated.

Ex. 63

The *Tartiniana Seconda*, a divertimento in four movements (Pastorale, Tempo di Bourrée, Presto, Variazioni), is a free adaptation of material by Tartini, with added (and sometimes very dissonant) counterpoints and accompaniments.

Dallapiccola's only other chamber works are the various groups of songs with mixed instrumental accompaniment, similar in conception (and sometimes in their brevity) to Webern's numerous groups of chamber-music songs. Among them are the Five Songs for baritone and eight instruments (1956), the six *Goethe-Lieder* for mezzo-soprano and three clarinets (1953), and Two Lyrics of Anacreon, with accompaniment for two clarinets, viola, and piano (1945). In this work the first song is a series of canons, in two, three, and four parts, on a lyrical twelve-note theme entirely of small intervals, and the second a set of variations on a contrasting, vehement twelve-note theme, with large intervals and consecutive melodic leaps, taken from the composer's earlier song-cycle, Five Fragments from Sappho for voice and chamber orchestra (1942). He quotes this same theme also near the beginning of the *Sex Carmina Alcaei*, for voice and eleven instruments (1943). These songs, dedicated to Webern on his sixtieth birthday, are described on the title-page in Latin: 'Canones diversi, motu recto contrarioque, simplices ac duplices, cancrizantes, etc., super seriem unam tonorum duodecim.' An earlier work, 'Divertimento in quattro esercizi' (1934) for soprano, flute (piccolo), oboe, clarinet, viola, and 'cello, is in the neo-classical vein of Casella, to whom it is dedicated. The four movements are: Introduction (Recitative), Arietta, Bourrée, Siciliana.

Among the younger Italian composers the outstanding contributors to chamber music are Luciano Berio (b. 1925) and Riccardo Malipiero (b. 1914). BERIO has written a single-movement String Quartet (1955), with spare but attractive thematic material, euphoniously treated in a relatively simple post-Webernian manner, with frequent echoes of traditional harmony, and scored with many imaginative effects of instrumental colour. The same is true of his triptych of songs, *Chamber Music* (1953), a setting of poems by James Joyce for female voice, clarinet, 'cello, and harp, but his later song-cycle *Circles* (1960), a setting of poems by E. E. Cummings for soprano, harp, and two percussion players (each surrounded by fifteen groups of instruments), commissioned by the Fromm Foundation, is a landmark in the development of chamber music with voice comparable in originality with its two great predecessors, *Pierrot Lunaire* and *Le Marteau sans Maître*. The medium and the use of it are even more revolutionary than in either of those works, and so is the notation, which presents both the singer and the players with a series of new symbols which must be specially learnt. In addition to singing exactly and approximately at indicated pitches, the singer has to speak, to whisper, changing from one method of delivery to another sometimes in the middle of a word or syllable. She must also for different sections of the work take up different positions in relation to the players, and from time to time play glass chimes, wood chimes, claves, finger cymbals, clap her hands, and give the beat. The two percussion players, with the harpist between them, from time to time whirl rapidly round the complete array of instruments encircling them (a reference presumably to the title of the work), and are also required here and there to contribute vocal sounds to the work, intended not to be heard as such but 'to colour the different kinds of instrumental attack in the

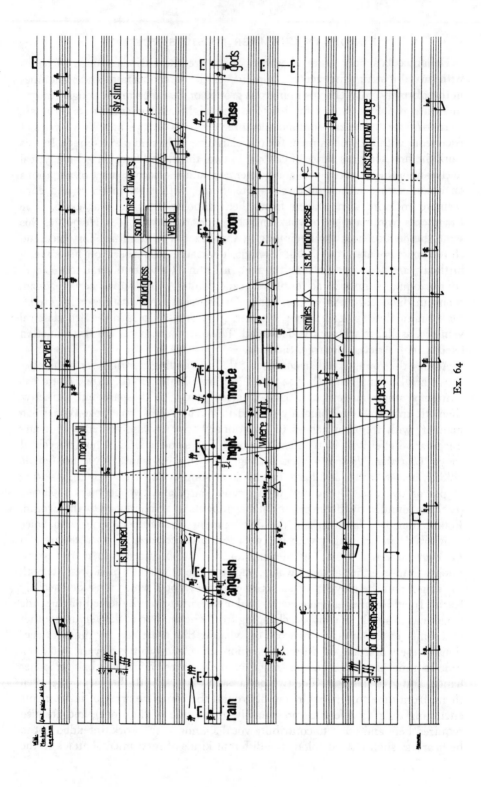

Ex. 64

different registers'. A page of the score is reproduced as Ex. 64. Here the words printed in boxes in the percussion parts are to be spoken by the singer, while the percussionists are required to 'play' them—that is to devise the nearest possible imitation of them on the instruments indicated.

In form and musical content, by contrast, *Circles* is rather more traditional and accessible than *Le Marteau sans Maître*. There are five movements, of which the fourth and fifth are varied settings of the texts of the second and first. A condensed and heavily varied but at certain points instantly recognizable musical recapitulation also takes place in the last two movements, though this does not always coincide with the recapitulation of the words. The beginning of the repetition of the text of the second movement is set in the fourth to a recapitulation not of its own original melodic line but to a rhythmic transformation of the singer's line from the beginning of the first movement. On the other hand, the word 'rose' in the last movement is ornamented with the same melisma (slightly changed in rhythm) as at its original appearance in the first movement. The fourth movement, like the first, is accompanied for the most part by the harp alone, with some percussion entries towards the end. More percussion instruments are used in the second and fifth movements, and the third, in which, as in Cummings's poem, the words are split up without regard either for their sense or for their normal articulation, is in the nature of a sustained cadenza for both the percussion players and the singer—the vocal part being mostly spoken or half-spoken, with very few notes of definite pitch. Except in this movement *Circles* is more conspicuously and continuously dominated than either *Pierrot Lunaire* or *Le Marteau sans Maître* by the singer, whose ornately lyrical line is the main musical thread of the work. But it is the imaginative and entirely musical writing for the percussion, always in the spirit and dimensions of chamber music, that gives it its unique distinction—not only in the field of chamber music but as an example of the new uses of percussion.

Riccardo MALIPIERO, a nephew of the older Malipiero, has written two string quartets (1941 and 1954) and a Sonata for violin and piano (1956), attractive and excellent works, eclectic and relatively conservative in idiom.

EASTERN EUROPE

The outstanding East European contribution to chamber music since **C** has been the last four quartets of BARTÓK (**C**, d. 1945), which with the earlier two discussed in **C** have become the first and still the only string quartets since Ravel's to enter the popular repertory. It has even been claimed for them that they are the most important series of works in this medium since Beethoven's.

As there is already an abundant literature on all these works, including several detailed analytical studies, the method followed here will be simply to illustrate briefly the nature of their thematic material and to observe Bartók's changing methods of thematic unification in them.

No. 1 is in three movements (Lento, Allegretto, Allegro vivace), material from which is quoted in **C**. They are linked by thematic derivation from the opening phrase of the 'Lento' (Ex. 65), which in the second movement, transformed into Ex. 66, becomes an important subsidiary thematic element, and in the third movement grows into the principal thematic motive, first heard as Ex. 67.

Ex. 65

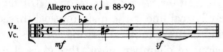

Ex. 66

Ex. 67

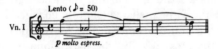

No. 2 (see also **C**) also has three movements, but in an even more unconventional order, opening with a sonata movement, followed by a scherzo, and ending with a slow movement. These are linked, less closely than those of any of the other quartets, by the exploitation of the intervals of the perfect fourth and augmented fourth, which are, however, not so much definite thematic components as merely prominent melodic and harmonic features of the general idiom. As in No. 1, the opening melodic phrase with its two ascending fourths (Ex. 68)

Ex. 68

functions as a source-motive. In the second movement, which is in the character of a wild dance-like interlude between the lyrical first movement and the intense, enigmatic third, the tritone is thematically more conspicuous than the perfect fourth, which, however, appears aggressively in a brief middle section (sections 22–23 in the score). Both intervals are thematically prominent in the last movement. Ex. 69 echoes the opening of the first movement (Ex. 68), and Exx. 70a and 70b are important harmonic motives in the last movement.

Ex. 69

Ex. 70A

Ex. 70B

In No. 3 (1927) the problem of thematic unification of several movements does not arise, as it is in one movement only, falling into four sections: the lyrical, opening 'prima parte', the quick, rather angularly contrapuntal, mainly canonic, middle section (seconda parte), an abbreviated 'ricapitulazione della prima parte', and a quick coda related to the middle section. The material presented in the 'prima parte' is diffuse almost to the point of athematicism, despite the close canonic and imitative texture of the music and the multiplicity of small, sometimes similar, but rarely closely related, melodic shapes. Each short section is potentially a rich source of distinctive thematic material, but no well-defined

Ex. 71

'theme' emerges until the sustained tune in octaves on the second violin and viola, with a simple chordal accompaniment, at the end of the 'prima parte' (Ex. 71). The canonic writing is carried over into the 'seconda parte', which has been described by different analysts as a sonata structure and as a set of variations. It is distinctly sonata-like, and the slight suggestion of variations is due to the similarity of the opening theme of the second subject (Ex. 73) to that of the first (Ex. 72). The subsequent phrases diverge widely. Another important theme

Ex. 72

Ex. 73

in the first subject is Ex. 74, which emerges clearly after various anticipatory figures. The semiquavers of this tune dominate the development and the first

Ex. 74

part of the reprise. In the whole of this 'seconda parte' the canonic writing is very strict, in obviously deliberate contrast with the 'prima parte', where, although canonic writing is equally prominent, it is very free. A long transition based on one fragment of the 'prima parte' leads to the recapitulation of the 'prima parte' itself. Here not only is the material very diffuse again, but it is almost unrecognizably transformed and greatly condensed, and such sections as are recognizable appear in a different sequence. A sustained ostinato canon at the tritone, for instance, is recapitulated simply as a held tritone, and the harmonic content of Ex. 75, which goes on for four bars, is summarized in the recapitulation as Ex. 76. The coda recapitulates with similar condensation,

Ex. 75

but more recognizably, the material of the 'seconda parte', with an increase in the tempo and in the brilliance of the writing making clear its function as a coda. In 1928 this work won Bartók half of the substantial prize (Casella was the joint winner) in a competition organized by the Musical Fund Society of Philadelphia.

For the String Quartet No. 4 (1928) Bartók adopted a symmetrical five-movement form. He may have been influenced in this by Hindemith's Clarinet Quintet, which he had probably heard (or heard about) at its first performance at

Ex. 76

Salzburg in 1923. Hindemith's work is in five movements of which the last is an exact cancrizans repetition of the first—a device that he used again in the Septet for wind instruments (see p. 15). Bartók does not apply the principle of symmetry so rigidly as this, but he uses it more extensively and in a freer way. The last movement of this quartet uses the same themes as the first (compare Exx. 77 and 78), the fourth movement the same as the second (Exx. 79 and 80), and the entire thematic material of the whole work is derived from the first 6 bars of the middle movement (Ex. 81). The tonal plan of the work is

Ex. 77

Ex. 78

Ex. 79

also symmetrical, the first and last movements being in C, the second and fourth in E and A flat, respectively a major third above and below C. The central movement is ambiguous in tonality, but much of the melody suggests C, and there are several main cadences on C. In many details of harmony and counterpoint, too, there is a clear symmetry of structure which was clearly intended by Bartók to serve as one of the main principles of harmonic and tonal as well as formal organization of the work.

Ex. 80

Ex. 81

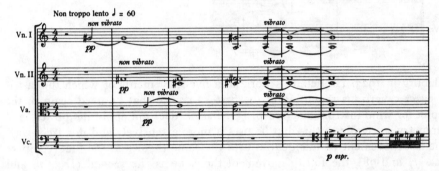

The idea of symmetry is prominent again in the formal plan of the String Quartet No. 5 (1934), which is again in a five-movement 'arch' form, very similar to that of the fourth quartet, except that there a central slow movement was set between two scherzos, whereas here there is a central scherzo and trio between two slow movements. The very central section of the work, the trio of the scherzo, is one of Bartók's 'nature' pieces, with shrill 'insect-noises' above and around a rather indefinite tune. Like the scherzo which precedes and follows it, the trio is in one of the so-called Bulgarian rhythms that Bartók began to make considerable use of at this period. Its time signature is $\frac{3+2+2+3}{8}$ (with variants), and that of the scherzo is $\frac{4+2+3}{8}$. Again there is a close correspondence between the second and fourth movements (Adagio molto and Andante), much the same in degree as that between the two scherzos in No. 4, their thematic

Ex. 82

material being closely related (see Exx. 82 and 83) and their form almost identical. The relationship between the first and last movements is slightly different from that in No. 4, and rather more remote, the first theme of the first movement (Ex. 84) and the main theme of the last movement (Ex. 85) being

Ex. 83

Ex. 84

Ex. 85

recognizable as variants only by their barest outline—their respective ascent and descent of an octave, and their emphasis during that ascent and descent on the central tritone. In the course of the last movement, however, there is a fugal episode on the original first-movement form of the theme. The relationship of the main theme of the last movement to that of the first also represents in this work the principle of tonal symmetry, expressed in No. 4 in the key sequence of the movements. In the first movement the theme ascends from B flat to the octave, with an intermediate emphasis on the central E, and in the last movement descends from E to the octave, with intermediate emphasis on the central B flat. This work was commissioned by the Elizabeth Sprague Coolidge Foundation.

In the String Quartet No. 6 (1939) Bartók abandoned the 'arch' form and returned to a more traditional design and method of thematic unification, as well as to a milder and more traditional idiom. The unifying element here is a motto-theme (Ex. 86) first played by the viola alone at the beginning of the work,

Ex. 86

then used in a two-part setting (both violins and viola playing in unison) as an introduction to the second movement—a strange march, which has a hint of similarity to the 'Alla marcia' of Beethoven's A minor Quartet—then in a three-part setting (first violin and viola in unison) before the third movement—an eccentric burlesque—and finally in a full four-part setting, much extended and developed, as the serene fourth movement itself. This motto figures in the work more considerably and more subtly than as mere introductory material to each movement. Its rhythm permeates the thematic material of the first movement, which is also pervaded by its mood. The 'Burletta' has two short episodes that recall the first movement, and hence the motto. And the main themes of the first movement appear during the development of the motto theme in the last movement. In its basic idiom this is the most traditional of Bartók's quartets, after the first. What does conspicuously remain here of the technical methods of the third, fourth, and fifth quartets is the extraordinary use of the four instruments to produce astonishing new sounds. In the trio section of the 'Marcia', Bartók makes much use of an unusual kind of portamento, a slow and heavy slide along the string, through fairly small intervals—a device he had first used prominently, with an abundance of single- and double-stopped glissandos, in the third quartet. In the 'Burletta' the violins are directed at certain points to play a quarter-tone flat, and elsewhere Bartók specifies a strong pizzicato 'so that the string rebounds off the fingerboard'—first used in the fourth quartet. Other unusual instrumental effects that he added to the language of chamber music are pizzicato glissandos, in the fourth and fifth quartets, and a pizzicato 'with the nail of the first finger at the upper end of the string', in the first slow movement of the fifth quartet. The Quartet No. 6 was commissioned by Zoltán Székely for his own string quartet, but owing to the outbreak of war they were unable to perform it. The first performance was given in New York by the Kolisch Quartet, to whom Bartók dedicated it.

Like most other modern quartets, Bartók's are unfortunately almost completely inaccessible to the amateur player, owing to their great technical difficulty. His only concerted work which is accessible to domestic players is the series of 44 Duos for two violins unaccompanied. Although intended essentially for educational and domestic use, these little pieces, even the most elementary of them, are fully characteristic of the composer in their musical language, and are an endless source of interest and pleasure to the players. For ambitious and assiduous violinists the more advanced duos could well serve as a preparation for the demands of the quartets.

In all his other chamber music Bartók employs the piano, which was his own instrument. The two violin sonatas, briefly described in C, were the works in which he came nearest, as he himself pointed out, to Schoenbergian total chromaticism or so-called atonality, and even leaned towards the twelve-note method that Schoenberg was at that time evolving (but had not yet formulated). They also contain several passages (see Ex. 87 from the first sonata) in which Bartók tried out the idea of symmetrical melodic and harmonic construction which he later carried much farther in the String Quartet No. 4 (see above). Nevertheless, they do not move completely away from traditional tonal concepts, and Bartók considered them as being, very freely, in the keys of C sharp and C

respectively. In later years he expressed some dissatisfaction with them, especially with the first, on account of their extreme tonal and formal freedom. The
form his criticism took, however, was no more than an observation to the effect

Ex. 87

that if he ever came to write another violin sonata he would not solve the problem in this way—which any composer might say of almost any of his works.
They are in fact among the most successful and convincing of the relatively few
large-scale abstract instrumental works of the 'expressionist' period. They remain
outstanding among modern violin sonatas also for the originality of their treatment of the medium. Many commentators have noted the extreme independence
of the two instrumental parts, which are harnessed and driven together more by
sheer expressive force than by persuasion and adaptation to each other.

How Bartók would have solved the problem later he never demonstrated. His
only other violin sonata is the unaccompanied one written in America for Yehudi
Menuhin, which presented a totally different problem (superbly solved) and
does not fall within the scope of this book. He did prepare alternative versions
with piano of the two rhapsodies for violin and orchestra (1928), but these are
slighter works. Based partly on Rumanian instrumental folk-music, they are
both in the traditional two movements (slow–fast), and are relatively simple,
although florid and almost gipsy-like, in instrumental style. The first is also
published for 'cello and piano. In 1944 Bartók revised the second, making extensive alterations to the second movement.

Similar in character, but more successful, is the trio for clarinet, violin, and
piano, commissioned in 1938 by Benny Goodman at Szigeti's instigation and
designed for them to play with the composer. Bartók originally intended this too
to be a rhapsody in two movements, but later added the central slow movement
and changed the title to *Contrasts*. Although more personal and attractive in
style than the rhapsodies, it is essentially a display piece for the three brilliant
players, especially for the clarinettist and violinist, each of whom has a cadenza.
The idiom is purely Hungarian. The contact with Benny Goodman did not
stimulate Bartók to apply his invention to the idiomatic tricks of jazz. The three
movements are called 'Verbunkos' (Recruiting Dance), 'Pihenő' (Relaxation),

and 'Sebes' (Fast Dance). In the last movement the clarinettist is directed to change from a B flat instrument to one in A, and the violinist must also have two instruments, one normally tuned, the other with the G string tuned to G sharp and the E string to E flat.

There remains the Sonata (which Bartók originally intended to call a quartet) for two pianos and percussion (1937). The percussion comprises three timpani, xylophone, two side-drums (one with and one without snares), bass drum, a pair of cymbals, suspended cymbal, triangle, and tam-tam, to be played by two, or if necessary three, players. Of these the timpani and xylophone in particular have thematically important parts, while the others, sounded in many different ways, provide rhythmic emphasis or decoration, and flecks of tone-colour. In this work, which was written, like *Contrasts*, between the fifth and sixth string quartets, there is no attempt at thematic unification, but there is again a considerable amount of symmetry in the writing. The first movement is in sonata form, with a slow introduction that foreshadows the second part of the first subject proper. The movement is written in 9/8 throughout, but with the accents differently distributed in the various themes. The slow movement is in a simpler ternary form, with a 'nocturnal' middle section, some of the effects of which are carried over into the varied recapitulation. The finale is a gay sonata-rondo dominated by the opening tune (Ex. 88) or its rhythm. It is an attractive work,

Ex. 88

but owing to its demand for two skilled percussion players, and to its heavy sonorities, which are excessive in a small hall, it can hardly be regarded as chamber music in any accepted sense. It is nevertheless very effective, and has proved much more popular in this original form than in the version with orchestra that Bartók prepared some years later.

Of the older and younger East European contemporaries of Bartók considered in **C**, only one calls for detailed additional comment. In Hungary KODÁLY has written no major chamber work since the 1920's, and DOHNÁNYI (d. 1960) broke no new ground in his Sextet, op. 37 (1933). This is true equally of the various later works of NOVÁK (d. 1949), FOERSTER (d. 1951), SUK (d. 1935), ENESCO (d. 1955), and also of GLAZUNOV (d. 1936)—whose name fits more aptly into this summary list than into the Russian chapter. The String Quartet No. 2 (1927) of SZYMANOWSKI (d. 1937) is somewhat more interesting. It is similar in general style to his earlier one in the same medium (**C**), and like that work it is in three movements, the last of which is again partly fugal. A lyrical opening movement in ternary form, with a very free middle section and a straightforward reprise, is followed by a scherzo and trio in which the reprise is tonally varied and thematically elaborated. In the third movement the fugal exposition is immediately followed by a second exposition, in diminution, with a different rhythm.

There is a lengthy non-fugal development and a final reprise-like variant of the second fugal exposition.

More important than any of these are the later chamber works of JANÁČEK (**C**, d. 1928), who in the last two years of his life produced two further important works that were published only posthumously and could not be included in Max Brod's short account. These were the Capriccio for solo piano (left hand) and seven instruments (1926), and the String Quartet No. 2 (1928). The list of earlier works should also be supplemented by a very early Suite for string quintet (with double bass), published in 1926, and *Pohádka* ('Fairy Tale') for 'cello and piano (1907–8), published in 1924. The correct Czech title of the suite for wind sextet, 'Youth', is *Mladí*, not as given in **C**.

The most valuable and important of Janáček's works, as far as the normal chamber-music repertory is concerned, are the two string quartets and the Violin Sonata, which are among the most extraordinary works ever written for these traditional ensembles. In the sonata and the first quartet, both briefly described in **C**, there are still some gestures of observance of convention. The first movement in each is in a concise and tonally traditional sonata form, and in other respects these two works have slightly more in common than the two quartets. Exx. 89 and 90 show the main themes of the third movement of the sonata and the second movement of the quartet, which have an obvious resem-

Ex. 89

Ex. 90

blance. The harmonic style of the sonata, although utterly personal to Janáček, is not quite so free and wilful as in the quartet (there are several harmonic and thematic echoes of his much earlier and best-known opera *Jenufa*), and there is

a continuity of mood and texture sustained throughout each movement, rarely
found in his later works. The first movement is in effect monothematic, the
second subject being a continuation of the first (see Ex. 91), with a short new

Ex. 91

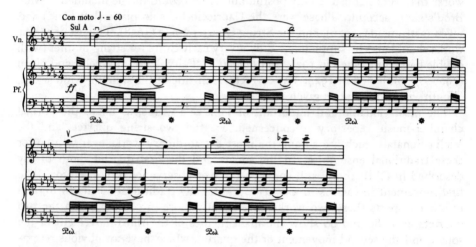

theme in the coda, which becomes prominent in the development. A double-bar
repeat of the exposition is marked. The second movement, headed 'Ballada', is
in ternary form, with a varied and developed recapitulation. In the third movement, also in ternary form, the folk-song-like theme quoted in Ex. 89 is contrasted in the middle section with a slower one of great harmonic beauty. The
final movement, an 'Adagio', is again in an almost monothematic sonata form,
the short second subject making no reappearance in either the development or
the recapitulation. Ex. 92 shows the beginning of the recapitulation, where the
melody played in the exposition by the piano, with only decorative interjections

Ex. 92

from the violin, is now given to the violin, while the piano provides an accompaniment new in harmony as well as in texture.
The examples quoted clearly illustrate the remarkable instrumental texture

throughout the work, in particular the very original writing for the piano and the unusual relationship of the two instruments.

The two string quartets are both programmatic, and the second, like Smetana's two quartets, is autobiographical. In the first, inspired by Tolstoy's *Kreutzer Sonata*, Janáček made use, as Max Brod pointed out in **C**, of material from an earlier unpublished Piano Trio (composed in 1908–9), also inspired by Tolstoy's story. As this trio now appears to have been lost or destroyed, it is impossible to establish how much was taken over from it, but a comparison with the 'Fairy Tale', written at about the same time as the trio, suggests that very little in the quartet belongs to that date. In the sonata-form first movement the folksong-like 'cello melody in Ex. 93 is the principal theme, and the two bars which precede it recur frequently, at the transitions, as a kind of ritornello. A similar

Ex. 93

folksong-like phrase is the principal theme (see Ex. 90) of the second movement, which is in binary form, with two subjects, and curious coda-cum-development at the end. In the third movement, in ternary form, the first part is built up by varied repetitions of the opening canonic phrase (Ex. 94). A contrasting theme is then introduced, and followed by a very free and rhapsodic development of the canonic theme and a few final bars of recapitulation. The fourth movement, which also has a fairly clear and simple ternary outline, slightly obscured by the internal repetitions and developments within the sections, is a kind of summing up. It opens with the ritornello theme from the first movement, which has much the same thematic function here. The other thematic material faintly echoes themes from all the preceding movements. No detailed 'programme' is provided for the work, beyond the subtitle 'inspired by Tolstoy's *Kreutzer Sonata*', though in a letter to Mrs. Kamila Stössl, quoted in *Letters and Reminiscences*, the composer wrote: 'I had in mind an unhappy, tortured, beaten woman, beaten to death as Tolstoy described her.'

In the String Quartet No. 2 traces of traditional formal outlines are more difficult to discern, and are not profitably to be sought. It bears the title *Intimate*

Letters, a later substitution, for the purposes of publication, for 'Love Letters', which was what the composer originally intended, and what is on the manuscript. The work is a record of events and feelings connected with his love affair

Ex. 94

in old age with a much younger woman, Mrs. Kamila Stössl, and on the manuscript the composer originally prescribed the viola d'amore for the viola part. It was his last work, composed in three weeks in the last year of his life.

The first movement describes the impression of his first meeting with Mrs. Stössl. Like that of the first quartet it opens with a harmonic theme, followed by an unaccompanied melodic phrase like a very distorted folksong melody

Ex. 95

(Ex. 95), several repetitions and variations of which form the exposition. This is followed by two further main sections, each introduced by a new melody which is then simultaneously developed with the themes of the exposition. In the second movement, which 'concerns the summer events at Luhačovice Spa in Moravia', the main theme is a lyrical melody of a smoother and less remarkable outline than most of Janáček's themes, though still characteristic in the brevity of its phrases. The middle section is a wild dance-like episode in 5/8 time, with a whole-tone melody (see Ex. 96). A very brief recapitulation of the first theme

Ex. 96

is followed by a reappearance of the main themes of the first movement (the first one accompanied by a new, folk-like melody on the viola) and a brief coda. The third movement similarly opens with an unusually smooth and regular dance-like theme in an unhurried 9/8. This is followed by a long slow episode recalling the later themes of the first movement, and this in turn by a new and wild theme (presto) with an ostinato accompaniment. Finally, the first two themes of the movement are briefly recapitulated, the phrases of the first one interrupted by quick, angular variants. This is formally the most baffling of the four movements, and the 'programme' does not throw much light on it.

The last movement opens with another folk-like tune (Ex. 97) which is one of two recurring themes in a kind of rondo. At the end of the first section it is

Ex. 97

combined with the other recurring theme, which is based on a four-note motive in which every note is always trilled (see Ex. 98). The thematic weight of the movement is very evenly balanced between these themes and the 'episodes', which in the first part of the movement are varied and unconnected, but in the second part are confined to the development of the important theme that emerges from them.

Ex. 98

In this work almost the only survival from the 'classical' string quartet is that it is in four movements. Neither in form nor in character do these movements observe any established convention. It is impossible in either of the quartets to speak of a 'slow movement' or 'scherzo'. Every movement has extreme and frequent fluctuations of tempo—though very slow passages are rare. (Janáček's most frequent tempo-marking is 'con moto'.) Nevertheless, in their extraordinary personal style the two quartets do make formal and absolute musical sense, and do not depend for intelligibility, any more than Smetana's quartets (or Janáček's own Violin Sonata, which has no avowed 'programme'), on extra-musical explanations.

The works for mixed ensembles are still more extraordinary and remote from anything previously (or since) composed as pure instrumental chamber music —though the composer curiously adheres even in these to a four-movement plan. The suite for wind sextet, *Mladí*, and the Concertino, written soon after it (both briefly mentioned in **C**), are both autobiographical. An editorial note in the score of the Concertino states that it is a 'sort of sequel' to *Mladí*. 'It too is an intimate expression of the artist's reminiscences of his youth, but—in contrast to the suite for wind instruments—of serious experiences, among them the bitterness and difficulties at the beginning of his creative work.' The first movement, a curious kind of prelude, is for piano and horn only, and the second, a scherzo, is for piano and E flat clarinet. In the last two movements all five accompanying instruments play, but in the fourth movement the strings and wind instruments are used only in alternation until they are finally combined in the short coda. The piano has by far the most prominent part, with a very sparse accompaniment from the horn in the first movement, and solo cadenzas in the third and fourth.

In the Capriccio the piano part (for left hand only) is clearly marked in the score 'Solo Piano'. This work was written, rather reluctantly on Janáček's part, at the request of the pianist Otakar Hollmann, whose right arm was paralysed during the 1914–18 war. A note in the score states that 'according to the correspondence and some authentic statements, Capriccio expresses a revolt against the cruel destiny'. It is one of Janáček's most baffling and eccentric works.

The two early works call for little comment. The 'Fairy Tale' for 'cello and piano is an attractive piece in three movements, not yet very characteristic of the composer as we know him by his later works, but by no means conventional in expression or in its use of its very rich, sweet, and consonant harmonic vocabulary. It is certainly well worth a place in the repertory. The very early Suite for string quintet, in six movements, shows no trace of Janáček's personality, and is chiefly remarkable for the tonal scheme of the six movements: G minor, G major, G major, D minor–G minor–G major, B flat major, B minor. A curious feature of all the later works is Janáček's obsession with the most remote flat keys—which may be among the reasons for players' resistance to them. In the 'Fairy Tale' all three movements are in G flat major (turning to F sharp minor in the first movement). The keys of the four movements of the Violin Sonata are D flat major, C sharp minor–D flat major, A flat minor, G sharp minor. In the first quartet the four movements are in E minor–major, A flat minor, G flat minor, A flat minor. After this the composer abandoned key signatures but continued to write, though more freely, in these favourite keys. In the second quartet the principal keys of the four movements are D flat major, B flat minor, A flat minor, D flat major.

Since Janáček and Bartók very little chamber music from east Europe has made any international impression—partly on account of a quarter of a century of continuous political difficulties that have denied the composers in these countries adequate communication with other countries. The Czech Alois HÁBA (C) and his younger brother Karel (b. 1898) have failed to make any headway with their microtonal systems, and the group of gifted young composers living in voluntary exile in Paris, sometimes known as the 'École de Paris', have been more prolific than distinguished. Among them are the Pole TANSMAN, the Czech MARTINŮ (d. 1959), the Hungarian HARSÁNYI (d. 1954), all briefly mentioned in C, the Rumanian Marcel MIHALOVICI (b. 1898) and the Hungarian László LAJTHA (1892–1963), who alone in the group kept up his association with his native country, although most of his works are published in Paris.

There are few national traits, either of their native or of their adopted country, in the works of any of these composers, who are all accomplished, eclectic romantics, more fluent than original. Only Martinů has become widely known, partly as a result of his second emigration, in 1941, to America. The list of his chamber works, like Lajtha's, is enormous. Their idiom is amiably neo-classical, their invention often attractive but uneven. A fairly consistent characteristic of his music is a lively rhythmic wit, shown in Ex. 99, from the last movement of his Violin Sonata No. 1.

A notable younger émigré is the Hungarian Sándor VERESS (b. 1907), now living in Switzerland, who stands out as the only Hungarian composer of his generation to resist successfully the overpowering influence of Bartók, Kodály, and folk-song. Among his chamber works are several early sonatinas (violin and piano, 'cello and piano, and woodwind trio) and his first string quartet, which are in a melodically attractive but contrapuntally very dissonant neo-classical style;

Ex. 99

the second string quartet and second violin sonata, in which the national flavour is stronger and the idiom more relaxed; and the String Trio, in which the use of the twelve-note technique restores something of the grittiness of idiom of the early works.

OTHER COUNTRIES

As far as the international chamber-music repertory is concerned, the contribution of the smaller and remoter nations can be surveyed fairly quickly. Switzerland's is the most considerable, but of the two major Swiss-born composers neither is a completely 'neutral' Swiss. Honegger is identified with France, and Bloch with America and Jewish music, and the works that they have composed. since C are discussed in the French and American chapters. Besides these two, Frank Martin and Othmar Schoeck (d. 1957), both briefly mentioned in C, have continued to hold a place. SCHOECK added to the list of his works given in C a Sonata for violin and piano op. 46 (1931), two works for voice and chamber ensemble (opp. 42 and 47), and an unusual Sonata for bass clarinet and piano op. 41 (1928), which exists also in versions for bassoon and for 'cello. MARTIN's contribution has been more slender and long in appearing. After the early works briefly mentioned in C he wrote a second Violin Sonata (1931–2), a String Trio (1936), and a Rhapsody for two violins, two violas, and double bass (1935), but publication of these began only in 1959, with the Violin Sonata. In this work, which is in a well-defined E major, the melody is of a neo-classical cut, and the harmony fairly dense, complex, and conservative. Among its interesting features is the continuous, non-symmetrical form of each of the three movements, the second of which is a chaconne in a very baroque style. This movement has also been published separately for 'cello and piano. Martin has also written several Ballades, each for a solo instrument (flute, trombone, and 'cello), to be played with orchestral or piano accompaniment, and a 'Sonata da Chiesa' for viola d'amore and organ (1938), which was later arranged with string orchestral accompaniment and also exists for flute and organ.

Slightly less widely known than Martin, but more prolific in chamber music, are Conrad Beck (b. 1901) and Willy Burkhard (1900–55). BECK's works include two string quartets (Nos. 3 and 4), two string trios, a Sonata for violin and piano, sonatinas for violin, 'cello, and oboe, all with piano, and a Duet for violin and viola. They are all in a witty and rhythmically lively style, and in a harmonic idiom that effectively combines sophisticated neo-classical asperity with romantic lushness. BURKHARD, similarly prolific, was more conservative, except possibly in his forms. His String Quartet and Piano Trio are both in one movement, of fairly extended and free design. His other chamber works include a Sonata and a Sonatina for violin and piano, Sonata for 'cello and piano, the *Lyrische Musik* (in memoriam Georg Trakl) for flute, viola, 'cello, and piano, in five movements, and the Divertimento for string trio, in which the third movement, marked 'Dialogo', is an accompanied solo for the 'cello, the dialogue being between the high and low registers of the 'cello. There are also numerous smaller works that are both easy and attractive.

An outstanding figure among the younger Swiss composers is Klaus HUBER (b. 1924), whose published chamber works include the cantata *Des Engels Anredung an die Seele*, for tenor, flute, clarinet, horn, and harp (1957), which was awarded a prize at the ISCM competition in Rome in 1959. Its seven movements are symmetrically grouped around the central one. The seventh is the strict retrograde of the first, the sixth contains a straightforward recapitulation of the second, and in the fifth the voice-part of the third is heard in retrograde motion (though the accompaniment differs). In style, like other works by Huber, it shows some influence of Stravinsky's serial and immediately pre-serial period, in particular of the *Cantata*. A similar structural method is used in Huber's *Auf die ruhige Nachtzeit* (1958), for soprano, flute, viola, and 'cello, which is also in seven movements. Among Huber's other chamber works are a Partita for 'cello and harpsichord (1955), 'Three Movements' for seven brass instruments (1957/58), 'Three Movements in two parts' (Drei Sätze in zwei Teilen) for wind quintet (1958/59), and *Noctes Intelligibilis Lucis* for oboe and harpsichord (1961).

From the other European countries the Dutch Willem Pijper (**C**, d. 1937) and Henk Badings (b. 1907), the Norwegian Fartein Valen (**C**, d. 1952), and more recently the Greek Nikos Skalkottas (1904–49) and the Danish Vagn Holmboe (b. 1909) have gained the most considerable international following.

PIJPER's music, like that of most other Dutch composers, shows a strong French influence, particularly that of Ravel, to whom his String Quartet No. 4 is dedicated. In addition to the handful of early works described in **C**, he wrote five string quartets, the last of which was left unfinished, a Sextet for wind and piano, a Septet for the same ensemble plus a double bass, a Wind Quintet, and a Wind Trio (flute, clarinet, and bassoon). With the exception of the unfinished String Quartet No. 5, on which he was working in 1946, the year before his death, all of these works were completed before 1930. They are concise in form and clear and simple in texture. In several of them an initial basic motive, in various transformations, provides the thematic material for all the movements, or serves as a 'motto' recurring in each movement. The effect, enhanced by his unemphatic cadences, is often of a single-movement work. Technically they are not difficult, though Pijper sometimes creates needless problems in the notation by his fairly frequent use of conflicting metres, which rarely involve any real rhythmic complexity.

BADINGS, a pupil of Pijper, has been more resistant than most Dutch composers to the French influence. In general he favours a more sombre and chromatically more intense harmony, and has sometimes used a system based on a scale of alternating major and minor seconds. His musical thinking is of a more German character, and there is sometimes a faint similarity in tone and style, and in a certain mechanical element in the writing, to Hindemith—though without any significant similarity of idiom. In his industry, too, Badings resembles Hindemith, having written over thirty major works of chamber music alone, including three string quartets, at least six trios and four quintets of various sorts, an octet, and many sonatas. Some of the ensembles are unusual. One of the trios is for two oboes and cor anglais, one for two violins and piano, and one for flute, violin, and viola.

Of the same generation as Badings is Rudolf ESCHER (b. 1912), another pupil of Pijper, who has rather more in common with his teacher, particularly in his admiration of Ravel. One of Escher's most important chamber works is *Le Tombeau de Ravel*, for flute, oboe, string trio, and harpsichord, a suite of seven movements in a symmetrical grouping slightly similar to that of Bartók's fourth and fifth string quartets, or of Hindemith's Clarinet Quintet and Septet. This symmetry is particularly evident in the scoring of the movements. The first and last (Pavane and Hymne) and the central movement (Sarabande) are scored for the full sextet, the second and sixth movements, both marked 'Air', are for solo 'cello and solo flute respectively, and the third and fifth movements (Forlane and Rigaudon) are both for quintet, the one omitting oboe and violin, the other flute and harpsichord. There are also many thematic relationships linking the movements, though these are not symmetrically organized. Other important chamber works by Escher include a remarkable Wind Trio (oboe, clarinet, and bassoon), and sonatas for violin and piano, 'cello and piano, and 'cello solo. Much of his music is extremely fragile and delicate in texture, with every note weighed almost as in Webern. Small as his output is, it commands attention and proclaims an originality perhaps more noteworthy than either Pijper's or Badings's.

Fartein VALEN, whose Sonata for violin and piano, op. 3 (1916), is briefly referred to in C, added to this in later years only four chamber works—the Piano Trio, op. 5 (1924), two string quartets, op. 10 (1929) and op. 13 (1931), and the Serenade for wind quintet, op. 42 (1947). The Piano Trio is the last of his 'early' works, more mature in style than the Violin Sonata and nearer to total chromaticism, but still with a strong harmonic interest. After that he abandoned purely harmonic writing almost entirely, in favour of a continuous counterpoint made up of a free canonic treatment of relatively short melodic motives which have something of the function of Schoenbergian note-series. The third movement of the String Quartet No. 1, a scherzo with very rapid 'buzzing' figurations, is one of the very few movements where there is a prominent harmonic interest. Otherwise it is only at the final cadences in each movement that the flow of the counterpoint is immobilized into anything like 'chords'. Like many serial composers Valen makes almost 'classical' use of inherited forms, often complete with double-bar repeats. The first movement of the String Quartet No. 1 is in sonata form, with a double-bar repeat of the exposition and a long coda, and in the last movement, headed 'Rondo', the form is of almost primitive simplicity. The 'Adagio' is in simple ternary form, the third section combining the recapitulation of the first with the continuation of the second. In the String Quartet No. 2, which has only three movements, the opening one is a slow fugue on a theme which, unlike many of Valen's, includes all twelve notes. The second movement, marked 'Tempo di Minuetto, grazioso', is in traditional minuet form, with a double-bar repeat of the first part of the minuet and a da capo after the trio. The last movement is in sonata form, again with a double-bar repeat of the exposition and an extended coda, in which the emphatic reappearance of the main theme gives the movement a suggestion of rondo form. The Serenade for wind instruments, which is in one movement, is very similar in form, except for the discarding of the double-bar repeat.

In Danish music the most prominent international figure since Nielsen is Vagn HOLMBOE, who has been prolific in chamber music as in most other forms. His mature output includes at least five string quartets and a Piano Trio, in addition to a series of chamber concertos. They are excellent and effective works in a spontaneous eclectic style, thematically inventive, widely varied, and well sustained, combining expansiveness with concentration. There is a strong Bartókian flavour, accounted for by Holmboe's having spent some time studying in Transylvania (1933–4). His second and third quartets are in a five-movement form probably suggested by Bartók's fourth and fifth quartets, and the middle movement of the String Quartet No. 1 is like a set of free variations after a design often found in Bartók—a slow movement with a quick scherzo-like central section. Within a forthrightly tonal idiom Holmboe also makes some use of twelve-note material. The third movement of the String Quartet No. 3 (Andante quasi una giacona) is based on a chromatic theme in C, beginning with a twelve-note series which appears in the course of the movement both in inversion and in retrograde inversion. A related twelve-note theme occurs in the fifth movement, a kind of epilogue which alludes also to the first movement. The first movement of the String Quartet No. 2 makes prominent use, in the middle section, of the BACH motive.

Of SKALKOTTAS's large output of chamber music too few works have so far been published to confirm the high claims made for him in some quarters since his death.

CHAMBER MUSIC IN BRITAIN
SINCE 1929

By COLIN MASON

WHEN the first edition of the *Cyclopedic Survey* was published in 1929, the established British composers who were still active were Bax, Bridge, Delius, Elgar, Holbrooke, Holst, Ireland, Scott, and Vaughan Williams. Of the younger generation Bliss and Walton were those of whom most was expected, and Benjamin, Bush, Finzi, Howells, Moeran, Rubbra, Van Dieren, and Warlock all had their champions or claimed attention for their promise.

ELGAR (d. 1934), HOLST (d. 1934), and WARLOCK (d. 1930) wrote no more chamber music. The names of BRIDGE (d. 1941), HOLBROOKE (d. 1958), and VAN DIEREN (d. 1936) are now rarely seen. The numerous later chamber works of BAX (d. 1953) contributed nothing new to his music and have not made their way into the repertory. This applies equally to those of Cyril SCOTT, which include a String Quartet No. 3 and a Sonata for flute and piano, both composed in his eighty-first year. The only one of this group of romantic harmonists whose reputation has not faded is the earliest of them, DELIUS (d. 1934), whose last chamber work, the short Violin Sonata No. 3 (1930), has found a modest place in the repertory beside his earlier two works in this form. (The works listed in **C** as the second and third sonatas for violin and piano are published as Nos. 1 and 2. The true No. 1, composed in 1892, is unpublished, as is the first string quartet, of 1893.)

John IRELAND (d. 1962) made two additions to the works listed in **C**—the Piano Trio No. 3 (1938), which is dedicated to Walton, and the Fantasy-Sonata for clarinet and piano (1943), written for Frederick Thurston. Both preserve the note of crispness which in his music, as in Bridge's, has enlivened the romantic idiom, and has kept some of his piano music, including the Piano Concerto, alive in the concert hall. The chamber works have not held their place so well, possibly because of Ireland's preference for the relatively unpopular medium of the piano trio. The Piano Trio No. 3 is based on material dating from 1913.

VAUGHAN WILLIAMS (d. 1958) also added two major chamber works to his output in the last decades of his career, after a gap of a quarter of a century. These were the String Quartet in A minor (1944) and the Sonata for violin and piano, in the same key (1954). He also wrote, just before 1939, a Partita for double string trio, which was performed several times at the National Gallery concerts during the war, but after various revisions was transformed into the

Partita for double string orchestra. It has never been published in the original version.

The String Quartet in A minor bears the dedication 'For Jean on her birthday', and was written for Jean Stewart, the viola player in the Menges Quartet. The viola part is particularly prominent throughout, beginning each of the four movements unaccompanied, and carrying a good deal of the melodic weight of the work. Like Vaughan Williams's earlier quartet, it has not established itself in the repertory, although an equally characteristic work, of considerable importance in his output. The title 'Prelude' for the first movement is belied by its extent, its thematic weight, and its clearly recognizable sonata form with condensed recapitulation. Ex. 100 shows part of the development of the main theme.

Ex. 100

The second movement, 'Romance', is equally extended and elaborate in form, a kind of variations-cum-rondo, with some harmonic passages of a sophistication and elegance unusual in this composer. Third comes a scherzo, which opens with a theme from Vaughan Williams's music for the film *49th Parallel*, played by the viola against a counterpoint played tremolo, muted, and sul ponticello by the other three instruments in unison. The form again is not the straightforward one of scherzo and trio, but more resembles that of the first movement— a sonata with condensed recapitulation. Finally, there is an 'Epilogue', subtitled 'Greetings from Joan to Jean', a short, serene, almost hymn-like piece of very simple, pure, and smoothly flowing four-part counterpoint. The subtitle refers to the composer's using for this movement a theme that he had written for a projected film of St. Joan.

The Violin Sonata, although completed and first performed in 1954, contains earlier material. It is in Vaughan Williams's blunter style, with rather thick and heavy but not ineffective piano-writing. The first movement, Fantasia, is of unusual form, consisting of a lengthy yet not very far-ranging pursuit of one main thematic idea, with infrequent and minor interruptions by a secondary theme. This is followed by a scherzo, of a rhythmic interest exceptional in Vaughan Williams, in a steady 4/4 time but with irregular accents (see Ex. 101).

Ex. 101

This also has an asymmetrical, continuously developing form, and is unexpectedly exciting and wild in character. The last movement is a set of six variations and coda, which contains a short cadenza for the violinist, and reverts also to the main theme and mood of the first movement. The theme of the variations, according to the composer, is adapted from a work which he had written some years earlier, and later discarded.

Besides these two main works, Vaughan Williams wrote a Romance for viola and piano, which appeared only posthumously, a Suite for pipes, a set of 'Six Studies in English Folk-Song', for 'cello and piano (1927), and a set of three preludes on Welsh hymn-tunes, under the title *Household Music* (1942). These last two works are also adapted for various other instruments. On the fringe of chamber music there are two song-cycles from his later years, with unusual solo instrumental accompaniment. *Along the Field* (1954, but dating partly from the 1930's), for high voice and violin, is a beautiful set of eight Housman poems, which on its smaller and still more intimate scale is as original and imaginative a masterpiece as *On Wenlock Edge*. The other cycle, one of his very last works, performed and published after his death, is 'Ten Blake Songs' for tenor and oboe. Some of the songs may also be sung by a soprano, and a note in the score permits (but does not advise) the performance of the oboe part on a violin or a B flat clarinet. The fourth, sixth, and ninth songs are unaccompanied.

As in the senior group, there are several also among the younger English composers included in C whose subsequent work needs little comment. The contributions of BENJAMIN (d. 1960), FINZI (d. 1956), and HOWELLS are not among their most characteristic works, and are of little importance. Howells has added a pair of sonatas, for oboe and piano (1943) and clarinet and piano (1949), and Benjamin a String Quartet No. 2 (1952, rev. 1956), a Sonatina for 'cello and piano (1938), a suite of 'Valses-Caprices' under the title *Le Tombeau de Ravel* for violin (or clarinet) and piano (1949), and a Sonata (consisting of an Elegy, Waltz, and Toccata) for viola and piano (1945). Finzi's only chamber works are a Prelude and Fugue for string trio (1942), an Interlude for oboe and string quartet (1936), and Five Bagatelles for clarinet and piano (1945). With these composers may be grouped the more sophisticated Eugene GOOSSENS (d. 1962), who added only the Violin Sonata No. 2 (1930) and String Quartet No. 2 (1942); and Gordon JACOB, whose String Quartet was briefly mentioned in the Appendix to C. His later works include an Oboe Quartet, a Clarinet Quintet, and *Six Shakespeare Studies* for string trio.

The later works of MOERAN (d. 1950) are of slightly more account. They include a Sonata for two violins unaccompanied (1930), a String Trio (1931), a Fantasy Quartet for oboe and string trio (1946), a Sonata for 'cello and piano (1947), and a String Quartet in E flat (an early work discovered after his death). In the conservative romantic tradition to which they belong these works have something of the accomplishment, strength, and consistency of John Ireland's chamber works.

The one other composer in this group who received substantial mention in C was BLISS, who has followed up the dashing early works mentioned there with a series of more sober and traditional works in which the seemingly sharp distinction that existed in 1929 between him, a cosmopolitan experimenter, and his more conservative and provincial English contemporaries has become very blurred. His most important later chamber works are the Clarinet Quintet (1931), the Sonata for viola and piano (1932), and the String Quartets Nos. 1 and 2 (1941 and 1950). In all of these he writes in the very accomplished, fluent, and lush romantic idiom of his maturity, which in the second quartet in particular (as in the Violin Concerto) is very close to Walton's both in the flexible, sinuous, nostalgic melodies and in the dissonant sweetness of the harmonies. The forms are expansive and unselfconscious, without any experimental or unusual features. Sometimes they are closely worked, like the first movement of the second quartet, dominated by one theme, sometimes more rhapsodically lyrical, like the first movement of the Clarinet Quintet. This work, with a fulsome part for the clarinet (particularly in the floridly expressive slow movement), has proved more popular

than either of the quartets or the sonata. Ex. 102 shows the principal motive of
the first movement of the String Quartet No. 2.

Ex. 102

The development of Walton, Bush, and Rubbra, who all received a very brief
mention in **C**, has been similar to Bliss's. After *Façade* (**C**) WALTON produced
no chamber music until the String Quartet in A minor (1947) and the Sonata for
violin and piano (1949). These belong to the leanest years of his output, between
the Violin Concerto (1939) and *Troilus and Cressida* (1954), during which period
he composed no other work of major dimensions. Both are in a predominantly
lyrical vein, and there is much in them to admire, especially in the quartet, in
which his gift for sustained melody, supported by tirelessly springy rhythms,
is exemplified at its best. The first movement, in a clear-cut sonata form on a
large scale, and the slow movement, an extended asymmetrical design of continuous thematic development, carry the main weight of the work, with a terse and
lightweight scherzo between them, and a concluding movement of more or less
simple ternary design, mainly crisp and rhythmical, with a very brief central
section of flowing melody. It is a finely balanced work, attempting no formal
innovations. Ex. 103 shows a fugato theme from the development section of
the first movement, based on a rhythmic variant of the principal motive of the
movement and a subsidiary motive from the first subject.

Ex. 103

The Violin Sonata, written for Yehudi Menuhin, is formally more unusual,
consisting of only two movements, of about 12 minutes' duration each, in sonata
and variation form respectively. The first movement is similar in character to

that of the quartet, but rather less rich in thematic interest and texture, and
perhaps too exclusively concerned with its first subject, which is itself dominated
by a typically Waltonian rhythmic quirk that he works almost to excess. The
theme of the second movement begins with two eight-bar melodic phrases in the
same melodic vein, but the melody of the third and final eight-bar phrase consists of two statements of a twelve-note series, which acquires more prominence
as the movement progresses. In Variations 1 and 2 it remains an eight-bar
codetta, but in Variation 3 the codetta is extended, and Variation 4 is almost
wholly based on the twelve-note theme, which disappears only in the central
six bars. This is the central variation, and the process is then reversed, the
twelve-note theme reverting in Variations 5, 6, and 7 to the function of codetta,
before the extended coda to the whole movement, which is in effect a final
variation, recapitulating first the codetta-like eight bars and then the sixteen-
bar main section, both speeded up, extended, and completely transformed. The
extremely 'cerebral' conception evident in this strictly symmetrical formal
scheme, in Walton's experiment with twelve-note technique, and in his use of
such a deliberately and symmetrically constructed note-series (it consists in fact
of a sequence of three identical four-note groups, the second a tone higher
than the first and the third a tone lower) is very little reflected in the actual
musical content and style. Walton does draw attention to the symmetrical
arrangement of the variations by the unusualness of the writing in the central
one, which is in unison throughout except for the central six bars in which the
twelve-note theme is abandoned. Otherwise he does not specially mark either
the form or the twelve-note melody, which is given a rich chromatic harmonization that disguises its very deliberate construction (see Ex. 104). Walton has also
written Two Pieces for violin and piano—a Canzonetta (based on a troubadour
melody) and a Scherzetto.

Ex. 104

Alan BUSH has also toyed with the twelve-note method. Soon after the early
works briefly mentioned in **C**, new influences led to rapid development in his

style and the abandonment of his relatively conservative English idiom for a more cosmopolitan one of greater intellectual severity. The best-known example of his work at this period is *Dialectic* (1929), a movement for string quartet, which won acceptance as a landmark in modern English chamber music. As its title implies, it is an essay in logical musical argument, and it is a very strict example of what Bush later called his 'thematic' method of composition, in which every note is thematically derived. The movement is in a recognizable sonata form, with development and recapitulation combined. The material is expounded in seven sections, related by the melodic predominance in them all of the interval of the perfect fourth. A brief unison passage, recalling the unison opening, leads immediately to the recapitulation of these sections in a different sequence, with different key-relationships and some development of the material. The musical argument now seems a good deal less tough than when the work was first heard, but it has lost none of its strength, and remains one of the finest of modern English string quartets. Ex. 105 shows the end of the fugato that closes the exposition.

Ex. 105

No less impressive is Bush's Concert Piece for 'cello and piano (1936), in a more Bartókian vein, but this, like his earlier Five Pieces for clarinet, horn, and string trio (1925) and his original and inventive Three Concert Studies for piano trio (1947), has remained in manuscript. His only other published chamber work of importance is the 'Lyric Interlude' for violin and piano (1944), written at the time when he was trying to get back again to a simpler and less severe style.

The lyrical quality postulated in the title is sought in a serene, flowing melodic line, harmonized almost entirely with gentle dominant discords, treated as consonances, in unusual and elliptical progressions, giving the work a sustained warmth and soft richness of harmonic colour, continuously beguiling to the ear. In form it is subtle and elusive, a relaxed but finely shaped rhapsody with rudimentary sonata-features, in which the melodic field is gradually extended in the manner of developing variations. It is one of Bush's most successful solutions of the problem that he set himself, as a composer temperamentally inclined to intellectual experiment and an austere idiom, of writing in a more accessible style, reconciling the closeness of argument of *Dialectic* with a less forbidding language.

An austerity of another kind characterizes most of the chamber music of Edmund RUBBRA. Many of his works have a rhapsodic expansiveness of form somewhat similar to that of Bush's 'Lyric Interlude', and the same prevalent consonance of harmonic language, though only rarely with the particular sensuous delight in the harmonic sound as such. His chamber music is in two widely separated groups bounded by the original (1933) and revised (1946) versions of his String Quartet No. 1. Having won early attention with the Fantasy for two violins and piano described in **C**, he worked in relative obscurity until after 1940, and it is only since the war that most of his early works have become available. An exception is the Violin Sonata No. 2 (No. 1 is withdrawn), composed in 1931, which quickly found a publisher and was later recorded under the auspices of the British Council. With a vigorously lyrical opening movement, a slow middle movement headed 'Lament' (Lento e dolente), and a toccata-like finale (Allegro vivo e feroce), it is not altogether characteristic of Rubbra, whose works rarely show such an emphatic emotional contrast of movements. The Fantasy for two violins and piano (1925) is in a single pastoral 6/8 movement marked 'flowing', and the 'Lyric Movement', op. 24, for piano quartet (1929) has only a short middle section at a brisker tempo. Rubbra returned to what he calls a one-movement form in the Piano Trio, op. 68 (1950), though this is unmistakably in three movements played without a break. The first is a lyrical rhapsody, of moderate tempo, the second an 'Episodio scherzando', at the end of which a new slow theme appears, followed by three short meditations on it, forming a third movement. The main justification for describing the work on the title-page as being in one movement seems to be the presence in the themes in the first two movements of a four-note figure with a prominent rising fifth, which is also reintroduced in the coda to the last movement. Such cyclic methods are not part of Rubbra's normal practice in his other chamber music. The First Quartet is in three movements, of which the third is a later addition, made when the first and second were revised. Both this and the Second Quartet (1952), which is in a more or less traditional four-movement design, show in Rubbra a certain temperamental and technical affinity with Hindemith, though it is in the sobriety rather than the actual flavour of the counterpoint that the similarity lies. Both quartets contain episodes (in No. 2 it is the entire second movement, marked

'Scherzo polimetrico') in which the parts are independently barred. Ex. 106 is a fragment of the scherzo of the String Quartet No. 2. Another important chamber

Ex. 106

work by Rubbra is the Sonata, op. 60, for 'cello and piano (1946), in three movements, the first nearer to rondo than to sonata form, the second a scherzo, the last a set of contrapuntal variations ending with a fugue. This sonata is notable among Rubbra's works for the variety in the general texture and in the writing for the piano. In spite of his being a good pianist himself, Rubbra rarely writes gratefully for this instrument, though there is some attractive piano-writing also in the slighter Sonata in C, op. 100, for oboe and piano (1958). This is unusual among works for oboe in its avoidance of the 'pastoral' convention. It is in three movements, of which the first and second (the latter marked 'Elegy') are both lyrical in character, with a simple but fairly florid melodic line, and an equally simple harmony, lit up with subtle touches of beauty. The third movement is a gay and witty 'Presto', with brilliant, darting scales in the piano part. Although the title-page says 'Sonata in C', there are key-signatures of three flats for the first movement and four flats for the last. In addition to these and various smaller instrumental works, Rubbra has written numerous songs with chamber-music accompaniment, among them the *Amoretti* to five sonnets by Spenser, for voice and string quartet.

Walton was the youngest English composer included in **C**, which was published when he was twenty-seven. He was exceptionally precocious, and if yearly supplements to **C** had been published it would have been some years before any new name had appeared in them. When it did appear it would have been not that of any of his nearest contemporaries—Lennox Berkeley (b. 1903), Michael Tippett (b. 1905), and Alan Rawsthorne (b. 1905)—who were as late in establishing themselves as he was early, but that of the considerably younger and still more precocious Benjamin BRITTEN (b. 1913), who attracted attention with his first two published instrumental works while his three seniors had nothing yet to show. These works were the Sinfonietta, op. 1, for ten instruments, and the Fantasy Quartet, op. 2, for oboe and strings, both written in 1932, while Britten was still a student at the Royal College of Music. Op. 1 was publicly performed in London early in 1933, and Op. 2 in the following year, first in London and then at the ISCM Festival in Florence, when the composer was still only twenty years old. Berkeley reached the ISCM Festival only in 1936 (when Britten was represented for a second time, with the Suite, op. 6, for violin and piano, composed in 1935, in which he played the piano part himself with Antonio Brosa), and Rawsthorne in 1938. Britten followed up the Suite for violin and piano with the string quartets Nos. 1 and 2 (1941 and 1945). Since the war his absorption in opera has deprived us of any other instrumental chamber music except the *Lachrymae* for viola and piano (1950), the Sonata for 'cello and piano (1961), written for the Russian 'cellist Rostropovich, and the Canticle No. 3 'Still falls the rain', for tenor, horn, and piano (1954).

The large instrumental ensemble used by Britten in the Sinfonietta is strictly a chamber orchestra, and the work does not properly fall within the scope of chamber music as defined by Cobbett, who set the limit at the nonet. The Fantasy Quartet, on the other hand, is very much a Cobbett work—a late successor to the many modern English fantasies inspired by the Cobbett competitions (**C**). Britten shows great inventiveness and originality in the design of his single movement, which, to justify the title Fantasy, avoids any of the traditional sonata types. In the opening 'Andante alla marcia' a first section concerned mainly with the interval of the minor third is followed by a melody for the oboe, in which the interval of the fifth is prominent. Both intervals play an important thematic part in the work. A short transition leads to the 'Allegro giusto', in which a new theme is presented and developed in the manner of variations, the last of which, with a change of tempo to 'Andante', reverts to the oboe tune of the first section, now contrapuntally treated by the strings, with the oboe providing only an accompaniment derived from the 'Allegro' theme. The oboe then remains silent during an extended and intensive development of the 'Andante' tune, re-entering only as the development begins to subside, with its own florid and sustained extension of the 'Andante' tune. The development is then resumed, simultaneously with the recapitulation of the materials of the 'Allegro', and the form is completed by a slightly varied recapitulation of the opening 'Andante'. Ex. 107 shows the recapitulation of the 'Allegro' theme (violin) together with a development of the 'Andante' theme (oboe).

The Suite, op. 6, for violin and piano has not yet found the place in the repertory that it deserves. It is similar in spirit to the 'Variations on a Theme of Frank Bridge', a light-hearted display of virtuosity and invention. The four movements are: March, Moto perpetuo, Lullaby, and Waltz. The March is preceded by a brief introduction, to which there is a reference in the course of the Waltz.

The first of Britten's two string quartets was written in America, and is dedicated to Mrs. Elizabeth Sprague Coolidge. It opens arrestingly with the passage quoted in Ex. 108. After 24 bars a 'Tempo secundo' (Allegro vivo) introduces the theme quoted in Ex. 109, which is then twice repeated, with canonic imitations first at the third above, then at the third and fifth. The development begins with rapid scale-like passages against variants of the opening motive of Ex. 109. After a recurrence of the opening material, now in F, the

Ex. 107

Ex. 108

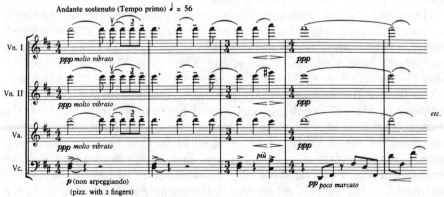

development of the second theme is resumed, and continues throughout the recapitulation, in which the 'Tempo primo' is represented, at the 'Tempo secundo', as in Ex. 110, simultaneously with the development-cum-recapitulation

Ex. 109

Ex. 110

of the 'Allegro' theme. A brief coda reverts to the original form of both themes. The second movement, 'Allegretto con slancio', is a scherzo-like study in dynamics, in the form ABABABA. It begins with staccato crotchet chords, *ppp*, spattered with increasingly frequent interjections of abrupt fortissimo triplets. A gradual crescendo throughout this section leads to B, a rhythmically irregular melody, *fff*, marked 'con esagerazione', accompanied by trilled scales. The process is twice repeated, with some thematic, tonal, and dynamic variation, the second A section being a development of the first, the third reversing the dynamic progress, from loud to soft. At the end of this the melody in the third B section is marked '*pp* delicatissimo'. The slow movement, 'Andante calmo', in 5/4 throughout, is in a simple song-like ternary form with a thematically related middle section and varied (inverted and condensed) recapitulation. A very similar form is found in the brisk last movement, with a more contrasted middle section, and a coda based on both thematic groups.

Britten wrote his second quartet in 1945 to commemorate the 250th anniversary of Purcell's death. It was first performed on that date (21 November) at Wigmore Hall, London. The quartet is in three movements, in the first of which Britten carries still farther the methods of simultaneous and developing recapitulation of subjects, observed in the preceding works. He presents the entire thematic material of the movement within the first 40 bars. This consists of three short sections of melody, each introduced by a rising tenth—the first on the

tonic, C–E, the second on the dominant, G–B, the third on the dominant of the
dominant, D–F sharp. In the analysis by Erwin Stein printed with the miniature
score, these are referred to as first, second, and third subject, but they form
a continuous and coherent melody which may equally well be regarded as the
single main theme of the movement. Development begins immediately, first on
the interval of the tenth, then on the various sections of the theme, in turn or
together, in various keys. A further section based on the tenth leads to a further
phase of development in which new melodic material is introduced, marking
this as the development proper, as distinct from the expository development
previously heard. With a further section of tenths, the new material is abandoned,
but the development of the various sections of the original theme continues, and
leads abruptly into the recapitulation, where the three melodic sections are now
presented simultaneously (see Ex. 111). There is a short coda in which the interval
of the tenth, and section three of the theme, are prominent.

Ex. 111

The second movement, 'Vivace', is another brilliant dynamic scherzo, muted
throughout, with some striking similarities to the second movement of Bartók's
fourth quartet. It is in the form of a scherzo and trio, elaborately organized, with
a hint of sonata form in that the trio may be regarded as a development section,
since its main theme is a variant of the scherzo theme. The two are shown in
Exx. 112 a and b. In the reprise of the scherzo the material undergoes very considerable transformation. The third movement, which carries the main burden

of the homage to Purcell intended in the work, is entitled 'Chacony'. There are twenty-one variations on the theme (Ex. 113), the first eighteen grouped in three

Ex. 112A

Ex. 112B

Ex. 113

sixes, with unaccompanied cadenzas for 'cello, viola, and violin, in that order, between the groups. In the first group the variations are of harmonization, in the second of rhythm and texture, and in the third a counter-subject to the theme is developed. The final three variations present the theme first in the bass, below a chromatic progression of triads, then on the violin, above seventh-chords leading up to a massive dominant suspension, and, finally, in unison on all four instruments, with pedal-like interjections of the tonic (C major) chord.

In his next chamber work, the *Lachrymae* for viola and piano, written in 1950 for William Primrose, Britten, as in his earlier instrumental duet, the Suite for violin and piano, avoids the sonata form. It is sub-titled 'Reflections on a song of Dowland', and consists of a theme and ten variations. The theme consists of the first 8 bars of Dowland's song 'If my complaints could passions move', set in the bass on the piano in a context of perfect and augmented triads in first inversion, derived from the first phrase of the song. The succession of triads, with some alteration of the augmented into perfect ones, is the basis of most of the variations, which in other respects range very far afield. In Variation 6 the viola quotes a short phrase from another Dowland song, 'Flow my tears' (at the words 'Never may my woes be relieved'). The last variation leads to an extended coda, based on the remaining 16 bars of 'If my complaints', with the original bass, and closer in style to Dowland than anything in the variations.

Having studiously avoided the sonata in his two earlier works for two instruments, in the 'Cello Sonata Britten casts the first movement, headed 'Dialogo', in a model sonata form, complete with double-bar repeat of the exposition. Another new element in the work is the conspicuous influence of Bartók, not formerly one of the composers most admired by Britten. The sonata is in five movements (Dialogo, Scherzo pizzicato, Elegia, Marcia, Moto Perpetuo), and although these are not thematically related as in Bartók's five-movement works, some of the themes in different movements can be related to the same source. Adjacent major and minor seconds are among the conspicuous thematic elements (as in Bartók's String Quartet No. 4), and Peter Evans has pointed out in an article in *Tempo* that much of the work is based on scales of alternating tones and semitones.

Ex. 114

Ex. 114 shows the opening theme. Both the complete scale on the piano and the major second (i.e. a single unit of the scale) so prominent in the 'cello part are thematically important throughout the movement. All the main points of transition (end of the first subject, end of the exposition, etc.) are marked by the appearance of this major second as a harmonic instead of a melodic interval. There are three contrasting subsidiary themes, closely but well-disguisedly derived from the opening material (rather as in the Second String Quartet), and all are worked on in the development, but in the recapitulation only the principal

theme (in augmentation) and the coda-like fourth theme appear in full, the other
two being allusively included in the restatement of the principal theme.

The second movement, pizzicato throughout, begins with the theme quoted
in Ex. 115. The slightly Bartókian character of this becomes still more marked in
the 'trio', where the devices of mirror inversion and polymodality are exploited
in a very Bartókian kind of stretto (see Ex. 116). There is no real recapitulation,
only a coda-like return of the theme of the scherzo.

Ex. 115

Ex. 116

The same kind of Bartókian mirror inversion is to be found in the third
movement, when at the climax the theme (shown in Ex. 117) appears inverted
on the 'cello in a high register, against the outline of its original form in massive
bass chords on the piano. After this climax the 'cello makes a long and very
Brittenish descent in steps of a third to a sustained bass C which enables him to
put on the mute. The two aspects of the single theme presented in the exposition
are brought closer together in the recapitulation, in alternating phrases against
a 'cello ostinato.

Ex. 117

The fourth movement again recalls Bartók, not so much in technique as in
its wry humour, which is like that of the marches in the Sixth Quartet and

Contrasts. In form it is a straightforward march with trio, though in the 'da capo' the march appears in an entirely new guise.

The fifth movement is again monothematic, all its material being derived from, or closely related to, Ex. 118.

Ex. 118

The Canticle No. 3, 'Still falls the rain', for tenor, horn, and piano, written in memory of Noel Mewton-Wood, belongs to the same year as the opera *The Turn of the Screw*, and is designed on a closely similar principle. There are six song-verses, corresponding to the opera's sixteen scenes, linked in a similar way by instrumental variations on an introductory theme. The theme consists of a 16-bar melody on the horn, which introduces all twelve notes and is symmetrically constructed in pairs of phrases. The first phrase, introducing five notes, is answered by its inversion, introducing five more. The remaining two notes occur in the third and final phrase, in which again the first five-note sequence (discounting repetitions) is answered by its inversion. The piano harmony passes through a highly dissonant chromatic progression and ends on a high bare fifth (B flat–F) above the horn's long-held low B flat. In the variations that follow, the structural principle of the horn's melodic line is consistently adhered to, while the actual melodic content is varied. Whereas in the theme the first five-note phrase opened with a whole-tone tetrachord, in the variations it becomes successively a dominant-seventh arpeggio, a chromatic scale-fragment, an arpeggio of rising perfect fourths, a quintuplet on one note, and an arpeggio of rising perfect fifths. The piano harmony starts each time from the same point, makes its way through similar but not identical progressions to an identical short coda over the horn's sustained low B flat, resolving on to the original fifth on B flat. The six verses, all firmly anchored to this B flat chord, all begin with an identical refrain ('Still falls the rain'), and then from verse to verse gradually extend their tonal and melodic range in directions suggested each time by the preceding instrumental variation. Finally, instrumental variation and song-verse are combined in Variation 6, where above the horn's melody, built up still in five-note phrases and their inversions, consisting now of diatonic scale-fragments in B flat major, the voice in rhythmic unison sings the inversion of each of the horn's phrases—a device similar to that with the two voices in the Canticle No. 2 (*Abraham and Isaac*), and used for the same purpose, to suggest, with a serene and impersonal effect, the voice of God. During this section the piano is silent, until horn and voice resolve at last on to their unison B flat, over which the piano finally repeats the recurring harmonic coda to the variations.

The chamber music of Michael TIPPETT (b. 1905) consists of three string quartets (No. 1, 1935, revised 1943; No. 2, 1942; No. 3, 1946) and a Sonata for four horns (1955). The best known of these is the String Quartet No. 2, which has been recorded for the British Council, and is relatively popular, as modern string quartets go. Its success is well deserved, although it is a pity that it has been at the expense of the other two quartets, both of which are among the most beautiful and original of modern English chamber works.

No. 1 is in three movements, of which the first is in sonata form. Both the exposition and the recapitulation end with an unaccompanied cadenza for the 'cello. Following this is a monothematic slow movement of great melodic beauty, with a rich and lyrical contrapuntal texture. The third movement, like many in Tippett's works, has features suggestive of a variety of traditional forms. In character it is scherzo-like. The main theme, of 21 bars (Ex. 119), consisting of

Ex. 119

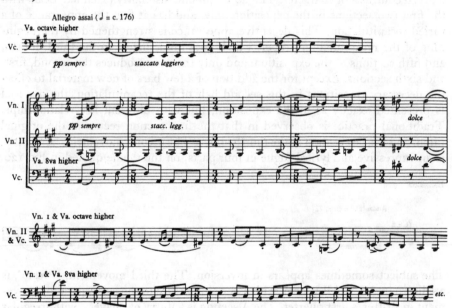

two sections (8 bars and 13 bars), is played eight times, in a contrapuntal texture of changing content but consistent style. The fourth and eighth appearances of it are in the same key as the first. After the fourth appearance there is a long episode of nearly 100 bars which contains references to both sections of the main theme, as well as new material. The remaining four statements of the main theme thus have a reprise-like function in relation to the 'expository' first four state-ments, but after the sixth statement there is a second, shorter episode (36 bars), thematically loosely related to the first, which introduces a suggestion of rondo form. This fascinating and wholly successful movement is an early example of Tippett's highly individual technique of perpetual repetition without repetitiveness.

In the score of the String Quartet No. 2 (in F sharp), a prefatory note draws attention to the rhythmic characteristics of the work, and particularly of the first movement, which, it states, 'is partly derived from Madrigal technique where each part may have its own rhythm and the music is propelled by the differing accents, which tend to thrust each other forward. The bar-lines are thus sometimes only an arbitrary division of time, and the proper rhythms are shown in the notation by the groupings of the notes and by the bowing.' Of the fourth and last movement it says that it 'needs a decisively sprung rhythm on which virtually the whole movement is based'.

This quartet is one of Tippett's most beautifully shaped works, at once clear, simple, and subtle. The first movement (Allegro grazioso) is in sonata form, with an extended exposition in six well-defined but unified sections that present no marked contrasts of character. The development, also fairly extended, deals with the first two sections of the exposition only, and has at first the appearance of a varied recapitulation. This deceptive appearance is strengthened by the beginning of the recapitulation proper, which goes immediately to the third, fourth, and fifth sections of the exposition, and only then reintroduces the second, first, and sixth sections. Except for the addition of a few bars of new material to effect the necessary transitions in this second half of the recapitulation, the material is presented exactly as in the exposition, but with different key-relationships. Traditional practice is observed in that the first section recurs at the original pitch, and the last section at the fourth above. The second movement, 'Andante', is an expressive and lyrical fugue in four parts, on the theme quoted in Ex. 120.

Ex. 120

The subject sometimes appears in inversion. The third movement, 'Presto', is a scherzo in ABABABA form, with some similarities to the corresponding movement in Britten's first quartet. The A section is a flurry of quavers, with irregular accents and intermittent hints of an emerging tune, and is stated three times on different instruments with a varying accompaniment texture. The whole process is twice repeated, section A rising in pitch each time by a third (first minor, then major), section B changing pitch more freely and undergoing other variations. The final A section is condensed into twelve cadential bars. The last movement is in regular sonata form, with material similar in character to that of the first movement, except for a contrasting central thematic section (i.e. the beginning of the second subject) dominated by poignant falling ninths (see Ex. 121).

Tippett's String Quartet No. 3 is more complex and unusual in design. Fugal technique is prominent in three of its five movements, but their form is much more elaborate than that of the fugue in the second quartet. In the first movement

Ex. 121

Tippett seems to have been influenced by Beethoven's C major Quartet, op. 59, No. 3. It begins with a similar chordal passage and then leads through a florid cadenza for all four instruments to a lengthy fugue subject in rapid notes, followed by a counter-subject, both extensively developed, with several 'episodes', including a recurrence of the introductory material. In the second movement the principal melody is in 3/2 throughout, against a varying accompaniment which is always in 3/4 (see Ex. 122). The movement is marked 'Andante (♩ con moto, ♩ tranquillo)'. Its form is simple though difficult to describe. The

Ex. 122

scheme is ABABA, the A sections being a short ritornello-like introduction, interlude, and coda. The B sections are more extended, and each presents the principal melody three times—the first repetition at the original pitch, the second a fifth higher. In the 'recapitulation' the whole section goes into the minor, with some other slight variations. Ex. 123 shows a fragment from the first B section. The scherzo, a brilliant contrapuntal movement, combines the characteristics of sonata, fugue, canon, and round. Both the first and second thematic groups of the sonata exposition are fugal expositions of different subjects and counter-

subjects, the first in four parts, the second in two. There is a lengthy development
section making use of all four of these themes, and a full recapitulation, with the

Ex. 123

second subject transposed. Nearly all the counterpoint in the movement is
canonic. Ex. 124 illustrates the texture. The fourth movement, 'Lento', is a kind

Ex. 124

of interlude, recalling the introduction to the first movement, opening very
quietly and slowly, then leading through a very florid and increasingly rapid
accompanied cadenza for the 'cello to a declamatory, recitative-like passage.
This is then twice repeated, with the cadenza first on the viola, then on the first
violin. The violin cadenza leads not to a second repetition of the declamatory
passage but to a cadenza of swirling fourths and fifths for all four instruments.

The fifth movement is rather like an epilogue, detached from the rest of the work. The marking is 'Allegro comodo'. In form it is elusive and indefinite, with no symmetrical design. The main musical argument lies in the quasi-fugal presentation of three fairly short melodic themes at many different pitch levels.

Tippett's only other published work of chamber music is the Sonata for four horns, written for Dennis Brain. The following is the composer's note written for the first performance at Wigmore Hall:

> The first movement of the Sonata is strophic; like three verses of a song. The cadence of each strophe is echoed with mutes. The second movement is a sonata allegro. The slow movement has the traditional a-b-a form of a nocturne. The finale is a fugue, where the subject is set against changing counter-subjects. All the movements contain characteristic calls and arpeggios. Sometimes the call is the text of the music itself, e.g., in the fugue; sometimes the calls make accompaniment to a solo, e.g., in the nocturne

Alan RAWSTHORNE (b. 1905), like Britten, sounded a strongly individual note with his very first works, which appeared just before the 1939–45 war and immediately made his name. Two of these were chamber works—the Theme and Variations for two violins unaccompanied (1937), played at the ISCM festival in London in 1938, and the Theme and Variations for string quartet (1939), which was originally part of a quartet in several movements. The original score was lost, and this was the only movement that Rawsthorne reconstructed. The distinctive idiom of these works won immediate attention and admiration, and served Rawsthorne, with scarcely any discernible development, for almost twenty years. Ex. 125, the opening of the quartet, is characteristic.

Ex. 125

As variations these two works call for little further comment on their form. In the two-violin work the last variation is a developing rondo with references to some of the earlier variations as the episodes. His sonata-form works all diverge considerably from the traditional patterns. They are all brief, generally under 20 minutes in total playing-time, and often elliptical in form, with very compressed recapitulations. The Viola Sonata, written at the same time as the Theme and Variations for two violins, shows most of these features already fully developed, though it is not possible to know to what extent this may be due to later revisions. After its first performance in 1938 the manuscript of this work too was lost for many years, and rediscovered only in 1954, when the composer revised it thoroughly. Only an unusual weight and thickness in some of the piano-writing suggest an early work. In the first movement, a weighty and sustained slow introduction precedes a toccata-like 'Allegro'. There is a varied, lightened, and condensed reprise of the introduction and a quick coda based on the 'Allegro'. The second movement is a scherzo with two trios, the scherzo being played backwards at the first repetition and varied at the second. The viola is muted until the final section, and there is a C sharp pedal in the piano part sounded throughout much of the movement. The slow movement is a short set of variations, of great expressive intensity, leading straight into a gay and lively final rondo of straightforward design, with the main theme accompanied at its last appearance by its own inversion—a constructional contrapuntal device of a kind rarely found in Rawsthorne's later music.

He did not write another chamber work after the Theme and Variations for string quartet until the Quartet for clarinet and string trio (1948). This is in three movements, of which the first two are in ternary form with varied reprise, the first movement monothematic, the second with a contrasting middle section, in which the clarinet is silent. The third and last movement is an extended sonata-rondo of straightforward form, with a coda recalling the first movement. A first movement of very similar design, with the addition of a slow introduction, presenting the main theme, is found in the Sonata for 'cello and piano (1949), the three movements of which are closely linked. The second movement is in a simple ternary form in which both the main and the subsidiary theme are taken from the development section of the first movement. In the finale new themes are introduced and developed, and only the coda reverts to the main theme of the first movement.

The interest of Rawsthorne's formal designs in these works is offset, as in many of Hindemith's works, by some lack of variety in the thematic material. In his String Quartet No. 2 (1954), written for the Cheltenham Festival, he showed signs for almost the first time of some development in his language. The forms of the four movements, which this time are not thematically related, are again original. The first is in a terse sonata form with an abbreviated recapitulation of the second subject. Ex. 126, part of the first subject, shows the new style. The second movement has two 'allegro' and two 'adagio' sections, in the manner of alternating variations. The thematic material for the differing tempi is unrelated, but the first violin's opening phrase from the 'allegro' is introduced at one point into each of the 'adagio' sections. The third movement, a muted waltz-like intermezzo, has the same kind of ternary form as the first movements of the two preceding works, with a development as middle section. A theme, three variations, and coda form the finale, a slow and rather remote movement.

The Sonata for violin and piano (1958), dedicated to Joseph Szigeti, reverts to the cyclic procedures of the 'Cello Sonata and the Clarinet Quartet. Its motto-theme, or rather motto-chord, is thematically important in the outer two

movements, and makes conspicuous appearances in the middle two. All four
movements have Rawsthorne's typical conciseness and flexibility of form. The

Ex. 126

first movement opens with a slow, recitative-like introduction (see Ex. 127) beginning with the motto-harmony—a combination of the chords of D minor and E flat
(major or minor). The toccata-like sonata-form 'Allegro' which follows starts
with a transformation of the piano's two chords, which recur again in the long
development, against a line of more sustained, rhapsodic melody on the violin.
The coda recapitulates the introduction exactly. In the slightly waltz-like second
movement (Allegretto), marked 'poco misterioso', the motto-harmony occurs at
the end of the first theme, and again at the end of the movement when the first
theme, after a lengthy middle section in which two further themes are presented,
is recapitulated. The third movement, marked 'Toccata' (Allegro di bravura), is
again in a kind of sonata form, with two themes. Here the motto-chord appears
during the development section. The fourth movement, headed 'Epilogue'

(Adagio rapsodico), is closely related to the first movement, beginning and ending with close variants of the introductory recitative (with the motto-chord floridly arpeggiated), surrounding an aria-like middle section. The work ends with a kind of Tierce de Picardie on the combined chords of D major and E flat minor.

Ex. 127

Rawsthorne's latest chamber work, which does not strictly fall within the limits of the genre as defined in C, is the Concerto for Ten Instruments, commissioned for the 1961 Cheltenham Festival. It is in four movements (Preludio—allegro deciso; Andante poco doloroso; Allegro; Poco lento), of which the fourth is described by the composer as 'a kind of meditation on the preceding music, containing occasional snatches of ideas heard before'. The ensemble consists of a string quintet (with double bass) and the customary wind quintet. In his original programme-note Rawsthorne wrote that his aim had been 'not so much to contrast the timbres of the string ensemble with that of the wind, as to evolve passages in which the two will mingle into a colourful whole.'

There also exists a little-known Concertante No. 2 for violin and piano composed by Rawsthorne in 1935. The idiom is already mature and the form characteristic—a single movement with several sections of varying tempi, the alternation of which is robbed of effect by the similarity of figuration in all the sections, fast or slow: the tempo-indications might be interchanged without any great difference of effect. The Concertante No. 1, also for violin and piano (1934), and a Trio for flute, oboe, and piano (1936) are now lost.

The musical personality of Lennox BERKELEY (b. 1903) is not so distinctive. His major published chamber works are the String Quartet No. 2 (1940), String Trio (1944), Sextet for clarinet, horn, and string quartet (1957), Trio for horn, violin, and piano (1956), Concertino for recorder (or flute), violin, 'cello, and harpsichord (1956), Sonata for viola and piano (1945), Sonatina for violin and piano (1942), and Sonatina for recorder (or flute) and piano (1940). The String Quartet No. 1 (1935) and Sonata No. 2 for violin and piano, originally published in 1934, are now out of print, and the Sonata No. 1 for violin and piano, which has never been published, has been destroyed by the composer.

The predominant characteristics of these works are a reserved lyrical sentiment and a gentle wit, which effortlessly coexist in nearly all his music. Although neo-classical in idiom and spirit, many of his works have a certain emotional serious-ness and warmth that in his more recent works, such as the Horn Trio and the Sextet, have led him to a more outspokenly romantic expression. This has not been all gain, for in freeing his style in this way he has sacrificed some of the thematic incisiveness and clarity of the more pastiche-like works. In the Con-certino, written for Carl Dolmetsch for the Haslemere Festival, he combines very marked neo-classical appearances, in the use of recorder and harpsichord (the piano is not suggested in the score as a possible alternative), with a first venture in twelve-note technique. The work is in four movements, of which the middle ones, both slow, are called Aria 1 and Aria 11, the one for recorder and 'cello alone, the other for violin and harpsichord. Aria 1 consists of five statements of a twelve-note chaconne theme (the fourth appearance of which is in the treble), accompanied by variations, also serial, of a second melody, also containing all twelve notes, built out of a winding chromatic scale, first ascending an octave (B to B), then descending to E to include the two notes avoided in the ascent. The movement is very successfully fitted into a work that is otherwise closer than usual to the eighteenth century in the letter as well as in spirit.

His most convincing venture beyond his normal range of style is in the String Quartet No. 2, which has an occasional note of aggressive vigour and acerbity of language unusual in his music. Within the neo-classical style his finest and most expansive works are the Viola Sonata and the String Trio, both of a lyrical and sustained thematic beauty. The Sonatina for violin and piano and the Sonatina for recorder and piano are equally attractive works of similar thematic quality, on a slighter scale and more innocent in character. Ex. 128 shows the opening of the String Trio, with its possibly intentional reminiscence of Schubert's A minor String Quartet.

The form of Berkeley's works is in keeping with their character—terse, clear, modest in scale, and with no innovations of style or striking characteristics except the consistent avoidance of the scherzo, which appears only in the youthful String Quartet No. 1. All the other works described above, except the Concer-tino, are in three movements, the middle one slow, and the last generally scherzo-like in its material, often with some marked rhythmic characteristic, such as an uneven metre. In the Horn Trio, the Violin Sonata, and the String Quartet No. 1, the finale is a set of variations, and the finale of the Sextet combines variation-like and rondo-like features.

Ex. 128

Several others among the many talented English composers of the generation of Berkeley, Tippett, Rawsthorne, and Britten have contributed notably to chamber music. Arnold COOKE (b. 1906) is a composer with gifts of a similar nature to Berkeley's, with the difference that he was a pupil not of the Boulanger school but of Hindemith, to whose music his bears much the same relationship as Berkeley's to Stravinsky's. It has a similar emotional reserve, urbanity, and unassertive individuality, and it sounds a quietly distinctive note in English music. His numerous chamber works, not all of which are published, include two string quartets, two sonatas for violin and piano, one each for viola and 'cello, both with piano, a String Trio, an Oboe Quartet, and a Flute Quartet.

The works of Benjamin FRANKEL (b. 1906) are nearer in character to Rawsthorne's, similarly sombre, though less distinctive, in harmonic idiom. He has written four string quartets, two string trios, a Trio for clarinet, 'cello, and piano, a Viola Sonata, an interesting set of eight 'Inventions in major-minor modes' for 'cello and piano, and a Clarinet Quintet (1956), one of his finest works. A Clarinet Quintet by William WORDSWORTH (b. 1908), composed in 1952, has also made a stronger impression than any of his five string quartets. It is one of several of his later works in which this naturally conservative composer makes some use of twelve-note technique, which without proclaiming itself on the surface of his music has had the effect of refreshing and strengthening his invention. Among the more interesting of his many other chamber works are a Piano Trio and an Oboe Quartet.

The most consistent of the twelve-note composers in Britain is Elisabeth LUTYENS (b. 1906). Her published chamber music includes Nos. 2 (1938), 3 (1948), and 6 (1952) of her six string quartets, a Wind Quintet (1960), commissioned by the BBC for the first appearance of the BBC Chamber Ensemble, Nine Bagatelles for 'cello and piano, *Valediction* for clarinet and piano, marked 'Dylan Thomas, December 1953'. In addition she has written a set of Six Chamber Concertos, op. 8, of which the first, for nine solo instruments, comes within the category of chamber music proper. It is a light and attractive work in four short movements (Theme and Variations, Aria, Scherzo, Rondo). A more recent work in a similar category is the Six Tempi for ten instruments, op. 42 (1957). Her forms are generally concise and simple. The Quartet No. 6, for instance, is in a single movement in a 'da capo' ternary form. Such double-bar repeats are a common feature of her scores, and she also makes frequent use of the device of repetition in retrograde motion. When the opening section of the fourth movement of the Wind Quintet is recapitulated at the end, the first four bars are re-stated in reverse, then a further seven bars in their original form.

The seven string quartets of Elizabeth Maconchy (b. 1907) are effective and sustained studies in a very limited range of harmonic sonorities (as distinct from harmonic progressions), based on the exhaustive exploitation of slender thematic material, which varies comparatively little from work to work.

Priaulx Rainier (b. 1903) and Phyllis Tate (b. 1911) have been less productive. Rainier has written three string quartets, of which only the middle one (1939) has been published, as No. 1 (No. 1 proper, a very early work, has been withdrawn). A Suite for clarinet and piano (1943) and a Sonata for viola and piano (1945) are also published. These works are generally spare in harmony and texture, and their musical interest lies more in the extension and development of the melodic material. In Phyllis Tate's single String Quartet (1953), something of the wit and spirit of Haydn's quartets, rare in serious chamber music since his day, is recaptured. This is her most important instrumental work, disguising beneath an easy-going manner a musical content of some weight. Her other chamber music includes a 'Triptych' (Prelude, Scherzo, and Soliloquy) for violin and piano (1954) and a Sonata for clarinet and 'cello (1947), which have a slightly melancholy lyrical sentiment, slenderer thematic material, and a more decorative interest in the instrumental writing. There is also a certain element of pastiche in them, which is more prominent still in the Air and Variations for violin, clarinet, and piano (1957), consisting of six short character-pieces, variously scored. She has also written several works of vocal chamber music, principally the 'Nocturne' for four solo voices with instrumental septet, and 'Songs of Sundry Natures' for baritone with quintet.

Two other composers claim attention for isolated works that have established themselves. Howard Ferguson (b. 1908) wrote in 1933 an Octet, for the same ensemble as that used by Schubert, which has been frequently performed. Herbert Murrill (1909–52) wrote an excellent String Quartet (1939), of modest neo-classical character and proportions, to which he added an attractive Sonata for recorder and harpsichord, in the same vein, two years before his early death.

The extraordinary precocity of Britten, the youngest member of the pre-1914 generation, and the suspension of normal musical life during the 1939–45 war created a very wide gap between him and the next generation in English music. By dates of birth only seven years separate him from Peter Racine FRICKER (b. 1920), who was the first of his juniors to gain international recognition, but by the time Fricker had achieved this, with the performance of his String Quartet No. 1 (1949) at the Brussels Festival of the ISCM in 1950, the gap had more than doubled. Three years earlier Fricker's Wind Quintet (1947), the work by which he first became known, had won the Alfred Clements Prize. His subsequent chamber works are a Sonata for violin and piano (1950), String Quartet No. 2, commissioned by the Cheltenham Festival (1953), Sonata for horn and piano (1955), composed for Dennis Brain, Sonata for 'cello and piano, commissioned by the BBC for the tenth anniversary of the Third Programme (1956), Octet (1958), commissioned by the Virtuoso Ensemble, and two serenades, No. 1, commissioned by the Canadian Broadcasting Corporation, for flute, clarinet, bass clarinet, harp, viola, and 'cello, No. 2 for flute, oboe, and piano (both 1959).

The Wind Quintet already shows his powers of invention and the originality of his musical thought, although it is not otherwise representative. There is evidence still of student work about it, in a certain technical naïvety and literal-mindedness, and it has a gaiety and wit not characteristic of Fricker's later work, in which seriousness and technical subtlety are among the conspicuous qualities. They manifest themselves strongly in the String Quartet No. 1, which is a fully mature and assured work, in a concise single movement. It has three main tempi, and a complex form, which has suggestions of various traditional forms but eludes any precise definition. Even that useful label 'sonata rondo', which will cover almost anything, will not suffice for this movement. 'Fantasy-sonata-rondo' is perhaps as near as that kind of terminology can get to it. Canonic writing plays a considerable part in the work, but is now less obvious than in the 'Canonic Variations' that form the third movement of the Wind Quintet. There is one

Ex. 129

remarkable passage (see Ex. 129) in double mirror canon in block chords, a tender lyrical passage typical of Fricker in its disguise of the structural devices, or rather the highly expressive and free treatment of them. His increasing use of twelve-note technique in later works is similarly free, and often after propounding a twelve-note thematic idea he treats it in a free tonal manner. The String Quartet No. 1 has no key, but No. 2 is loosely anchored to E flat, both its outer movements ending on this chord. This is more traditional in design, except that it ends with the slow movement and dispenses with a 'finale'. Each of its three movements is in a sonata-like ternary form—the first quite straightforward, with a fugal development; the second a scherzo with a very short trio-like section instead of a development, a reprise varied in tonality and in parts rhythmically transformed, and a coda that almost turns it into a sonata-rondo; and the third a da capo aria with a development as middle section and a reprise again heavily varied. The carefully worked-out rhythmic device in the second violin and viola parts in Ex. 130, from the middle movement, and the symmetrical construction of the scales, are another example of intricacies of structure concealed by the simplicity of the effect, and in this case also 'thrown away' in an accompaniment.

Ex. 130

A somewhat similar design is found in the Violin Sonata, also in three movements, which become progressively slower. The forms of the movements here are less straightforward. The first is a sonata-movement (Allegro), very rich and closely packed with material, with an extended development section. In the reprise the first subject-group is abbreviated, the second subject-group extended and melodically rethought. The second movement, marked 'Allegretto', begins muted 'Come un valse distante'. It is elusive in form, and can best be described again as a fantasy-rondo in which the middle section of the opening theme functions as the 'refrain'. The last movement, as in the String Quartet No. 2, is again a da capo aria with an elaborated, extended, and tonally varied reprise. Each of the three sections in this movement leads through a short decorative cadenza to an identical complex chord, which is given a different resolution each time, the third a slightly jolting one on to a pure C major triad.

In the Sonata for horn and piano there is no true slow movement, and the nearest to it is again placed last. It opens with a sonata movement remarkable for its very brief development section. The first subject is inverted and condensed in the reprise. This movement leads without a break into the scherzo, which is of simple ABABA design, the two themes being varied at each appearance. The last movement, headed 'Invocation', is something like a rondo, in which the 'refrain' theme is a horn-call that takes a new form at each recurrence. The episodes are fairly extended, and are linked by certain thematic relationships. Each of the first two movements of this work opens with a clear twelve-note melodic statement by the horn, but any part that twelve-note technique plays in the continuation of these movements is very well concealed. Similar twelve-note passages occur even more prominently in the 'Cello Sonata, without apparently functioning as the thematic or structural basis of the work. This has four movements, of original design. The first is a variety of sonata-rondo, in which the exposition consists of an opening theme for unaccompanied 'cello, followed by a continuation with a harmonically elaborate accompaniment. The opening theme is then repeated, at the original pitch, in an extended and varied version, followed by a new episode. Finally, the two sections of the exposition are recapitulated simultaneously. The second movement is in sonata form with a suggestion of a da capo aria. The middle section, marked 'scherzando', introduces contrasting material in a 9/8 metre irregularly split up into beats of two plus three plus four quavers. In the reprise the second subject is melodically rethought, as in the first movement of the Violin Sonata. In the third movement there is another variety of sonata-rondo, of palindrome design. There are three statements of the main theme, the middle one a fifth higher than the first, and with a new accompaniment, the final one merely an ostinato-like repetition of its first phrase, more like a coda than a restatement of the theme. The second-subject material includes a short twelve-note melodic statement, the reappearance of which in the reprise, very much disguised, is the principal thematic identification mark of the second-subject material, which is otherwise still more thoroughly transformed. Exx. 131 and 132 show it as it originally appears and as it is transformed in the

Ex. 131

recapitulation. In the fourth movement the twelve-note writing is more conspicuous than in any of the earlier ones. After an opening piano theme, which grows progressively more chromatic, the 'cello makes its first entry, unaccompanied, with a twelve-note phrase that is present in much of the rest of the movement. Like the second movement this is in an aria-like sonata form, with a different emphasis. There the middle section was a simple contrast, not a development, but the reprise was sonata-like. Here the middle section is a strictly thematic development section, but in the reprise both subjects (based on the same material but distinguished by different tempi and texture), although very greatly transformed, reappear at their original pitch.

Ex. 132

The Octet is scored for flute, clarinet, horn, bassoon, violin, viola, 'cello, and double bass. It is in five movements, headed: Toccata, Nocturne, Scherzetto, Canto, and Finale. The first movement is in sonata form, with a thematic introduction consisting of a melody on the viola accompanied by sustained chords. Both the melody and the harmonic progression contain all twelve notes, and the melody is used as a quasi-serial theme in the Toccata that follows, the first phrase of which consists of the same sequence of notes in diminution and in a new rhythm. In the course of the exposition of the first subject this 'series' appears simultaneously on the flute in semiquavers and on the horn in augmentation at the fifth below (see Ex. 133). The more homophonic second subject

Ex. 133

begins with a melody presented in double mirror-canon on the wind instruments, to an accompaniment of symmetrical chords giving almost another double mirror-canon, which is sustained throughout the theme, while the melody is reduced to a single line. In the modified recapitulation the harmonies of the introduction reappear simultaneously with the first subject of the Toccata. The players are directed to play the Toccata as a soft staccato throughout. The Nocturne (Adagio) is a duet for clarinet and violin, with a ritornello-like theme on the horn, and an intermittent 'buzzing' accompaniment on the other instruments, which at the central climax of the movement develops into an agitated Bartókian 'night-music'. The scherzo, according to the composer, is based on Berlioz's 'Queen Mab' scherzo in *Romeo and Juliet*, and with this clue certain relationships can be discerned. In the exposition the form is defined by the three rondo-like recurrences of a single quasi-twelve-note melodic phrase, separated by lengthy and varying episodes. After the third appearance of the main theme there is a still longer episode, which is in effect the trio, followed by a vestigial 'da capo' in the form of a repeat of the opening melodic phrase and an athematic coda. The Canto (Andante) is the most complex movement in the work. It is an elaborate web of melodious counterpoint, rather in the manner of an early seventeenth-century fantasia. There is a principal melodic line sustained throughout, but its course is difficult to follow on account of the constant exchange of melodic motives between the principal and the subsidiary parts. In recognition of this difficulty Fricker has indicated the principal line in the score, for the benefit of the performers, by means of the signs used by Schoenberg for the same purpose. Ex. 134 shows a fragment of the texture, including a short passage in

Ex. 134

mirror-canon between the violin and viola—a favourite device of Fricker's, which has already been noted in the second subject of the opening movement, and appears again in the second subject of the finale. This movement begins with a reminiscence of the introductory harmonies to the first movement, to which it is closely similar in character and form, with a quick, syncopated, toccata-like second theme, a fugal development, and a reversed and varied recapitulation in which the first subject reappears as a varied restatement of the introduction to the first movement.

Among the other composers of Fricker's generation, Bernard STEVENS (b. 1916) has written a number of attractive and accessible works on a fairly small scale, including a Fantasia on a theme of Dowland, for violin and piano, a Fantasia for two violins and piano, a 'Lyric Suite' for string trio, a Theme and Variations for string quartet, as well as an early Piano Trio and Violin Sonata. Most of the earlier works of Humphrey SEARLE (b. 1915), composed under the influence of his teacher Webern, are similarly small in scale. They include a Quartet for clarinet, bassoon, violin, and viola, and a 'Passacaglietta in nomine Arnold Schoenberg', for string quartet. In later works his style has become more expansive and his idiom simpler. The most important of these is the Variations and Finale for ten instruments, commissioned by the Virtuoso Ensemble in 1957, in which each instrument in turn is treated as soloist.

All the chamber works of John ADDISON (b. 1920) include wind instruments. The most important of them is the Serenade for wind quintet and harp, commissioned by the BBC for the Cheltenham Festival in 1957, in which he slightly extended the emotional range of his music, which is otherwise almost exclusively light and jocular. His other chamber works include a Trio for flute, oboe, and piano (1950), and a set of Inventions for oboe and piano (1958). Much of the chamber music of Malcolm ARNOLD (b. 1921) is in a similarly light vein, and he too favours wind instruments. He has composed a Trio for flute, viola, and bassoon, a Divertimento for flute, oboe, and clarinet, Three Shanties for wind quintet, sonatinas for flute, oboe, clarinet, and recorder, all with piano, as well as two sonatas for violin and piano, one for viola and piano, a Piano Trio, and a String Quartet.

At the opposite extreme of temperament are the three string quartets of Robert SIMPSON (b. 1921), in which the thematic material is very exhaustively developed in massively designed movements. No. 2 is in one movement, and Nos. 1 and 3 are each in two movements. Peter WISHART (b. 1921) made an early impression with Four Pieces for violin and piano and a Cassation for violin and viola, both interesting and excellent works of a rather Stravinskian neo-classical character, but no chamber music by him has been published since.

Iain HAMILTON (b. 1922) has written a large number of chamber works, not all of which are published. It was with his Clarinet Quintet, op. 2 (MS.), and his String Quartet, op. 5, awarded the Alfred Clements Prize in 1950, that he first attracted attention. He then won the Edwin Evans Memorial Prize in 1951 with his Three Nocturnes, op. 6, for clarinet and piano. As a pianist he formed a duo with the clarinettist John Davies, and has written several other works for this combination—a Divertimento, op. 18 (MS.), and a Sonata, op. 22, as well as a Serenata for clarinet and violin, op. 31 (MS.). His other chamber works include a Sonata for viola and piano, op. 9, a Piano Trio, op. 25, an Octet for strings, op. 28 (MS.), and a Sonata for 'cello and piano. A compelling vehemence of expression and fierceness of harmony distinguish the best of the earlier works. The more recent ones, notably the Piano Trio, the Octet, and the 'Cello Sonata, begin to show a more disciplined invention. In the Trio (1954) the harmony, although characteristically dense, has a diatonic clarity that is almost neo-classical, as may be seen in Ex. 135 from the first movement. The 'Cello Sonata (1959), in

Ex. 135

which the composer uses serial technique, is a continuous work of remarkable form, consisting of four cadenzas, marked respectively bizarre, fantastic, passionate, and tempestuous, separated by three 'movements', of progressively decreasing speed (allegro, con moto, placido), with no readily apparent thematic connexions between the seven parts. Among the other outstanding features of the work are the inventive 'scoring', which is very varied and includes some remarkable effects, and the combination of a dense and complex harmonic content with a serial texture of a post-Webernian kind. Both the Octet and the 'Cello Sonata were commissioned by the University of Glasgow out of the money left to them by Sir John McEwen (C) on his death for the encouragement of Scottish chamber music. Other interesting works commissioned from the same source include the String Quartet No. 2 by Robert CRAWFORD (b. 1925) and a String Quartet by Thea MUSGRAVE (b. 1928). In Miss Musgrave's terse and ingenious work the main theme appears prominently in all three movements, sometimes in inversion, and there is a skilful and effective use of alternating tempi. The attractive idiom is eclectic and without marked individuality, as is true also of Crawford's slightly more expansive and conservative work. His String Quartet No. 1 was performed at the ISCM Festival at Frankfurt in 1951. Miss Musgrave's other works include a one-movement Trio for flute, oboe, and piano (1960) and an engaging *Colloquy* for violin and piano, written for the 1960 Cheltenham Festival. In the composer's original programme-note the four short movements of the later work were headed 'Disagreement', 'Digression', 'Development', and 'Agreement', but she has since discarded these titles.

The Welsh composer Alun HODDINOTT (b. 1929) has written several large-scale chamber works for mixed ensembles, including a Septet, op. 10, for clarinet, horn, bassoon, piano, violin, viola, and 'cello (1956), commissioned for the tenth anniversary of the BBC Third Programme, a Sextet, op. 20, for flute, clarinet, bassoon, and string trio (1960), Variations, op. 28, for flute, clarinet, harp, and string quartet (1962), and a 'Rondo Scherzoso' for trumpet and piano (1957), which is the only one yet published.

One of the most prolific of the younger composers is Kenneth LEIGHTON (b. 1929), whose published chamber music includes his String Quartet No. 1, Sonata No. 2 for violin and piano, and 'Fantasia on the name BACH' for viola and piano. These are very fluent neo-romantic works on a large scale, also in a conservative eclectic idiom, effectively sprinkled with favourite modernisms, including some twelve-note themes. Joseph HOROVITZ (b. 1926), also fairly prolific, writes formally and emotionally more modest music, leaner in texture and more impersonal, but less derivative in idiom. His published chamber works include a String Quartet No. 4, Oboe Quartet, Sonata for 'cello and piano, and Sonatina for oboe and piano.

The South African composer John JOUBERT (b. 1927), now living in England, started his career with an inventive and accomplished String Quartet in A flat (op. 1), a work of some distinction, strongly influenced by Walton. This was followed by a Sonata for viola and piano, op. 6, of similar character, and much later by the String Trio, op. 30 (1959), which is more mixed in style.

Outstandingly gifted among the generation born after 1930 are two composers who belonged originally to the group of pupils of Richard Hall at the Royal Manchester College of Music, briefly known as the Manchester New Music Group. The more prolific of them is Peter Maxwell DAVIES (b. 1934), who first attracted attention in his early twenties with a Sonata for trumpet and piano (1955). Two of his later chamber works, *Alma Redemptoris Mater* (1957), for flute, oboe, two clarinets, bassoon, and horn, and 'Ricercar and Doubles' (1959), for flute, oboe, clarinet, bassoon, horn, viola, 'cello, and harpsichord, were performed at the ISCM festivals of 1958 (Strasbourg) and 1960 (Cologne). The 'Ricercar and Doubles' had previously been heard at the 1959 Dartmouth Festival (USA), for which it was commissioned.

Like other works by Maxwell Davies, both these were inspired by medieval English music. The sextet is based on a motet by Dunstable, and the 'Ricercar and Doubles' on the carol 'To Many a Well'. The relationship between the works and their medieval sources is defined by the composer in his programme-note for the 'Ricercar and Doubles', in which he describes the opening slow Ricercar as a contrapuntal fantasy on a cantus firmus derived from the carol. The wind and strings have the main argument, the harpsichord 'adding comment in the form of chordal elaborations, or of occasional free melismas growing out of a note already sounding in the main parts'. The two Doubles, or variations, 'use the same sequence of transpositions of the basic material, with its chordal and isorhythmic structure', the first of them, which is quick, 'developing the rhythmic characteristics of the basic material', and the slow second one 'dwelling on the expressive qualities of the carol'.

Maxwell Davies's only work for a traditional chamber ensemble is the String Quartet (1961), in which he uses a similar technique to that of the 'Ricercar', with one slow melodic line (written in red ink in the manuscript score) to which the other three parts add ornamentation, frequently starting in unison with the main part, then branching off. This technique is used chiefly in the first and third sections of the work, in which the traditional four movements are compressed into one. Both these sections are slow, the first the most extended in the work, the third brief. Between them comes a dance-like scherzo of essentially rhythmic interest, and finally a brief march and coda, in which the harmonic nature of the material is explored. There is a strong 'tonal' element in the work. The melody moves for the most part in diatonic modes, and the tonality is extended only gradually. The interval of the minor third, A to C, is several times underlined in the first movement, and still more conspicuously in the third, which begins with a long pedal A on the viola. Maxwell Davies's use of the medium is highly original, and this very beautiful work is remarkable also, among modern string quartets (and among works of 'post-Webernian' technique), in being technically not excessively demanding.

The most important chamber work of Alexander GOEHR (b. 1932) is the Suite op. 11 for six players—flute, clarinet, horn, harp, violin (doubling viola), and 'cello—commissioned for a concert by the Melos Ensemble at the 1961 Aldeburgh Festival. It is in five movements—an extended opening 'Allegro'; an Intermezzo (Andante) of 'nocturnal' character, in which the harp is treated as a solo instrument; a scherzo and trio in which, since the scherzo has palindromic features (its second half being a variation of the first in retrograde motion), the composer dispenses with a 'da capo', making instead only a four-bar allusion to the scherzo at the end of the trio; an Arietta (Lento e misterioso) in which the flute is the soloist (the composer's original idea was for a work for chamber ensemble with solo flute); and finally a Quodlibet, which has cadenzas for harp (accompanied) and flute (unaccompanied), and recapitulates in varied form some of the material of the earlier movements against a refrain-like recurring theme on the horn.

Goehr's earlier works include a set of Variations for flute and piano (1959), a cantata *The Deluge* (1958), based on a draft of a film scenario by Eisenstein, for soprano, contralto, and eight instruments, a String Quartet (1956), which is withdrawn for revision, and Fantasias op. 3 for clarinet and piano (1952).

A third composer of the Manchester group, Harrison BIRTWISTLE (b. 1934), has written a wind quintet of original form under the title 'Refrains and Choruses' (1957), a 'Monody for Corpus Christi' (1960) (soprano, flute, violin, and horn), in which two vocal movements are separated by one for the instruments alone, and an instrumental motet *The World is Discovered* (1961), based on Heinrich Isaac, in which three 'verses', for solo flute, clarinet, and oboe in turn, alternate with 'choruses' for the full ensemble of ten wind instruments, harp, and guitar.

Richard Rodney BENNETT (b. 1936), the outstanding composer of this generation outside the Manchester group, is more conservative in his choice of media and in his approach to the techniques of Stockhausen and Boulez. His chamber works are all instrumental, and his preference has been for wind instruments. Particularly successful among them are the brilliant early Sonatina for unaccompanied flute (1954), in which his purely melodic use of a single twelve-note series shows remarkable resource and invention, and the attractively lyrical Sonata for oboe and piano (1961), in which the four movements have greater contrast and definition of character than the three movements of his *Winter Music* (1960) for flute and piano. In his Quintet for clarinet, piano, and string trio (1961) a single movement encompasses the contrasts of several, including slow movement and scherzo. For larger chamber ensembles he has written *The Approaches of Sleep*, for four solo voices and ten instruments, and *Calendar*, for twelve players.

Of the several distinguished refugee composers working in Britain, the Hungarian-born Mátyás SEIBER (1905–60) had an outstanding success in chamber music with the third of his three string quartets. His other chamber music includes a Divertimento for clarinet and string quartet, Serenade for wind sextet, Sonata da Camera for violin and 'cello, Concert Piece for violin and piano, Sonata for violin and piano, commissioned by the BBC for the 1960 Cheltenham Festival, Improvisation for oboe and piano, *Permutazioni a cinque* for wind quintet, written for the Virtuoso Ensemble, and a Fantasy for 'cello and piano, which was later incorporated into the Three Pieces for 'cello and orchestra. The String Quartet No. 1, Serenade, and Divertimento, all written in his late teens and early twenties, are attractive, technically masterly, witty, and astonishingly mature works, variously influenced by Kodály (Seiber's teacher), Hindemith, and Stravinsky. The 'Sonata da Camera', written during the same period, is more experimental and less euphonious in idiom. In the String Quartet No. 2, which followed in 1935, he brilliantly reconciled a strict use of twelve-note technique with a general idiom and in some cases an actual thematic material very close to that of Bartók's fourth quartet, as may be seen in the opening bars (Ex. 136). The second of the three movements, headed 'Intermezzo alla "Blues"', exemplifies another influence to which Seiber had responded (he had taught jazz at the Frankfurt Conservatory), and also demonstrates, within a work deeply influenced by two composers both completely uninterested in jazz, Seiber's remarkable power of assimilating and unifying the most diverse musical elements. His String Quartet No. 3 (1948–51), called 'Quartetto Lirico', combines, like No. 2, a Bar-tókian idiom with twelve-note technique. The three-movement form resembles

Ex. 136

that of Bartók's second quartet in tempo-sequence (Andante amabile, Allegretto scherzando e leggiero, Lento espressivo), and there is also some similarity in the lyrical tone of the two works, though there is nothing in Seiber's light and delicate scherzo of the ferocity of the corresponding movement in the Bartók. In the Concert Piece for violin and piano (1954), which like the 'Sonata da Camera' has a conspicuous element of technical experiment, Seiber uses a series of twelve notes arranged in three identical groups of four (each consisting of a perfect fourth enclosed within a perfect fifth). The complete series has only one possible transposition—a semitone away. From it Seiber derives a great variety of melodic and harmonic formations, and an equal variety of musical textures, providing several contrasting themes, developed in a free ternary form with a complete reorganization of the material in the recapitulation. The Improvisation for oboe and piano (1957) is evidently a by-product of the Concert Piece, being based on an almost identical series. It is a small-scale and simple ternary movement of sonata-like features, with an exposition of several short 'themes', a very brief scherzo-like middle section, and a transposed and partly inverted recapitulation. The Violin Sonata is in three movements, the first vehement, with complex per-cussive harmonies on the piano, alternating with agitated declamatory flourishes on the violin, the second a kind of intermezzo, described by the composer as 'measured and dance-like', and the last a lyrical slow movement in which the conflict of the two instruments in the first movement is resolved.

Roberto Gerhard and Egon Wellesz, who were both briefly mentioned in C, and have since made their home in England, suffered a greater setback to their careers as composers by their uprooting. WELLESZ has written a further four string quartets, an Octet, for the same ensemble as Schubert's, commissioned by the Vienna Philharmonic Octet, a Suite for viola and piano, and a Suite for wind instruments. They are distinguished and inventive works in a conservative and slightly austere romantic idiom, in which Wellesz makes use of twelve-note themes (but not twelve-note technique) more naturally and convincingly than most composers who attempt this kind of compromise.

After the early Piano Trio (1918) listed in **C**, an accomplished but immature work showing strong French influences, GERHARD, like Wellesz, became a pupil of Schoenberg. Since then his most important chamber works have been a Wind Quintet (1928), a String Quartet (1955), and a Nonet (1956) for wind instruments. The Wind Quintet was Gerhard's first major work completed after his studies with Schoenberg, and was influenced to some extent by Schoenberg's own Wind Quintet, written two years earlier, though it is nearer in character to Schoenberg's Serenade op. 24. The opening phrase for solo bassoon presents a seven-note series which remains melodically prominent throughout the first two movements, and in the second of them is used as the theme of a rather free passacaglia. In the third and fourth movements new themes, also treated serially, come into the foreground, but the original melodic series returns in the middle section of the finale, in combination with the main theme of the scherzo.

Gerhard's String Quartet and Wind Nonet are similarly in the traditional four movements, which are also less revolutionary in internal structure than those of some of his other later works, in which he has tried to break away from familiar concepts and to achieve intelligibility without the symmetry of even the vestigial reprise. In the Quartet, the first two movements have fairly plain traces of recapitulation, and in the third movement there is a tiny three-note figure which recurs three times like a shadow of a ritornello, and gives an appearance of familiar shape to a movement in which more substantial thematic relationships are not easily discerned. Ex. 137 shows the beginning of the recapitulation of the

Ex. 137

first movement, with the theme in canon. Gerhard makes some use in this work of a rhythmic series, derived from the pitch series, but in musical and rhythmic character the Quartet is totally unlike the work of post-Webernian composers who have been most closely associated with the idea of rhythmic serialization, and is much more like Bartók's in general dynamic and rhythmic effect. When the second movement was published separately in the special issue of the periodical *The Score* devoted to him (September 1956), it was headed 'Capriccio', but this title is not reproduced in the complete published miniature score.

The brilliant Nonet is nearer in character to the Wind Quintet. Gerhard has made an important innovation here by introducing the piano accordion into the wind ensemble. Combining the characteristics of a wind instrument with some of those of a keyboard instrument, it is more useful for ensemble-music than any of the pitched or unpitched percussion instruments that have lately been recruited, and far more agreeable than the vibraphone, which comes nearest to rivalling it in potentiality. The snatched sforzando chords, the quick and slow crescendos and diminuendos, even the occasional dynamically level single note, that Gerhard has written for it here, all immediately catch the ear as new and fascinating sounds. In form the Nonet shows a certain pre-classical inspiration. The ceremonial introductory movement, with its sharp repeated notes, has something of the manner of a French overture about it, and the last movement harks back allusively to the rhythm of the 18th-century gigue. The third movement is a slow contrapuntal aria, with an expressive oboe line and single melodic notes from other instruments, which are then absorbed into the harmony, and the second movement is a kind of dance-scherzo, the melody darting across the parts to a percussively concerted rhythmic accompaniment.

Other chamber works by Gerhard, as yet unpublished, include a Sonata for viola and piano (1950), which was later (1958) revised and re-worked for 'cello and piano, 'Seven Hai Kai' for voice with piano and four wind instruments (1922), Sardanas for wind ensemble (1928), a Capriccio for solo flute (1949), a Fantasia for solo guitar and a Chaconne for unaccompanied violin (both 1958). The early string quartet mentioned in C has not survived.

The youngest of the refugee composers in England is the German-born Franz REIZENSTEIN (b. 1911), who differs from all the others in not having been influenced by Schoenberg. He was a pupil of Hindemith, and uses an idiom very close to that of his teacher's later and milder music. His early, pre-war chamber music included a Clarinet Quintet, a Wind Quintet, and a Divertimento for string quartet. In his later works he has generally used the piano, and as an excellent pianist himself has frequently performed in them. Among them are a Piano Quintet, Piano Trio, Trio for flute, oboe, and piano, a Sonata and a Fantasia Concertante for violin and piano, a Sonata for 'cello and piano, and a Sonatina for oboe and piano. Soon after coming to England Reizenstein studied for a time with Vaughan Williams, for whose eighty-fifth birthday the Piano Trio was written. He absorbed very little English influence, however, and there is hardly a trace of it in his mature instrumental music—unless the use of the tune 'Daisy Bell' in the last movement of the Trio for flute, oboe, and piano is allowed as an example. The only other is his use of Morley's tune 'Now is the month of Maying' as a theme for a set of variations in the finale of the very early Divertimento for string quartet. The less serious tone of this slight and entertaining work (in which the other three movements are headed 'Chorale', 'Capriccio', and 'Romance'), is one that Reizenstein does not often sound. He does so again, with similarly attractive effect, in the Sonatina for oboe and piano.

RUSSIAN CHAMBER MUSIC

STRAVINSKY. *By* COLIN MASON

THE last work of Stravinsky's discussed by Arthur Lourié in C was the Octet of 1923. Nearly ten years passed before he wrote another chamber work, and then a further twenty before he returned to this medium again. In 1932 he wrote the 'Duo Concertant' for violin and piano, which has become by far his best-known and most frequently played work of chamber music. This is in five movements (Cantilène, Eglogues I and II, Gigue, and Dithyrambe) and in his autobiography[1] he gives the following account of its conception:

Its composition is closely connected in my mind with a book which had just appeared and which had greatly delighted me. It was the remarkable *Petrarch* of Charles Albert Cingria, an author of rare sagacity and deep originality. . . . 'Lyricism cannot exist without rules, and it is essential that they should be strict. Otherwise there is only a faculty for lyricism, and that exists everywhere. What does not exist everywhere is lyrical expression and composition. To achieve that, apprenticeship to a trade is necessary.' . . . These words of Cingria seemed to apply with the utmost appropriateness to the work I had in hand. My object was to create a lyrical composition, a work of musical versification, and I was more than ever experiencing the advantage of a rigorous discipline which gives the taste for the craft and satisfaction of being able to apply it —and more particularly in a work of lyrical character. . . . The spirit and form of my 'Duo Concertant' were determined by my love of the pastoral poets of antiquity and their scholarly art and technique. The theme which I had chosen developed through all the five movements of the piece which forms an integral whole, and, as it were, offers a musical parallel to the old pastoral poetry.

What the 'rules' are Stravinsky does not explain, nor what the theme is, or how it develops. There is no apparent melodic theme common to all five movements, though a tenuous relationship, hardly amounting to more than a consistency of style, might be discovered in the harmonic technique which could be read as suggesting that the 'rule' was the avoidance of pure consonance, and the 'theme' the continuous simultaneous use of at least two diatonic chords, keeping in continuous play all or most of the diatonic notes of the key of the moment. For the composition of a lyrical work this seems a severe enough rule to satisfy all Stravinsky's longing for 'rigorous discipline'. Exx. 138 and 139, from the Cantilène and the Gigue respectively, give an idea of the general harmonic style.

The nine-year gap between the Octet and the 'Duo Concertant' was followed by an even longer one, of twenty-one years, before the next chamber work, the Septet (1953). A new chamber-music phase now began in Stravinsky's development, similar in character to the period begun by the Japanese songs in 1913, in that the composer again showed himself particularly interested in the combination of voice with small instrumental ensemble, rather than in pure instrumental

[1] Published by Max Steuer.

chamber music. It was in these works that, under the influence of Webern, he gradually made his transition to serial technique, and did so by Webern's own route, by an ever-increasing use of the technique of canon (see p. 6). In the

Ex. 138

Ex. 139

first movement of the Septet, which is in sonata form, the opening theme on the clarinet appears simultaneously in free imitation, augmented, both on the horn (in inversion) and on the bassoon (Ex. 140). The whole texture of the exposition and recapitulation is thick with imitative counterpoint of this kind, which in the development turns into a strict and complex fugue on a subject that has emerged at the end of the exposition, derived rather remotely from the main subject. In the other two movements, entitled Passacaglia and Gigue, which are both thematically related to the first movement, contrapuntal devices of this sort are even more prominent, and suggest that the themes of the first movement were derived from them rather than vice versa. The Passacaglia is built on a sixteen-note theme (Ex. 141), the first half of which is the obvious source of the first clarinet theme of the first movement, the bare outline of this (i.e. excluding all repeated notes) being identical with it (see Ex. 140). It is in this Passacaglia that Stravinsky comes nearest, in this work, to true serial writing, for instance at the third rotation of the ground (on the 'cello), above which first the clarinet, violin, and viola, and then the clarinet, horn, and bassoon, simultaneously complete one statement each of the same theme in diminution, the horn part in retrograde form, and all in different rhythms. The fourth rotation of the ground is even more complex, and again strictly serial, the ground appearing in octaves, divided among all seven instruments, while the piano at the same time also runs twice through all four forms of the theme (i.e. basic theme, inversion, retrograde, and retrograde inversion), in rapid figurations of two-part counterpoint, each form being played simultaneously with its particular inversion. Such strictly serial passages alternate with statements of the ground over which, although serial

Ex. 140

writing is not abandoned, free parts are added. At the ninth rotation the ground is played simultaneously with its other three forms, all in approximately the same note-values, and at the tenth and final one simultaneously with the retrograde inversion, both divided among the instruments.

The theme of the Passacaglia is also the theme of the Gigue, which consists entirely of fugues on this subject in various forms and rhythmic transformations. First there is a three-part fugue for the string trio, in the gigue rhythm, followed by a repetition of this fugue on the piano, against which the three wind instruments play another fugue on a more expansive version of the subject; then another fugue for the string trio, on the inversion of the original subject, again followed by a repetition on the piano, against another fugue for the wind instruments, on a different form of this same subject (i.e. the inversion), this time in yet another expansive rhythmic variant. Ex. 142 shows the beginning of this final double fugue.

Despite the tendency towards serialism, the Septet is essentially a neo-classical tonal work (in A major), rather similar in tonal and general character to the 'Duo Concertant', only with the quantity and conflict of the 'wrong notes' much increased by the complex contrapuntal texture, in which there are often six or more parts—though each part is melodically clear, simple, flowing, and tonally well-defined.

Ex. 142

In the two vocal works with chamber-music accompaniment which followed the Septet, Stravinsky moved on from these strict contrapuntal techniques to serial writing proper. These works were the *Three Songs from Wm. Shakespeare* for mezzo-soprano, flute, clarinet, and viola (1953), and the *In Memoriam Dylan Thomas*, for tenor, string quartet, and four trombones (1954). The first of the Shakespeare songs, 'Musick to heare', is built up almost entirely on a four-note series, used with the strictest serial technique, except that the first and last eight bars have an additional accompaniment of scale-passages up and down between the tonic and dominant of C major, to provide the song with a tonal 'frame'. (The only other divergence from the serial order is in the voice part on the last note of bar 26 and the first three notes of bar 27, where the order is 4, 2, 3, 1.) Ex. 143 illustrates the serial method. The second song, 'Full Fadom Five', is slightly less strict. The main section is based on a seven-note row, but the introduction and coda, although closely related, are free, and there are a few free notes in the accompaniment during the main section. This song shows also Stravinsky's fondness for cancrizans writing. In the voice part the seven-note row (line 2 of the poem) is immediately followed (line 3) by the retrograde form. Then, for lines 4 and 5 of the poem, the inversion and retrograde inversion of the series are used, giving the inverted cancrizans of lines 2 and 3, though with a change of pitch half-way through (see Ex. 144). This song, unlike the first, has no tonal 'frame' in the accompaniment, but there is a strong suggestion of tonality in the melodic line, which is on the scale of (though not *in*) G flat major, with excursions on to that of A flat major. The harmony does not confirm this suggestion, and

Ex. 143

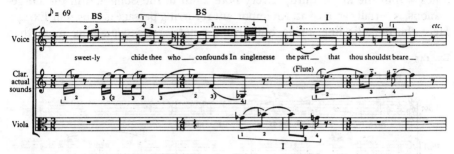

Ex. 144

the song remains tonally ambiguous. The last song in the set is freer than the other two, but here again an approximate cancrizans technique can be observed in the structure of the vocal line. Bars 3 and 4 are a slightly varied retrograde version of bar 1, and similar approximate relationships exist between the larger units of the song. The main part of the vocal line is entirely on the scale of A flat major, with a brief modulation to that of C major in the middle, but again the harmony does not confirm the key. The accompaniment here is not serial, but moves almost entirely in melodic intervals of the fourth, fifth, and minor second, in a prickly counterpoint that continually contradicts any sense of an A flat tonality by sounding the tonic and dominant notes of the key remotest from it (D and A).

In the Dylan Thomas song Stravinsky made his final step to total serialism. Thomas was to have written an opera libretto for him, but died in New York on his way to California to discuss the project. The *In Memoriam* was composed shortly afterwards, to Thomas's poem 'Do not go gentle into that good night', written in memory of his father. In a note on this work Stravinsky wrote: 'Here my music is entirely canonic. It requires a tenor voice and string quartet. Having thus composed the song I decided to add a purely instrumental prelude and postlude (called Dirge-Canons) which are antiphonal canons between a quartet of trombones and the string quartet.' The technique is not canonic in the ordinary sense, but purely serial, a continuation of that of the first of the Shakespeare songs. The series itself is almost identical, having the same total compass of a major third, but consisting of five notes instead of four (i.e. using all the semitones within the major third). Every note, both in the Song and in the Dirge-Canons, is serially arrived at. An important recurring passage is shown in Ex.145. Here the melodic line, being built from a note-series containing more than

Ex. 145

two adjoining semitones, cannot observe the scale of, or suggest, any one key, but as in 'Musick to heare' Stravinsky provides a rather arbitrary tonal 'frame' of C major. He does so this time by means of a recurring cadence in the Dirge-Canons, in which the four parts are led to the triad C–D–E (see Ex. 146).

Ex. 146

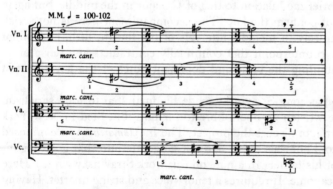

Two further small chamber works, also both 'in memoriam', followed in 1959. These were the *Epitaphium für das Grabmal des Prinzen Max Egon zu Fürstenberg*

(the patron of the Donaueschingen Festival), for flute, clarinet, and harp, and the Double Canon 'in memoriam Raoul Dufy' for string quartet. The *Epitaphium* consists of eight varied statements of a twelve-note series, in seven phrases, played alternately by the harp and by the pair of wind instruments. (The sixth phrase, played by the flute and clarinet, contains two statements of the series.) All four forms of the series are used, without transpositions, in the following carefully-planned order: basic series (harp), basic series (flute and clarinet), inversion (harp), retrograde inversion (flute and clarinet), retrograde (harp), retrograde followed by inversion (flute and clarinet), retrograde inversion (harp). For the first time in any work by Stravinsky the harmony is serially ordered throughout. In all the works so far described he had in general used the series only melodically, the several contrapuntal parts each following one form of the series without regard (from the serial point of view) to the harmony. Only intermittently, in brief cadential or ritornello-like passages, had a single rotation of the series been split up among several contrapuntal parts, and he had hardly ever written chords built up from a single form of the series. In the *Epitaphium* in contrast the series is used harmonically throughout. The harp part is mainly harmonic (chordal), not contrapuntal in conception, and the contrapuntal lines in the sections for flute and clarinet are serially complementary throughout, never independent. There is no complete melodic statement of the series in any one part, and only in three places does a single part contain as many as three consecutive notes of the series. Two consecutive notes occur more often, but equally often the series crosses from one part to the other with every note. As in several of Stravinsky's serial works, there is a single divergence from the strict serial order at one point (the beginning of the fifth statement). The harmonic arrangement of the series is changed at every statement, and the work is in effect a miniature set of variations. Its playing time is one minute.

The Double Canon is similarly brief (a minute and a quarter). It is based on a very characteristic twelve-note theme, in which the first five notes are almost identical with the Dylan Thomas series (in its retrograde inversion), and the next five notes, which again are all within the compass of a major third, are a more remote permutation of it. There are twelve statements of the theme, of which only three forms are used (i.e. not the inversion). The two violins play the theme in canon four times, at the major second (below), at the unison, then the retrograde inversion at the major second (above) and at the unison. Against the second and third of these canons the viola and 'cello play the retrograde form in canon first at the minor seventh (below), then at the octave. It is canonic in the strict traditional sense, not in the modern serial sense. There are no octave transpositions, and the note-values are unaltered throughout.

During this period Stravinsky also transcribed for voice and small instrumental ensemble several of his earlier songs, originally written with piano accompaniment. These are the 'Two Poems' (1911, texts by Balmont), now arranged (1954) for soprano, two flutes (one doubling piccolo), two clarinets (one doubling bass-clarinet), and string quartet, and published in one score with the 'Three Japanese Lyrics'; and Four Songs for soprano, flute, harp, and guitar (1953), which were originally Nos. 1 and 4 of 'Quatre Chants Russes' (1918) and Nos. 1 and 2 of 'Trois Histoires pour Enfants' (1915 and 1917). Another important transcription of this period is that of the Concertino for string quartet (see C), for violin, 'cello, and ten wind instruments (1952).

One other work that calls for mention, although not strictly within the definition of chamber music, is the Elegy for viola (or violin) unaccompanied, composed in 1944 for one famous chamber-music player, Germain Prévost, to play in memory of another, Alphonse Onnou (founder of the Pro Arte Quartet, of which Prévost was also a member). It is a miniature prelude, fugue, and postlude, in two-part counterpoint throughout, simply and beautifully expressive, in the Phrygian mode on C.

SOVIET CHAMBER MUSIC. *By* I. I. MARTINOV[1]

CHAMBER music has always held a particular fascination for Soviet composers, who have devoted considerable attention to this genre, and have produced a series of works which have achieved wide recognition. This phenomenon stems partly from personal inclination, partly from the interest in chamber music which is shown by the public at large, and partly from the wealth of performers available in the country.

There are in the USSR a considerable number of string quartets giving regular performances. One of the oldest is the Beethoven Quartet, whose membership has remained unaltered ever since its original formation in 1923— a remarkable record. Among the best-known quartets, mention must be made of the Bolshoi Theatre Quartet, the Armenian Komitas Quartet, the Georgian Quartet, and, among those more recently inaugurated, the Borodin Quartet. There are also numerous competitions for string quartets held within the territories of the USSR, the first of which took place in 1925. Besides these various quartets, there are also a number of trio and sonata ensembles which give regular performances.

Soviet composers of chamber music are primarily concerned to assimilate the experience and traditions of the major Russian classics. These traditions hark back to the great masters, Glinka, Tchaikovsky, Taneyev, Borodin, and Glazunov —composers who, while drawing their inspiration directly from sources in the national cultural heritage, managed, nevertheless, to establish an original style of their own in the field of chamber music. The continuity of tradition between the classics and their Soviet descendants becomes still more apparent when we remember that the leading composers of the older Soviet generation, Prokofiev, Myaskovsky, and Glier, had themselves been pupils of Rimsky-Korsakov, Lyadov, and Taneyev. Inevitably, however, Soviet composers have followed new lines in the development of this classical tradition, and have set themselves artistic aims which reflect the particular character of modern Soviet art.

The period of intensive development in Soviet art and music begins in the

[1] Translated by Richard Coe.

thirties. Ever since that epoch, composers such as Myaskovsky, Shostakovich, Shebalin, Prokofiev, Kabalevsky, and Khachaturian have turned out score after score in rapid succession—not to mention the contribution made by the younger generation, Babadjanian, Tzintzadze, &c. In chamber music we find a range of mood and feeling identical with that which characterizes Soviet music as a whole, yet skilfully adapted to meet the requirements of the particular medium. The finest works in the field are characterized by the urge to exploit a wide range of expressive means, by the desire to achieve clarity of form and sharpness of musical idiom, and by an attempt to assimilate the vast wealth of Russian folk-music, yet without destroying the style of the individual composer.

The form which has held the greatest attraction for Soviet composers has been the string quartet, together with all those other various instrumental combinations which include the piano. Works for solo instruments, whether string or wind, are rarer, although even here we find quite a few works, particularly recent works, well worthy of attention.

It should be added that if, in the past, Moscow and Leningrad provided the national centres for chamber music, the picture has changed considerably within the last twenty-five years. Today there is activity in every corner of the Soviet Union; in the Ukraine, in the Republics of the Baltic, in Central Asia, and in the Transcaucasus the output of new chamber works is progressively increasing, while new chamber ensembles are constantly being formed. Such factors testify to the rapid growth of musical culture within the framework of the Soviet Republics.

We should turn now and consider some of the best-known compositions for chamber ensemble by Soviet composers.

Arno BABADJANIAN (b. 1921). Armenian composer and pianist. Among his works to date, the most remarkable is the Piano Trio in F sharp minor, written in 1952. This work is full of romantic excitement and dramatic pathos; it is conceived in free and sweeping lines, and is richly imbued with colour and energy. Technically, there are traces of the influence of Rachmaninoff, but the composer uses an idiom which is highly original, yet at the same time closely allied with the tonalities and rhythms of his native folk-song tradition. This trio has proved a fascinating challenge to all who have performed it, and possesses great melodic charm combined with considerable depth of feeling.

Reinhold GLIER (C, d. 1956). One of the most prolific Soviet composers of the older generation. During the entire course of his life Glier showed a consistent interest in chamber music. At the very outset of his career as a composer he wrote a Sextet in C minor, op. 1, for two violins, two violas, and two 'cellos (1898). This sextet, with its profound roots in Russian folk-music, received high praise from Rimsky-Korsakov, Glazunov, and Lyadov, and was awarded the Glinka Prize. The masterly treatment of scoring, the sure handling of polyphony, the brilliance of national tone-colour—these are characteristic of many other chamber works belonging to this early period: the Quartet No. 1 in A major, op. 2 (1899); the Sextet No. 2 in B minor, op. 7 (1904); and the Sextet No. 3 in

C major, op. 11 (1905). Glier also wrote a large number of works for 'cello and piano and for double bass and piano, as well as duets for two violins, &c. However, if we consider his output of chamber music since the beginning of the Soviet period, the most important single item is his fourth string quartet.

The Quartet No. 4 in F minor (op. 83) was written in 1944. It is a fine example of the mature style of a composer who was fascinated by clear melodic lines and complex polyphonic structures. In this respect the finale, with its polished handling of counterpoint, is unusually interesting. In the second movement the composer displays no less mastery in the handling of a set of variations. Considered as a whole, this quartet, which never breaks the restraint imposed upon it by the spirit of the classical tradition, creates a striking effect by the assertive optimism of its musical texture and by the virtuosity of its scoring, all the technical intricacies of which Glier had completely at his finger-tips.

Dmitri KABALEVSKY (b. 1904). Composer of two string quartets, and of an Improvisation for violin and piano.

The Quartet No. 1 in A minor, op. 8 (1931), was written while the composer was still a young man in search of his own personal style and idiom. The Quartet No. 2 in G minor, op. 44 (1945), must rank among his finest musical achievements. It is profoundly lyrical in character, and this lyrical quality is emphasized by the humorous treatment of certain isolated episodes, and by the vivacity of the dynamic finale. The second part of this finale consists of a set of variations on two original themes, whose tonality clearly reveals their close relationship to the traditions of Russian folk-song. It would be true, however, to apply this latter comment to the quartet as a whole, no less than to the Twenty-four Piano Preludes based on themes from Russian folksongs, which were composed at roughly the same period. This second string quartet by Kabalevsky is a masterly composition, bearing the clear stamp of his own characteristic style. Ex. 147 shows the beginning of the third movement.

Ex. 147

The Improvisation for Violin and Piano, op. 21 (1934), is an extract from the music which he composed for the film *A Petersburg Night*, and tells the tragic tale of a serf-violinist. This is highly emotional music with a strong sense of dramatic development, which is intensely rewarding in performance, and it has grown to be a firm favourite in the Soviet concert repertoire.

Boris LYATOSHINSKY (b. 1894). One of the most prominent among Ukrainian composers. Lyatoshinsky was a pupil of Glier, and inherited from his teacher the latter's love of chamber music. His compositions include a Quartet No. 1 in D minor, op. 1 (1915); a Quartet No. 2 in A major, op. 4 (1922); a Trio, op. 7 (1922); a Sonata for Violin and Piano, op. 19 (1926); a Quartet No. 3, op. 21 (1928); a second Trio, op. 41 (1944); a Quartet No. 4, op. 43 (1943); and the Ukrainian Quartet in G minor, op. 42 (1942–5). This last has found signal favour among many different audiences, and has been widely acclaimed.

Lyatoshinsky's Piano Quintet was written during the war, and plainly reflects the dramatic experiences of the time. Its thematic material has all the striking brilliance of tonal colour which is characteristic of Ukrainian music, with its broad rhythms and sweeping melodies. His music abounds in contrasts; his treatment is tuneful and direct in its impact; and his compositions are scored in a finely controlled concerted style.

Nicolaï MYASKOVSKY (C, d. 1950). Composer of thirteen string quartets. The best of these, together with his symphonic compositions, occupy a place of considerable importance in the general catalogue of his works. He also wrote two sonatas for 'cello and piano.

This composer first caught the general attention in 1930, when three of his quartets (op. 33) received public performance. When the scores of these were printed, that of a fourth quartet was added. It must be realized, however, that Quartets Nos. 3 and 4 had been written as far back as 1910 and 1909 respectively, and had merely been revised by the composer towards the year 1930. Quartets Nos. 1 and 2, on the other hand, had been composed in 1929 and 1930, during the years of an intense quest for new means of creative expression which culminated in a far-reaching stylistic renovation. This new style was to become the hall-mark of Myaskovsky's finest works in the thirties and forties.

The Quartet No. 1 in A minor and the Quartet No. 2 in C minor abound in sharp dramatic contrasts and offer a rich field of psychological tensions. Their idiom makes heavy demands upon the listener's attention (particularly in the case of No. 1), and is full of fierce and strained dissonances. The execution of the score makes no less severe demands upon the performers. Ex. 148 shows part of the principal theme of the first movement.

Ex. 148

Allegro non troppo

The Quartet No. 3 in D minor and the Quartet No. 4 in F minor are more readily understandable and more transparent in texture. It is interesting to note that the Finale of the D minor quartet takes the form of a set of variations on Grieg's 'Cradle Song' (op. 66, no. 7), developed with an impressive fertility of invention. Of the four quartets which make up this opus number it is No. 4, with its clearly defined, plastic material, which presents the most interesting features. Yet taking a general view, all four scores may be said to represent a steady progress in the craftsmanship of quartet-writing.

Myaskovsky's ultimate mastery in this genre is brilliantly displayed in the Quartet No. 5 in E minor, op. 47 (1937–8). This work received its first performance in 1939, and has remained ever since a firm favourite with all lovers of chamber music. It is divided into the traditional four movements, but the music itself reveals an intense individuality. The first movement (Allegro) is dominated throughout by a mood of unbroken lyricism (see Ex. 149); the second (Scherzo)

Ex. 149

is full of subtle elegance; the third (Andante) maintains a steady, epic quality; while the fourth (Finale) is possessed of tremendous verve and swing. The music of this fifth quartet contains a great wealth of emotion, and the score is remarkable for its clean lines and for the plasticity of its themes, with their unmistakable tonal relationship to the traditions of Russian folk-song. The composer repudiates the over-complex technique which had been so marked a feature of Op. 33, but his brilliant exploitation of instrumental possibilities and rich variety of instrumental tone remain unaffected by this change.

The Quartet No. 6 in G minor, op. 49, composed between 1939 and 1940, is in many ways related to the fifth quartet, but is more concentrated and perhaps reveals a deeper sense of self-analysis. This work is unusual, both in the character of its different movements and in their mutual relationship. Thus the first movement is an Elegy, whose luminous strain of sadness is reminiscent of the *Yellowed Pages* cycle by the same composer. The second movement (Burlesque) is a miniature toy march. The culminating point of the whole quartet is reached in the third movement (Tristesse), a rather sombre composition of great harmonic complexity. The fourth movement (Rondo) concludes the work in a cheerful and lighthearted mood.

The Quartet No. 7 in F major, op. 55 (1941), was directly inspired by the grandiose scenery of the Caucasus and by the musical traditions of the Kabardà (the slow movement, for instance, incorporates a Kabardà folk-song). On the whole, the music possesses an essential clarity of texture; the first movement is in pastoral mood, while the finale is brisk and hymn-like.

The Quartet No. 8 in F sharp minor, op. 59 (1942), which is dedicated to the memory of a dead friend, is a serious and deeply contemplative work, permeated with a sense of wistful sadness. This is one of Myaskovsky's finest compositions in the field of chamber music. The first movement is an Elegy charged with powerful currents of emotion; the second, a free-developed 'Adagio', remarkable for its skilled handling of polyphony. The finale is intensely dynamic in conception, but here again particular stress is laid upon episodes whose structure is directly inspired by folk-traditions. Especially interesting is the passage where the two themes of the finale are combined with the main theme from the first movement. This score deserves particular attention, not only on account of its sheer musical beauty and its depth of content, but also on account of its striking formal originality, which bears witness to the composer's untiring quest for new means of creative expression. Ex. 150 shows the beginning of the last movement.

Ex. 150

The Quartet No. 9 in D minor, op. 62 (1943), is another highly successful composition. Compared with those works which have hitherto been discussed, it attains an impressive and individual stature of its own, thanks partly to the broad scale on which it is conceived and partly to its free and sweeping lines, far transcending those moods of pure lyricism which characterize the fifth, sixth, and, to some extent, the eighth quartets. The dynamic principle becomes apparent as early as the first movement, with its typically Russian themes. The second movement would appear to combine the functions of both slow movement and scherzo. The finale, which proceeds with an air of solemn majesty, is a grandiose and brilliant conception.

The Quartet No. 10 in F major, op. 67, no. 1 (1945), is a revised version of a score composed as far back as 1907, and preserved for all those years among the composer's manuscripts. Its idiom and technique are devoid of complexity, and it represents a kind of intermezzo—a nostalgic memory of youth on the part of a composer already declining into old age.

The Quartet No. 11 in E flat major, op. 67, no. 2 (1945), bears the title

'Reminiscence', which, according to Myaskovsky's biographer, Professor T. Livanov, indicates its connexion with the musical concepts of Myaskovsky's early works. The most striking feature of this score is the third movement, which takes the form of a waltz.

The Quartet No. 12 in G major, op. 77 (1947), is a thoroughly assertive and clear-cut composition, both in general conception and in thematic material. The first movement is based upon the opposition of two contrasting themes, one quiet, the other energetic—a common enough device in sonata-writing. The development, however, shows considerable originality, especially in the coda, which vanishes finally away into silence. The second movement (Scherzo) is rhythmic and resilient, and although its tone-colour may here and there be almost too exotic, it is scored with most telling effect. The third movement abounds in chromatic sequences reminiscent of an earlier period in Myaskovsky's work, when the harmonic texture of his scores was saturated with violent and disquieting juxtapositions. The finale, with its liveliness and *élan*, much in the manner of the great classics, is irresistible.

The Quartet No. 13 in A minor, op. 86 (1949), is one of the last works of a composer whose creative faculties remained unimpaired to the end, in spite of serious illness. Together with the Symphony No. 27, it represents the last will and testament of a fine artist, a great and meditative musical composer. In this work we return once again to a pervasive mood of lyrical serenity, expressed in finely chiselled line, in balanced structure, and in delicately sculpted melodic contours. The exposition is supremely economical, every note having its logical place and function in the musical texture; and every bar is rich with significance. The first movement, which combines the elements of sonata and rondo, is based upon a captivating central motive (see Ex. 151), which retains its predominance

Ex. 151

in subsequent movements throughout the development of the work. The brilliant and evocative 'sunlight' of the first movement is set off against the eerie and fantastic 'night music' of the ensuing scherzo. The slow movement and finale merge with the two initial movements to form a single, harmonious entity. The sincere and profound poetry of this music has evoked an immediate response among the audiences of the Soviet Union.

All thirteen of these quartets by Myaskovsky bear the hall-mark of his great creative personality. They are infinitely varied in form and content alike, and their technique, in close response to each new demand for particular expression which is made upon it, varies accordingly.

Besides this output of quartets, Myaskovsky composed two sonatas for 'cello and piano. The first of these, Sonata No. 1 in D major, op. 12, was completed in 1912, and published in revised form in 1945. The Sonata No. 2 in A minor, op. 81, was composed between 1948 and 1949, and is also obtainable in an arrangement for viola and piano.

The second 'cello sonata is remarkable for its clear melodic lines, for the purity of its harmonic style, and for the arresting individuality of its instrumental technique. The outstanding characteristic of the first movement is the broad and leisurely exposition section, with its hauntingly beautiful thematic material, contrasted with the comparatively compact treatment of the development—a rare enough feature in the work of a composer who both loved and understood the process of developing his musical ideas. The second movement is likewise dominated by a free-flowing melody with occasional traces of pathos. The finale is cast in the form of a rondo-sonata with sharply contrasted themes. The whole score is instinct with freshness and originality; it offers no difficulties to an audience; and it possesses a number of characteristic features which will amply reward the attentive listener.

Sergei PROKOFIEV (C, d. 1953). Prokofiev made but infrequent excursions into the realm of chamber music. Nevertheless, his occasional contributions have left their highly individual mark upon the genre, and at each stage of his artistic evolution he produced works reflecting his development in this field—compositions scintillating with wit, breath-taking in the airy flights of their imaginative genius, and enriched with all the treasures of his magnificent talent.

His first work in the field of chamber music was a Ballade in C minor, op. 15, for 'cello and piano, composed in 1912 while he was still a student at the Conservatoire. Musically, this Ballade reveals a richly endowed imagination, and allows the listener to glimpse certain gifts of dramatic expression; but stylistically it is still immature. It represents the first steps of a young composer in an unfamiliar medium, and is considerably inferior to the piano works which had been appearing at the same time, amongst which we may already discover some genuine masterpieces of Prokofiev's art—e.g. the Toccata.

The year 1919 saw the composition of an 'Overture on Jewish Themes', in the form of a Sextet in G minor, op. 34, for clarinet, two violins, viola, 'cello, and piano, written in response to a chance request made by a group of fellow musicians. (In 1934 this same sextet was rearranged by the composer himself in an arrangement for small symphony orchestra.) Among all Prokofiev's compositions, this is the first in which he takes genuine folk-material and employs it as the basis of the whole work. It reveals a brilliant sense of craftsmanship. The combination of grotesque and lyric elements (e.g. the melodious second subject), the reiterated contrasts, the ingenuity of the exposition, with its passages of sparkling wit and its finely chiselled detail—all these features give the Overture-Sextet an interesting and original position in the field of chamber music.

Prokofiev's Quintet in G minor, op. 39, for oboe, clarinet, violin, viola, and double bass (1924), is, technically speaking, one of the most complex achievements of his whole career. In style, it bears a relation to his second symphony, with its passion for abstract structural logic ('constructivism') and its fondness for harsh and rigid harmonic complexes. The story of its composition is as follows: Prokofiev had begun work on a ballet, *The Trapeze*, which was to have been scored for the same combination of instruments as the quintet. Later, however, he abandoned the idea of the ballet, and incorporated such music as he had already written into the six-movement suite which now goes by the title of the Quintet in G minor. The score abounds in complicated melodic phrases superimposed one above the other, and in intricate rhythmic patterns, while the abstract character of the music as a whole seems rather untypical of Prokofiev, whose essential qualities lie precisely in the picturesque and evocative nature of his music and in the power of his imagination.

His Five Melodies for violin and piano, op. 35b (1925), are lyrical pieces, and constitute in fact a revised version of the 'Five Songs without Words' for solo voice and piano, composed in 1920 and published originally as op. 35.

The Quartet No. 1 in B minor, op. 50 (1930), was commissioned by the Library of Congress in Washington. Abandoning the heritage of tradition, Prokofiev composed a work in three movements only, consisting of a sonata-like 'Allegro', a scherzo, and a slow, melodious finale. Prokofiev's musical idiom is here of the simplest character, and the influence of Russian folk-sources can be discerned throughout the work, especially in the last movement. This quartet is also remarkable for the austerity of its style, for its avoidance of superficial effects, and for its mood of radiant gravity.

The Sonata in C major, op. 56, for two violins (1932), one of the works belonging to Prokofiev's 'constructivist' period, has never become generally popular.

The Quartet No. 2 in F major, op. 92, was written in 1942 during the composer's sojourn in the Caucasus, where he first encountered the influence of Kabardà and Balkarà folk-music. In his treatment of these folk-melodies, Prokofiev eschewed the well-trodden paths of musical orientalism, emphasizing instead the stern and virile qualities inherent in this type of material. It is this factor which gives the whole quartet its markedly individual flavour. The first movement evolves around the development of a pair of contrasting themes, both of which bear the familiar and unmistakable stamp of his stylistic personality; one is bold and sweeping, while the other is ponderous and solemn (see Exx. 152 and 153). In point of fact, however, both are genuine folk-melodies transmuted into the composer's own characteristic idiom. In the development section the listener is startled by violent polytonal juxtapositions and harsh chordal effects, while the whole music seems at times to take on an almost metallic timbre. The second movement is dominated by the graceful elegance of its melodic

sequences decorated with the fantastic arabesques which are the common
heritage of eastern music (see Ex. 154). The third movement (a rondo-sonata

Ex. 152

Ex. 153

Ex. 154

with two secondary themes and a slow central episode) is full of life and incident.
The effect which Prokofiev's second quartet inevitably produces upon the listener
is that of a series of vivid musical images suggested by the spirit of poetry inherent
in the Caucasian races, and the work is indeed an object-lesson in the creative
transmutation of original folk-material. These qualities combine to make it one
of the outstanding works in the repertoire of Soviet chamber music.

Prokofiev's Sonata No. 1 in F minor, op. 80, for violin and piano, was begun as
early as 1938 but was not completed until 1946. The composer himself has left us
a concise but vivid description of this work: 'The first movement (Allegro assai)

is severe in character, and represents a sort of extended introduction in sonata-form to the 'Allegro' which constitutes the second movement; this 'Allegro' is impetuous and wild, yet with a broadly-flowing secondary theme in the lower parts which constantly accompanies the principal melody. The third movement is slow-moving and mellow. The finale works up to a frenzied impetus in a highly complicated metre.' This sonata, like the music written for the cantata *Alexander Nevsky* (1938), was inspired by the traditions of the Russian heroic epic, and we may find many features common to both works. It is exceptionally original in its musical imagery and tone-colour, in its novel exploitation of the potentialities of chamber music as a genre, and in the technical richness of its scoring for both violin and piano. It deserves a place among the finest achievements of an outstanding modern composer, and has, indeed, earned a lasting position in the international concert repertoire.

The Sonata in D major, op. 94, for flute and piano, was written in 1943. In the year following the composer rearranged it as a violin sonata, and as such it was published as op. 94*b*, under the title of Sonata No. 2 for violin and piano. It differs widely, both in style and in character, from the first violin sonata (which in strict chronology is in fact the second). Its predominant feature is the graceful, delicate contour of its melody, reminiscent of the same composer's 'Classical Symphony'; yet there is, none the less, a generous influx of new elements. The first movement (Moderato) is lucid and serene. The second (Scherzo) is a thing of winged elegance—one of Prokofiev's finest achievements in this vein. The third movement (Andante), with its measured rhythm, and the sprightly, vivacious finale are both almost 'classical' in shape. Both versions of this sonata (flute and violin) are remarkable for the technical virtuosity of the scoring, while each exploits to the fullest extent the possibilities of the various instruments concerned.

The Sonata in C major, op. 119, for 'cello and piano (1949), is a fine example of the composer's later style—his vigorous and characteristic lyricism set off against a background of gentle humour. The first movement has a narrative quality, the second is a witty scherzo, while the third re-establishes a mood of typical lyricism. This sonata, like the previous sonata in D major, is outstanding for its wealth of technical resources in the scoring for both instruments.

Aram KHACHATURIAN (b. 1904). This composer has produced only a very limited number of chamber works. Leaving aside such youthful compositions for violin and piano as the Dance (1926), the Ballad-Song (1929), the Allegretto (1929), and the Sonata (1932), together with the unpublished Double Fugue for string quartet (1932), the only work which Khachaturian has produced in the field of chamber music proper is the Trio for clarinet, violin, and piano, which was written in 1932 while he was still a student at the Moscow Conservatoire studying composition under Myaskovsky.

By its form, the Trio reveals a clean break with the classical tradition. Not one of its movements is in sonata form, and the key-sequences flout the laws of unity: it begins in G minor and ends in C minor. The first movement is a duet of a highly poetic character between the violin and the clarinet, with accompaniment from the piano. Its singing melody is decorated with many characteristic touches. The second movement is remarkable for the transparency of its tonal colouring and for the sharp precision of its dancing rhythms. The third movement takes the form of variations on an Uzbek folk-tune. Elaborate coloratura passages for the clarinet, reminiscent of the style employed by virtuoso folk-musicians, are here exploited with remarkable individuality. Considered as a whole, the work bears all the flamboyant imprint of the folk-tradition, yet at the same time reveals a tendency towards picturesque juxtapositions of harmony and timbre, which are a favourite device with Khachaturian. In fact, this early trio clearly betrays all the stylistic idiosyncrasies which have become so familiar to those who know his music of a later period.

Vissarion SHEBALIN (**C**, b. 1902, Vissarion, not Vasily). A composer who has been extremely prolific in the field of chamber music. His quartets, and indeed all his other chamber compositions, are characterized by a high degree of professional competence, by an uncompromising standard of taste in the selection of his material, and by his expert handling of the medium. Shebalin is a noted craftsman in the art of polyphony, and employs the most intricate contrapuntal devices with consummate ease. These qualities are already discernible in the earliest of his chamber works: the Quartet No. 1 in A minor, op. 2 (1923), the String Trio in G minor, op. 4 (1924), and the Quartet No. 2 in B flat major, op. 19 (1934). The most attractive aspect of these compositions is to be found in the tuneful slow movements, which bring out the noblest features of his extremely melodic style.

Shebalin's finest achievement is his Quartet No. 3 in E minor, op. 28, written in 1939, with its captivating rhythmic impetuosity and its sharp contrasts in the development of striking thematic material. Here too, the slow third movement is the most effective, with its original harmonic and melodic twists. His Quartet No. 4 in A minor, op. 29 (1940), displays a rare gift of unconstraint and naturalness in its rhythmic structure, and makes free use of irregular metres, with bars of five and seven beats. These features hark back directly to the native traditions of Russian folk-music, which exercised a considerable influence upon the formation of Shebalin's characteristic individual style.

None of Shebalin's compositions in the field of chamber music has won wider popularity than his Quartet No. 5 (the 'Slavonic') in F minor, op. 38 (1942). Here Shebalin exploits elements of melody drawn from Russian, Ukrainian, Polish, Slovak, and Serbian folk-sources, and absorbs them, without destroying their individuality, into the intrinsic unity of his artistic conception. This quartet is a living symbol of the deep-rooted love for music, and of the intense interest in its manifestations, which reigns among the divers interrelated Slavonic peoples. Composed during those historic years of trial and tribulation, it assumed a particular importance in its context, and indeed still holds a position of some eminence among the most popular pieces in the Soviet repertoire. The 'Slavonic' comprises five movements. From the very outset, the composer introduces us

to the vast and varied range of mood and emotion which characterizes the traditions of Slavonic folk-song, and whose scope extends from dynamic dance-
rhythms to lyrical episodes of untroubled serenity alternating with melancholy
contemplation. In the subsequent movements Shebalin offers us a series of
musical pictures covering a rich variety of subjects, yet one and all of deep
emotional significance, and one and all composed with intense enthusiasm.

The Quartet No. 6 in B minor, op. 34 (1942), is shot through and through with
the native genius of Russia, although, in point of fact, not one of its four movements contains a single genuine folk-tune. Here the most striking feature is the
lyrical quality of the music, startlingly fresh and serene. Throughout, the sure
hand of the composer exploits those characteristic touches which are peculiar to
instrumental music in the Russian folk-tradition. Thus in the scherzo tremolo
passages on the violin imitate the sound of the *zhaleïka*, a wind instrument which
is widely played in many districts of central Russia (see Ex. 155). Considered as
a whole, this quartet is a work of undoubted interest, and is very typical of
Shebalin's style.

Ex. 155

Shebalin has also written a Sonata for violin and viola, op. 35 (1945).

Dmitri SHOSTAKOVICH (**C**, b. 1906—not 1908). Shostakovich, whose fame rests
largely upon his symphonies, has also devoted considerable attention to chamber
music. He has eight quartets to his credit, besides a Piano Trio, a Piano Quintet,
a String Octet, and a Sonata for 'cello and piano. Taken as a whole, his chamber
works have many features in common with his symphonic compositions; yet
they manage to retain their own individual style, in spite of having been composed concurrently with the larger works. Shostakovich is extremely sensitive
to the inherent subtleties of the genre, and his output in this field is fully as
assured as in the realm of orchestral composition.

The Octet for strings, op. 11, was written in 1924, when the composer was
still a student at the Conservatoire, and full of enthusiasm for 'linearist' and
'constructivist' theories. It has two movements, a Prelude and a Scherzo, both of
which bear the unmistakable stamp of his gift for polyphonic invention and of
his characteristic passion for experiment. At times, however, this gift of pure
inventiveness veers towards formalism, and the style is stiff almost to the point

of deliberate artificiality, especially in the Scherzo (see Ex. 156). This score, in
fact, remains as a memento of adolescent enthusiams, which the composer has
since learnt to control, and which will not be found to recur in similar shape
in his later chamber works.

Ex. 156

The Sonata in D minor, op. 40, for 'cello and piano (1934), testifies to the
artistic evolution of its author, and to the progress he was making at this time
towards the twin ideals of melodic clarity and harmonic transparency. The
thematic material upon which it is based is both plastic and expressive—qualities
which find their clearest illustration in the main theme of the first movement
and in that of the 'Largo'. The music is at once evocative and dynamic, while
the sense of style revealed in the instrumental scoring is highly individual (the
'graphic' handling of the piano part—a characteristic touch—is of special
interest). The first movement, which opens in a mood of elegiac contemplation,
later assumes a more dramatic character. Attention should be drawn at this
point to the serene and pensive melancholy of the coda, which foreshadows the
concluding section of the first movement of the fifth symphony. The second
movement (Scherzo) contains two features thoroughly typical of Shostakovich—
the broad, sweeping design and the rich, earthy humour. The third movement
is concentrated and severe in texture, while the fourth provides a lively and witty
finale. Although somewhat uneven in style, this sonata is of great artistic value,
and it well deserves the place of honour which it holds in the contemporary
repertoire for the 'cello.

The Quartet No. 1 in C major, op. 49 (1938), reveals Shostakovich in one of
his happiest moods. Few other works have such a wealth of lyrical serenity.

Incidentally, the source of his inspiration may be found in Mozart—a fact which grows abundantly clear later, from the finale of the Piano Quintet. The first movement (Moderato) proceeds at a quiet, unhurried pace, and its whole rhythm and character are those of a song. The second movement (similarly marked 'Moderato') is in a wholly different temper, with a strong tendency towards sadness. It is written in the form of a set of variations, and the main theme, which is stated first by the viola, is reminiscent of a traditional Russian lament. The third movement (Allegro molto) is a feather-light scherzo, with some exquisite polyphonic scoring. The finale re-establishes the unruffled serenity of the opening movement. The score as a whole shows harmony and balance, the contrasts are well-defined but not too harsh, while the economy of technique and the sparing use of expressive means belong to the realm of chamber music *par excellence*.

This string quartet presents a remarkable contrast to the dramatic intensity of the fifth and sixth symphonies, which, in strict chronology, lie closest to it. This strange disparity was hailed at the time as a newly discovered facet of the composer's creative personality; whereas, in reality, this lyrical quality has always been a fundamental constituent of Shostakovich's talent, although it may perhaps never have appeared before in so unmistakable a guise. This same lyrical constituent is easily discernible in some of his other chamber works.

The Quintet in G minor, op. 57, for piano, two violins, viola, and 'cello (1940), belongs to that select company of his works which, from the date of their very first public performance, have won instantaneous recognition and approval from every type of audience. This quintet is in five movements: Prelude, Fugue, Scherzo, Intermezzo, and Finale. Each section contributes to the formation of a single, harmonious entity within the framework and development of the general design. The composition as a whole is deeply significant in content, and in many ways echoes the concepts of the fifth symphony. Its dominant characteristic is lyricism; yet this lyrical mood is utterly different from that of the first quartet, and has attained to a profounder, more philosophical character. Stylistically, the quintet harks back to the traditions of the old masters of the seventeenth and eighteenth centuries. This, however, does not imply that the music is in any way archaic or retrospective, since the composer retains a firm and unrelenting grasp over his own idiom, and infuses a new content into the old forms. An outstanding example of this phenomenon may be seen in the Fugue, which takes for its theme a traditional Russian song in lyrical vein. Yet the development of this initial theme is highly original, and the polyphonic texture, for all its intricate complexity, achieves a clear, almost transparent tone. This Fugue is a superb example of the relationship between emotional concepts and structural principles, and demonstrates how the elements of living speech may be infused into pure polyphony. Prokofiev was keenly appreciative, at the time, of its intrinsic originality. The impetuous Scherzo is brimming with zest for life; the Intermezzo is imbued with an exquisite quality of poetry and a wealth of flowing and wondrous melody; while the Finale, with its graceful line and its fantasy in detail, is a sheer miracle of light and space. This Finale also sets off to great advantage the simplicity of the over-all harmonic structure.

The Trio in E minor, op. 67, for violin, 'cello, and piano (1944), originated during the war years, and, being closely related in time to the eighth symphony, similarly reflects the anxious, tense, and even tragic moods of that epoch. All four movements of this trio are intensely original conceptions, in style no less than in descriptive imagery—particularly the finale, whose awe-inspiring grandeur makes it a unique example of its kind. From the very outset of the first movement, the listener's attention is arrested by the unusual tonal quality achieved by combining tremolo passages in the 'cello with notes scored for the violin in a low register (G string only). This creates the impression that the instruments have changed places in the score. The pure and haunting melody carries tonal reminiscences of the lyrical quality of Russian folk-song. If the first movement may—with certain qualifications—be thought of as an elegy, the second would seem to be a scherzo of impetuous urgency, and the third a mournful dialogue between the violin and 'cello against a background of sombre choral harmonies on the piano. This latter movement leads directly into a broadly developed finale, introducing us to that world of eerie, foreboding shapes which invaded Shostakovich's music during the years of the war (cf., for instance, the opening movement of the seventh symphony). The theme of the finale (see Ex. 157) is angular and menacing, and it develops with a mechanical, rhythmic

Ex. 157

motion, accompanied by weird, automatic repetitions of contrapuntal elements —the combined effect of which evokes the image of a monstrous procession and fills the imagination with a frieze of cruel and sinister shapes. In the coda the theme of the first movement returns once more, but now imbued with a sense of mounting excitement, symbolic of the noblest aspirations of humanity and of the immutable will which can withstand the onslaught of the forces of evil and destruction. This trio is one of the most brilliant contributions to Soviet music during the war period.

The Quartet No. 2 in A major, op. 69 (1944), is a work of great originality, no less in its harmonic scheme than in its formal pattern. It contains four movements: Overture, Recitative and Romance, Waltz, and finally Theme and Variations.

The harmonic sequence of the movements is: A major, B flat major, E flat minor, A minor. Neither in its style, nor in its scale of development, nor even in its emotional range, does it bear the least resemblance to the first quartet, and in fact it both poses and solves a totally different set of artistic problems. This same disparity can be seen again and again throughout Shostakovich's later quartets, for with each new work the composer was seeking to discover new things to express and new ways of expressing it. This is the fundamental reason why his quartets show such amazing variety. In the second quartet, which we are at present considering, Shostakovich transports us into a world of musical imagery which is unmistakably and completely his own. He leads us, by way of the brisk and spirited Overture (where we may perhaps catch a glimpse, here and there, of the old 'constructivist' influence at work again), first to the broad and sweeping regions of the Recitative and Romance, with its air of lyrical contemplation most plainly apparent in the latter section, where the solo violin takes up the melody, while the movement itself develops against a background of unhurried accompanying chords (see Ex. 158); next, to the realms of the Waltz,

Ex. 158

with its strange tints, its ever-delicate melancholy, the exquisite lines of its coda and its suggestion of shimmering mists; and so on to the finale, the most developed of all the movements, made up of a series of variations in many moods upon a theme which is the very essence of song, and to which the composer returns ever and again, as though fascinated by its beauty.

The Quartet No. 3 in F major, op. 73 (1946), is remarkable for the expressive range of its idiom, for its determined quest for new means of expression, and for its masterly scoring. It is built up on the principle of dramatic contrast. The first movement is serene and luminous, while the three subsequent movements transport us into a world of tragic experiences, whose temper comes close to that of the eighth symphony. The slow concluding movement is immediately arresting.

The Quartet No. 4 in D major, op. 83 (1949), is, taken as a whole, a work in lyrical mood, shot through with a radiance of light somewhat reminiscent of the first quartet. This resemblance is carried further still in the juxtaposition of the different movements: a pastoral 'Allegretto' is followed by a tuneful 'Andantino', a scherzo, and a finale. Stylistically, however, the score of this quartet is infinitely more complex, and bears the stamp of the long process of creative evolution which had proceeded without interruption over the whole eleven-year span separating the two compositions.

The Quartet No. 5 in B flat major, op. 91 (1951), is the most important work that Shostakovich has ever written for this particular combination of instruments; similarly, it is the most monumental in its proportions. Not once does the composer overstep the strict bounds of chamber music, yet he manages to imbue the work with all the elements of pure symphonic writing: with a symphonic breadth and tension in development, and with a symphonic scope in the juxtaposition of single themes and of entire movements. This revolution strikes the ear most forcibly in the first and last movements, with their dramatic intensity of mood and with their full cycle of thematic development. These two movements, both of unusual length, and together containing all the essential elements which go to form the work, are separated one from the other by a lyrical 'Andante' whose character serves but to emphasize the monumental quality of the whole. The fifth quartet is a work of creative experiment, of vast complexity in content as in style; yet this in no way detracts from its persuasive artistry and power, nor does it weaken the impact which it makes upon the listener. This composition has made its mark as one of the outstanding masterpieces of contemporary music.

The Quartet No. 6 in D major, op. 101 (1956), is yet another 'lyrical intermezzo', which sprang into being, sandwiched between momentous symphonic concepts, each pregnant with complexity of thought. Its interesting peculiarity is the way in which every movement ends on the same cadence—a device which serves to unify a series of otherwise isolated episodes and to transform them into a coherent whole. In this quartet Shostakovich once more reveals his brilliant handling of the art of polyphonic writing, more especially in the passacaglia (on the theme quoted in Ex. 159), which constitutes the slow movement—a

Ex. 159

form in which his excellence had long since been established (cf., for instance, the passacaglia in the fourth movement of the eighth symphony). This quartet evolves in a mood of predominant lyricism; its tone is consistently serene. It is

Ex. 160

remarkable for the exquisite detail of its instrumental technique, for the graceful juxtaposition of various concerted passages, and for the plastic quality of its melodic material. Ex. 160 shows the theme of the last movement.

Shostakovich's seventh and eighth quartets,[1] both completed in 1960, are a complementary pair with many characteristics (and some material) in common. In each of them the last movement repeats part of the first, and all the movements in each are tightly linked by close and conspicuous thematic relationships. There is also a thematic link between the two quartets. No. 8 is dominated by the melodic motive D E flat C B (in German D S C H, for D. Schostakowitsch), which is thematically prominent, mainly at that pitch, in four of the five movements, and also appears, less prominently, in the bass, transposed a tone higher, at the beginning of the middle section of the remaining movement (the fourth). In No. 7 a close variant (in fact a permutation) of this four-note motive, with the order of the first two notes reversed (i.e. E flat, D C B), is similarly prominent throughout, but in this work appears in many transpositions, and also often in inversion (or in retrograde—the two forms being identical).

The Quartet No. 7 in F sharp, op. 108, which is in three movements played without a break, is similar in dimensions and character to the terse and good-humouredly lyrical Quartet No. 1. The first movement (Allegretto) is in a simple sonata form with no development section, and a transformation of the rhythmically capricious subject from 2/4 (with some 3/4 bars) in the exposition to a regular 3/8 in the reprise. The four-note motive appears rather tentatively in this movement in the codas to both the main thematic groups, though it later becomes plain that the principal theme itself is also derived from it. A descending phrase from the coda to the second subject provides the initial idea for the first theme of the slow movement (Lento), a simple ternary-form movement with an extremely abbreviated recapitulation. Here the four-note motive is confined mainly to accompanying parts, but becomes conspicuous in the closing bars, and provides the beginning of the vehement fugue-theme of the third movement (Allegro). A short introduction to the fugue recalls the first theme of the first movement, inverted, and the continuation of the fugue-theme is a retrograde variant of the main theme of the second movement. Both the constituent motives of the fugue-theme are extensively developed, after which the themes from the second and first movements appear in their original form (the latter in four parallel lines at different pitches). A quiet coda, also directly quoted from the first movement, seems to be bringing the music to an end, but like Roussel in the last movement of his String Quartet, Shostakovich follows up the fugue with a long 'finale'—in which, like Roussel, he incorporates the fugue-theme (transformed in rhythm from quick 2/4 semiquavers to 3/4 quavers, and extended into a quick waltz-like tune), in alternation with the main theme of the first movement (also in 3/4), to which he now adds an inverted pedal on the tonic. After the first reappearance of this theme from the first movement, Shostakovich transposes the waltz-tune from F sharp to C, and brilliantly lights up its relationship to the subsidiary material in the first movement, where, in the same key, the four-note motive with which it begins was first heard. The two themes are then drawn

---

[1] The section on these two works was added by the editor.

together in shorter alternating phrases until first tune and then accent fade away in Schumannesque syncopations.

Not all the subtle tonal and thematic links between the movements of this work have been mentioned in this formal description. Several of Shostakovich's earlier quartets (Nos. 3, 5, and 6) are distinguished by their original and masterly methods of thematic unification, but No. 7 is the finest example. The application of similar methods in No. 8 (in C minor, op. 110) is not so convincing, in spite of some striking similarities in the formal plan—both works, for instance, ending with a fugue followed by a reprise of parts of the first movement.

No. 8 has a large autobiographical element. In addition to the thematically predominant DSCH motive already mentioned it contains quotations from the composer's first and tenth symphonies and from his Piano Trio. According to an article by Yury Keldysh, the editor of *Sovyetskaya Muzyka*, published in English in *The Musical Times* (April 1961), the work is dedicated to the memory of those who fell in the fight against Nazism. Among its unusual formal features is the choice of slow tempi for three of its five movements—the first, fourth, and fifth, all of which are marked 'Largo'. The first is a kind of contrapuntal prelude, beginning immediately with the DSCH motive. This is followed by a powerful sonata movement (Allegro molto), which leads straight into a waltz-like 'Allegretto', where the incessant repetitions of the DSCH motive in diminution call to mind Janáček's technique. The fourth movement is a declamatory kind of recitative, in which Shostakovich quotes a patriotic song, 'Crushed by the weight of bondage'. This leads by way of the gradual reappearance of the DSCH motive at its original pitch into the final movement, which answers the opening contrapuntal prelude with a fugue based on the same theme, and in its coda recapitulates several passages from the first movement—strengthening the aural impression of the quartet as a work not in five separate movements but in a single monothematic movement containing several extended variation-like episodes of contrasting tempi.

Sulkhan TZINTZADZE (b. 1925). A young Georgian composer of outstanding merit in the field of chamber music, a form of composition for which he has shown preference from the very outset of his artistic career. Himself a 'cellist and sometime member of the Georgian Quartet (1944–6), he has had the opportunity to make a special study of the characteristic problems of chamber music, and early achieved considerable mastery in the field, as is evident from his Quartet No. 1 (1947), which received the award of the Union of Georgian Composers. His Quartet No. 2 and his cycle of 'Miniature Pieces' for string quartet (1950) earned a still greater measure of success (if such were possible), and the composer, who at the time was still a student, was awarded the Stalin Prize for Composition. In all these works, as well as in the beautiful 'Pieces' for 'cello and piano (1955), his finest talents as a composer are well in evidence—his striking gift of melody, which has developed under the influence of Georgian folk-music; the individuality of his scoring; his fine sensitivity to the characteristic qualities of the genre; and his marked ability to exploit the

III   L

abundant possibilities of an instrumental ensemble. The third and fourth
quartets amply illustrate the rapid development of his artistic intelligence and of
his skill as a composer.

The Quartet No. 3 was completed in 1951, and allows us to trace the later
development of a composer who was steadily broadening the horizon of his
chamber-music technique. If, in the first two quartets, we find a wealth of
'regional' episodes inspired by the dance and vocal traditions of the peoples of
Georgia, in this subsequent work we discover a deepening lyrical trend and a
more mature, more varied sense of form.

In his Quartet No. 4 (1955), Tzintzadze is unmistakably trying to extend the
boundaries of chamber music as a genre, and at the same time to overcome the
tendency towards miniature composition which had been so distinctive a feature
of his early work. To judge by its musical idiom, the quartet is closely allied to
the traditions of Georgian folk-song, but these latter elements are now seen
refracted through the complex structure of an individual creative personality.
His score abounds in colourful and picturesque episodes, yet it is dominated by
a strong unity of purpose which welds the work into a solid whole. Tzintzadze's
instrumental technique is interesting, carefully worked out, and reveals in-
numerable original touches, as, for instance, when the viola enters in a high
register in the finale. The fourth quartet has found appreciation in the composer's native land, and is often heard from the concert-platform in various
cities scattered throughout the USSR. Ex. 161 shows the beginning of the
last movement.

Ex. 161

This present survey has dealt chiefly with composers whose works appear
regularly in the concert repertoire. However, the following should not be passed

over entirely without mention: Anatoly ALEXANDROV (b. 1888): four string quartets. Stasis VAÏNYUNAS (b. 1909): one piano quintet and one trio. Andrei VOLKONSKY (b. 1933): a piano quintet, which attracted some public notice. Evgeny GOLUBYEV (b. 1910): three quartets and three piano quintets. Vladimir KRYUKOV (b. 1902): a sonata for violin and piano. Nikolaï NARIMANIDZE (b. 1905): three string quartets. Leonid POLOVINKIN (1894–1949): four quartets, a piano trio, and a string trio. Nikolaï RAKOV (b. 1908): a 'Poem' for violin and piano, a 'Poem' for 'cello and piano, &c. Arkady FILIPYENKO (b. 1912), whose Quartet No. 2 represents an interesting experiment in using a chamber ensemble for the purposes of programme music. Yuri SHAPORIN (b. 1887): a cycle of short compositions for 'cello and piano.

CHAMBER MUSIC IN AMERICA

By NICOLAS SLONIMSKY

UNITED STATES

WHEN the eccentric French conductor Jullien visited America in 1853, he presented several 'monster concerts' at the Crystal Palace in New York. As a patronizing gesture to the natives, he included in one of his programmes a String Quartet by George Frederick Bristow, a violinist of the New York Philharmonic Society. In a public statement Jullien pronounced Bristow 'a classical composer of European stature who successfully essayed the most difficult of all instrumental writing, that of the string quartet'. To an American musician such an accolade was the height of commendation. Bristow launched a subscription for a golden wreath, and presented it to Jullien as a token of gratitude.

European, and specifically German, models completely dominated the form and substance of string quartets, piano trios, and violin sonatas written by Americans during the nineteenth century. Most performers were German immigrants, and the best-known ensembles bore such names as the Germania Society and the Mendelssohn Quintette Club.

German musical hegemony in America began to weaken about the turn of the century. The aesthetic mode became neo-classical, superseding the inflated romantic genre; the Germanic form gave way to a more liberal construction, rhapsodic and impressionistic. Considerable stress was put on American subject-matter, with direct or indirect quotations from Negro, Indian, or cowboy tunes. The first piece of chamber music that became known as 'American' was Dvořák's String Quartet in F, op. 96, which he composed during his American visit in 1893. According to Dvořák's own statement, made to Franz Kneisel on the occasion of the world première of the work by the Kneisel Quartet, the themes were derived from Negro melodies. The eminent Boston music critic Philip Hale, reviewing the performance, observed tartly that 'the Negroes encountered by Mr. Dvořák have a singular habit of whistling Scotch and Bohemian tunes'.

Native American composers never succeeded in matching Dvořák and creating a popular piece of chamber music based on native themes. Arthur FARWELL (1872–1952) worked valiantly for the cause of American music, making use of Indian tunes in his chamber music. Another pioneer in American music, Henry Franklin Belknap GILBERT (C), the 'Uramerikaner' as he was called by a German critic, arranged several of his piano pieces conceived in an authentically American style for various instrumental ensembles. The only American composer who successfully applied American themes to works of lasting value, Edward MACDOWELL, wrote no chamber music at all.

The slow development of chamber music in America can be explained by the predilection of American composers for programmatic music. It required a radical departure from old-fashioned and flamboyant nationalism to initiate a chamber-music style, contrapuntal in essence and capable of expressing American ideas and moods in a communicative manner. The vigorous flowering of American chamber music from 1925 was made possible when American composers finally relinquished a narrowly programmatic style of composition.

An isolated and unique instance of the creation of chamber music of great distinction and originality, and in a nationalistic style, is presented by that extraordinary American Charles IVES (1874–1954). In his string quartets and other instrumental works, written early in the twentieth century, he introduced a variety of environmental material—hymn tunes, patriotic songs, marches, and popular dances. To Ives, music was an active part of social life, a meeting of freely expressed and often discordant utterances. He was impatient with academic rules governing form and development. He felt that music should partake of the spirit of improvisation, and in his characteristic remarks strewn through his works he emphasized this relaxed freedom. In one of his string quartets the part of the second violin bears this inscription: 'Join in again, Professor, all in the key of C!'

The paradox of Ives is that for all his emphatic Americanism, almost 'corny' in its sources, he was a highly original experimenter who made use of such modern devices as atonality and polytonality long before the terms came into use. In one remarkable passage, in his *Tone Roads No. 3*, for chamber orchestra, he made use of a complete twelve-note series, repeated in different registers and in different rhythms, a procedure typical of the orthodox twelve-note technique. And Ives wrote this work in 1915, thus anticipating Schoenberg's explicit use of the method by several years.

Polytonal and atonal usages in the works of Ives result from natural distortions of melody and harmony, natural because they mimic the actual playing of familiar tunes by untutored musicians. In the First Violin Sonata (1903–8) Ives furnishes the tune of Lowell Mason's hymn 'Watchman, tell us of the night!' with a dissonant diatonic accompaniment. In the Fourth Violin Sonata, sub-titled *Children's Day at the Camp Meeting* (1915), there is in the last movement a quotation from Robert Lowry's tune 'Gather at the River', in a similar modernistic harmonic setting (see Ex. 162). The Second String Quartet (1907–13) has three programmatic movements: 'Discussions', 'Arguments', and 'The Call of the Mountains'. Again American hymnology and country dances provide the material. In his Piano Trio (1904) Ives uses an Alberti bass *à l'Américaine*, a sort of walking bass, typical of many American dances. One movement is marked 'T. S. I. A. J.', the initials signifying 'This Scherzo Is a Joke'.

Apart from the phenomenon of Ives, aggressive Americanism is not conspicuous in American chamber music. The national characteristics are mainly expressed in propulsive and highly syncopated rhythms derived from ragtime, later tending towards idealized and compactly organized jazz forms.

Characteristic rhythmical inflexions inevitably affect melodic structures, even in works atonally conceived. In purely diatonic or polytonal works the American rhythms impart a certain ambience suggesting the broad geographical expanses of the New World.

Ex. 162

(Reprinted by permission of Associated Music Publishers, Inc., New York)

The technical idiom of American chamber music, at its point of stabilization about mid-twentieth century, is contrapuntal in essence, but not usually addicted to elaborate polyphonic development. The melodic patterns are often atonal, but the harmonic base is firm, often supported by organ points. There is an increasing spread of the dodecaphonic techniques. One after another, American composers, and naturalized citizens, succumb to the lure of various forms of serial writing. Particularly common in American chamber music is the use of twelve-note subjects as a melodic motto, without further development in the forms of inversion or retrograde motion.

Some American composers of chamber music use a sort of adumbrative dodecaphony by writing melodies containing 9, 10, or 11 different thematic notes; non-repetition of essential thematic units, inherent in integral dodecaphony, remains the principal idea behind such usages.

The emigration to the United States of several important European composers —Stravinsky, Schoenberg, Bartók, Hindemith, among them—influenced the development of American chamber music to a very great extent, through frequent performances of their works, through an increased interest aroused by their presence on the American scene, and through teaching. Hindemith taught at several American universities before returning to Europe in 1953, and his influence on impressionable young Americans was personal as well as doctrinal. Schoenberg lived in Los Angeles, far from the centres of American musical education in the eastern states, but a number of young (and even not so young) composers travelled to California to study with him. Schoenberg was anchoretic rather than peripatetic, and his influence, ever increasing even after his death, was that of a prophet. Bartók and Stravinsky did practically no teaching.

The presence of these composers in America divided the country, musically speaking, into warring groups: pure constructivists and tonal contrapuntalists (Hindemith), atonalists and dodecaphonists (Schoenberg), folkloristic rhythmicians and instrumental colourists (Bartók), and austere neo-classicists and styli-zers (Stravinsky). To be sure, there is a group of chamber-music composers who follow the trends of romantic music, using conventional techniques of the nineteenth century, and also some impressionists who imitate Ravel and Debussy, but they remain in the rearguard of musical action in America, and are all but ignored by the moulders of musical opinion. Ernest Bloch's music is widely performed in the United States, but he produced few followers among American composers, and his former pupils veered away from his stylistic precepts. Darius Milhaud was a resident of the United States for many years without becoming a citizen; he had many American students, but failed to form a school of adher-ents to his particular type of composition. Broadly speaking, the neo-classical and the dodecaphonic styles dominate the American musical scene; sophisticated projections of American rhythms are fitted naturally into the neo-classical framework.

The essence of American rhythm is vividly presented by Roy Harris, himself a composer of distinctive American works, in Henry Cowell's symposium, *American Composers on American Music* (1933):

Our rhythmic impulses are fundamentally different from the rhythmic impulses of Europeans; and from this unique rhythmic sense are generated different melodic and form values. Our sense of rhythm is less symmetrical than the European rhythmic sense. European musicians are trained to think of rhythm in its largest common denominator, while we are born with a feeling for its smallest units. That is why the jazz boys, chained to an unimaginative commercial routine which serves only crystal-lized symmetrical dance rhythms, are continually breaking out into superimposed rhythmic variations. This asymmetrical balancing of rhythmic phrases is in our blood. We do not employ unconventional rhythms as a sophisticated gesture; we cannot avoid them.

The chamber music of Roy HARRIS (C) offers numerous instances of rhythmic Americanism as described by him. Melodically, it possesses a broad songful line, which he conceives as an expression of the vastness of the American West (he was born in Oklahoma). Several of his significant works were written for chamber groups: Sextet (C) for piano, clarinet, and string quartet (1926), String Quartet No. 1 (1930), String Sextet (1932), Three Variations on a Theme (String Quartet No. 2), Piano Trio (1934), and String Quartet No. 3 (1937). The remarkable point about Harris's chamber-music idiom is the inconspicuous incorporation of European modernism into a highly individualistic style. Like many other modern Americans, he made a dutiful pilgrimage to study with Nadia Boulanger in Paris. He also avidly studied Beethoven's last string quartets, and Bach. He avoided the road to Stravinsky, and he had little interest in the development of atonal writing. He by-passed impressionism. There are no direct traces of any specific influence in his music. Yet the modern quality of his style is unmistakable.

If it were not for Harris's strong individuality, he would have become an eclec-tic composer, a follower of trends. Fortunately for him (and perhaps for Ameri-can music), Harris was preoccupied with his own personal musical message, which he also believed to be of universal validity. The aesthetic code which he elaborated in his String Quartet No. 3 has something of the medieval quality. It consists of four preludes and fugues, all couched in ecclesiastical modes, which Harris conceives as reflecting varying emotional qualities. The larger the initial intervals from the tonal centre, the brighter the mood. The Lydian mode appears, therefore, at the brightest end of the spectrum; its inversion, the Locrian mode, at the darkest. The Dorian mode, being invertible, is emotionally neutral, and also the most satisfying for the symmetrical sense. Like any other theory of melody, Harris's spectrum of modes is arbitrary, but he utilizes it with compelling personal logic.

The contrapuntal scheme of Harris's String Quartet No. 3 is determined by the process of fugal imitation, in the preludes as well as in the fugues. The imitation is rather strict, at the intervals of the fourth and the fifth, thus adhering largely to the classical tradition of responses in the dominant and the sub-dominant.

The fugal element is also prominent in his Piano Trio, the last movement of which is a fugue on the theme quoted in Ex. 163. Simple imitation at the octave

Ex. 163

(*Copyrighted 1940 Merion Music Inc. Used by permission*)

is used to great advantage in the first movement of this work; there are numerous instances also of rhythmic canon, with entries at a very close range; this is a favourite device of Harris, which provides him with an opportunity of creating strong cross-accents in progressions of notes of even value. Much of this type of technique is found already in his first important piece of chamber music, the Sextet for piano, clarinet, and string quartet. In his orchestral and choral music Harris often adopts American subject-matter, but not in his chamber music. The spirit of classicism is particularly strong in his Quintet for piano and strings (1936), consisting of three movements: Passacaglia, Cadenza, and Fugue. There is no literal adherence to the form of passacaglia in the first movement; this term is expanded by Harris to mean a strong central pattern, beginning with a

Ex. 164

short melodic and rhythmic motto (see Ex. 164), and developing into a highly ornamental movement, approaching the character of a toccata in the piano part. The Fugue also includes toccata-like episodes.

The harmonic scheme in the chamber music of Harris is triadic. He combines closely related triads into seventh-chords, but studiously avoids the dominant seventh. By superimposing triads without a common note, he builds poly-harmonic structures. In his chamber music the tonal element, in polyharmonic structures, remains very strong.

William SCHUMAN (b. 1910) comes closest to Harris (with whom he studied for a brief while) in writing chamber music of an essentially classical cast, polyphonic in essence, and marked by strong asymmetrical rhythm. In Schu-man's string quartets the harmony is tense and dissonant; this is alleviated by passages in unison and by a strong sense of tonality, particularly in the opening and concluding bars of a movement.

The first movement of Schuman's String Quartet No. 2 (1937), headed 'Sinfonia', builds up tension by a gradual expansion of the basic motive (see Ex. 165). The theme of the second movement, Passacaglia (Ex. 166), is interest-ing in its quasi-dodecaphonic construction; it is made up of eight different notes.

Ex. 165

Ex. 166

It should be observed, however, that in this instance, as in similar passages in other works by non-dodecaphonic Americans, the underlying thought is not atonal but is derived from the modulatory cycle of fifths.

The third and last movement is a Fugue. The building of the theme on fourths is characteristic, as is the nervous vigorous rhythm of the first subject (Ex. 167); the second subject is of a more flowing nature. The exposition in both cases is quite explicit.

In Schuman's String Quartet No. 4 (1950) the exhortation to the players, 'calm and relaxed', is made difficult by the harsh frictional discords of the open-ing 'Adagio', cast in two-part counterpoint (Ex. 168). The second movement, 'Allegro con fuoco', illustrates Schuman's technique of divergent harmonic pro-gressions; in the opening bars the 'cello moves consistently in contrary motion to the first violin (see Ex. 169). Here again we find an adumbration of a dodeca-

phonic theme; the initial nine notes of the principal theme are all different.
The second theme is fugal in nature, and its component elements are poly-
phonically developed with great skill. The third movement, 'Andante', establishes

Ex. 167

Ex. 168

Ex. 169

at the outset a solemn hymn-like mood; the harmony is strong and dissonant;
a powerful progression in the 'cello, in double stops, provides the tonal support.
The fourth movement, 'Presto', contains interesting rhythmic developments of
thematic fragments.

Perhaps the greatest American master of pure chamber music is Walter PISTON
(b. 1894). Throughout his career he has cultivated the type of instrumental
music devoid of all programmatic artifice, and dedicated to purposeful melodic,
harmonic, and polyphonic art. After a period of study with Nadia Boulanger in
Paris, Piston joined the faculty of Harvard University, and it is in this atmo-
sphere of enlightened academicism that his chamber music (as well as his
symphonies) originated. This is not to say that Piston himself is an academic;

his nineteenth-century predecessors would have been horrified at his modernism. But Piston's chamber music, more than that of any other American composer, is the result of an evolutionary process. A central tonality is clearly established and invariably carried through. Each of his chamber-music works begins and ends on the same tonic, or on the tonic of the related key. The final chord sometimes lacks a third. Terminal thirdless triads, in open fifths, are, of course, characteristic not only of Walter Piston's music but of many European composers of the neo-classical persuasion. Piston dispenses with the key signature.

The String Quartet No. 1 (1933) is precise in musical exposition, songful in slow melodic passages, and strongly rhythmical throughout. The String Quartet No. 2 (1935) is more ornamental, but presents no departures from the neo-classical genre. The String Quartet No. 3 (1947) is marked by a more strict and less florid musical discourse. Asymmetrical rhythms are virile and germane to the melodic patterns. The String Quartet No. 4 (1953) is similarly effective in design and technical execution.

One of the finest of Piston's chamber-music works is his Piano Quintet (1949). The first movement, 'Allegro comodo', is poetically conceived. The mood is almost romantic in its easy flow of harmonic figurations, against which the principal theme is projected (Ex. 170). Dynamic and harmonic tension marks the

Ex. 170

(*Reprinted by permission of Associated Music Publishers, Inc., New York*)

middle section, and here the intervallic structure is in fourths and fifths. The return to the simple thematic progression forms a natural conclusion. This movement is perhaps the most explicitly tonal piece of writing by Walter Piston; the key is plainly that of G minor, although the composer refuses to signify it by a key signature. The conclusion of the movement has all the three notes of the G minor triad.

The second movement, 'Adagio', is built on highly dissonant but ethereally light harmonies, supported by deep organ points. The melodic line is placed within narrow chromatic confines, then expands into diatonic progressions, while the dynamic curve leads from pianissimo to fortissimo, and back again.

The third and last movement, 'Allegro vivo', is a typical Pistonian dance, cast in ternary form, with a quasi-fugal middle section. The coda is in G major, but the third of the chord is evaded at the end.

An interesting work is Piston's Quintet for flute and string quartet (1942). It is much lighter in texture than his string quartets and the Piano Quintet, and the idiom is transparently diatonic.

Piston's Divertimento for nine instruments (1946) presents a remarkable display of his polyphonic mastery. As in most of his instrumental works, the Divertimento is in three movements, with a slow movement placed between two fast ones.

Of all chamber music written by American composers, that of Roger SESSIONS (b. 1896) is the most forbidding, the most uncompromisingly esoteric, and the most intricate in its construction. It is a philosopher's art, conceived in an unrelentingly logical yet passionate spirit. It is not dry, and it is certainly not pedantic. But it is the product of deep thought, sharpened by a quest for perfection of design and execution. The texture is primarily contrapuntal, and the counterpoint is dissonant. Yet tonality is affirmed, and focal points of melodic patterns are clearly marked. Sessions applies the method of composition with twelve notes in a very personal manner; in some of his themes he deliberately stops short of dodecaphonic completeness, even though the melodic design is typically dodecaphonic.

Sessions is not a composer of many works, but his chamber music is an important part of his output. In his String Quartet No. 1 (1936) he explicitly designates the key as that of E minor, but departs from it almost instantly upon stating the tonic triad in the opening movement, 'Tempo moderato'. The second movement is 'Adagio molto'; the third and last is 'Vivace molto'. The final chord is a full E major triad.

The String Quartet No. 2 (1950) is an austere piece of work in an emphatically classical form, even in outward peculiarities. It is in five movements. The opening 'Lento' is a fugue with a quasi-dodecaphonic subject, in which a note is repeated non-consecutively, thus disrupting the series, which is not completed until fourteen notes are sounded (see Ex. 171). Another fugal subject, brought

Ex. 171

out in 'Un poco agitato', is totally dodecaphonic; there is imitation in inversion, and the first fugal theme appears in diminution. The thematic elements of both fugues are very much in evidence in a development section, which is worked out with great skill. The third movement, 'Andante tranquillo', is an air with variations (see Ex. 172). The fourth movement, 'Presto', is a scherzo. After a pause, the last movement, 'Adagio', introduces an ornamented subject consisting of thirteen notes, eleven of which are different (see Ex. 173).

In his String Quintet (1958) Sessions writes absolute music of the most austere type, with dodecaphonic themes skilfully adapted to a non-serial general design; canonic imitation, exact as to rhythm but free as to component intervals, is

Ex. 172

Ex. 173

effectively applied. The Quintet consists of three movements: 'Movimento tranquillo' is built on several interdependent twelve-note rows and numerous rhythmic stretti; 'Adagio ed espressivo' is derived thematically from groups of six different notes; the employment of mirror-like progressions is deliberately non-literal; there is a rhapsodic quality in the expressive use of fragmented solo passages. The third movement, 'Allegro appassionato', is rhythmically potent, and maintains its pulse unswervingly, but the thematic treatment is fragmentary. The first statement contains eleven different notes of the chromatic scale, and to make up for this omission, the twelfth note is conspicuously placed on the very first beat of the movement. Sessions seems reluctant to follow the rigid outlines of dodecaphonic orthodoxy, but makes use of its technical devices for his own creative purposes.

Among other chamber works by Sessions, the Duo for violin and piano should be mentioned as an entirely utilitarian piece of music.

In the late 1920's a series of Copland–Sessions concerts of modern music attracted a great deal of attention in New York City. What united these two dissimilar composers was the eloquent precision of their techniques and the basic lyricism of their inspiration. Aaron COPLAND (b. 1900) has become one of the best-known American composers, and in his ballets and symphonic works created masterpieces of explicit folkloric American self-expression. In his chamber music he essayed the folkloric genre in a few pieces, but subsequently turned to a searching, esoteric, and at times brooding style of composition. His earliest instrumental pieces were Nocturne and 'Ukulele Serenade' (1926) for violin and piano, in which he displayed his acute sense of nostalgia and engaging grotesquerie. Copland's Two Pieces for String Quartet (1928) are of little interest. In 1929 he wrote a piano trio subtitled *Vitebsk*, inspired by a Jewish folk-song which he heard during a performance of Ansky's play *The Dybbuk*, and which Ansky himself had heard in Vitebsk. This is an expressive work; in the string parts Copland makes use of quarter-tones, not as independent fractional intervals, but as colouristic devices intended to sharpen an orientalistic melodic line, much as Ernest Bloch applied quarter-tones in his Piano Quintet.

In 1943 Copland completed a Violin Sonata in three movements. The first movement, 'Andante semplice', is a pensive elegy, austerely conceived; the second movement, 'Lento', is a tender modal air, reposing on organ points; the third movement, 'Allegretto giusto', a nervous dance, greatly varied in rhythm and dynamics. The opening motive of the first movement returns as a reminiscence at the conclusion of the sonata.

The urban American rhythms that animated Copland's earliest works were later enriched by Latin American inflexions. In 1933 he wrote a 'Short Symphony' for the Orquesta Sinfónica de México, dedicating the score to its conductor, Carlos Chávez. In 1937 he arranged it for string quartet, clarinet, and piano, and it was in this reduced form, as a sextet, that the work became popular.

The first movement of the Sextet, 'Allegro vivace', bears the designation 'in a bold rhythmic style throughout'. The rhythms are asymmetrical, in a manner typical of Copland, but the groupings are distinctly Hispano-American, with the alternation and superposition of implied metres of 3/4 and 6/8 very much in evidence. The second movement, 'Lento', is a slow incantation, modally and rhythmically redolent of Latin American chants. The finale, marked 'precise and rhythmic', is full of vitality; its rhythms are close to the Afro-Cuban *danzón*; the cumulative agitation in the piano part relates this movement also to jazz. But there is no concession to vulgarity; this music is a highly sophisticated and yet authentic stylization of primitive rhythmic and melodic patterns.

A signal departure from Copland's familiar style is his Quartet for piano and strings (1950). For one thing, he adopts here a serial technique, using an eleven-note row in the very opening theme of the first movement, 'Adagio serio' (see Ex. 174); the most conspicuous elements of the series are two mutually exclusive whole-tone groups. The second movement, 'Allegro giusto', retains the serial motto, but the fragmentation is such that the reference is not immediately apparent (see Ex. 175). The movement is greatly varied in rhythmic content, but the main pulse is steady throughout. The third movement, 'Non troppo lento', is in the nature of a soliloquy; fragments of mutually exclusive whole-tone scales constitute the thematic link with the original series (see Ex. 176); towards the end, ten notes of the series are presented in a figure of descending whole-tone scales, in parallel major sixths.

In 1960 Copland wrote a Nonet for three violins, three violas, and three 'cellos.

It is in a single movement cyclically constructed, opening and closing with characteristic slow episodes. The more energetic middle section is freely rhapsodic, and rhythmically variegated. The triadic and polytriadic formations, so typical of many of Copland's works in an American idiom, are peculiarly appropriate in the Nonet, scored as it is for three homogeneous groups of instruments.

Ex. 174

Ex. 175

Ex. 176

The economy of means and unprejudiced acceptance of several workable techniques in the chamber music of Copland are also characteristic of several other American composers. A remarkable range of such techniques, from simplest diatonic harmonies to the most complex and continuous discords, is found in the works of Wallingford RIEGGER (**C**, d. 1961). He combined the qualities of an experimenter and a teacher, and published numerous compositions, conventional in form and idiom, under many pseudonyms. His String Quartet No. 1 (1945) makes a leap into the realm of dodecaphony; it is based on a twelve-note series, which is exploited with great resourcefulness. The second movement of the work uses the retrograde series, the third the inverted form, and the fourth the inverted and retrograde.

Riegger's Quartet No. 2 (1949) is an essay in rhythm and atonal melody. The first theme of the first movement is a brisk 'Scherzando'; the second theme a lyric incantation. The interval of the tritone is basic to the melodic development.

The second movement opens with a slow subject, atonally angular, which is imitated canonically in a slightly altered intervallic form; there is a rapid middle section. The third movement is energetic and lively; there are two principal motives, one broadly outlined, the other chromatic. The fourth movement is light and rhythmic.

Riegger uses a twelve-note series for his Nonet for three trumpets, two horns, three trombones, and tuba (1951). The music develops freely, without slavish dependence on the declared serial progression. The wide intervallic skips in writing for brass instruments contribute to the peculiar effectiveness of the score. Riegger also makes skilful use of consecutive chordal progressions.

Many other chamber-music works by Riegger still retain their musical value, beginning with an early but effective Piano Trio (1919), written in a pre-impressionist French manner. The list continues with 'Canons for Woodwinds' (1931), Divertissement for flute, harp, and 'cello (1933), 'Duos for Three Woodwinds' (1943), in which the three instruments—flute, oboe, and clarinet—are successively paired, Woodwind Quintet (1952), and Piano Quintet (1959).

A close contemporary of Riegger, John BECKER (1886–1961), is a bold experimenter in musical sonorities, and, like Riegger, is free from prejudice against traditional techniques. Becker introduced the term 'soundpiece' to denote compositions for various instrumental combinations, in various styles. His 'Soundpiece No. 2' (1938) is subtitled 'Homage to Haydn'. It is scored for string quartet reinforced by the double bass, and represents a polytonal and atonal version of an eighteenth-century work.

The name of Henry COWELL (b. 1897) is associated with the period of American ultra-modernism. He is the founder of the quarterly *New Music*, which publishes modern works, and the co-inventor (with Leon Theremin) of the Rhythmicon, an instrument capable of producing simultaneous rhythms. As a very young man, he began to use so-called 'tone-clusters', columns of diatonic or pentatonic notes played on the keyboard with the forearm or the palm of the hand, according to the number of notes involved. He used tone-clusters in the piano part of his Suite for violin and piano (1927) (see Ex. 177).

Ex. 177

*All the chromatic tones between the octave are sounded with the flat of the same hand used to play the whole note octave. This octave is sustained while the cluster is played an eighth rest later.

(*Reprinted by permission of Associated Music Publishers, Inc., New York*)

The most curious of Cowell's pieces of chamber music is *Ensemble* (1924) for string quintet with thundersticks (**C**), instruments used in initiation ceremonies by south-western American Indians. There are three parts for thundersticks, and the composer leaves the rhythmic and dynamic details to the discretion of the performer, suggesting only a general outline (in canonic imitation) in the initial bars.

Unquestionably the most forceful and the most original innovator upon the American scene is Edgar VARÈSE (b. 1885) of Paris, who settled in New York as early as 1916. With the harpist Carlos Salzedo he founded there the International Composers' Guild. His only work that may come under the heading of chamber music is *Octandre*, for flute, oboe, clarinet, bassoon, horn, trumpet, trombone, and double bass (1924). The score is typical of Varèse's style and technique; thematic succession is agglutinative, and all formal development is avoided; technical discords are used as self-sustaining units; the melodies are atonal.

Carlos SALZEDO (1885–1961) composed a number of small ensembles for harp, or several harps, with other instruments. He also constructed new harp models capable of performing many special effects demanded by his highly complex technique.

While the Frenchmen Varèse and Salzedo were promoting modern music in America, the American composer George ANTHEIL (**C**, Appendix, 1900–59) was demonstrating his brand of American music in Paris. His *Ballet mécanique* created a sensation. When the fashion for ultra-modern music ceased, Antheil returned to America and devoted himself to the composition of practical music in an almost romantic vein. He wrote several string quartets, violin sonatas, and other chamber music, but these works received little attention. Antheil's name remains in the annals of American music as that of the bard of the machine age.

At the opposite pole from American ultra-modernists stands Virgil THOMSON (b. 1896), a resident of Paris for many years, whose modernism finds its expression in a unique genre of sophisticated simplicity and stylistic paradox. He is known mainly through his musical play to Gertrude Stein's text, *Four Saints in Three Acts* (in which there are many more saints than four, and one more act than three). He professes admiration for 'le lieu commun', while rejecting 'banalité', and is not at all embarrassed by the unmodern and sometimes lowly character of his thematic material.

Thomson's String Quartet No. 1 (1931) could be passed for a work by a minor composer of the Mannheim School, with a minimum of adjustments. His String Quartet No. 2 (1932) is equally conventional. Much more interesting is his *Stabat Mater* for soprano and string quartet (1931), to French words by Max Jacob. Here Virgil Thomson's neo-archaic counterpoint bridges the gap of the centuries, and creates a distinct poetic impression.

An earlier work, a 'Sonata da Chiesa' (1926) for clarinet, trumpet, viola, horn, and trombone, is the product of Thomson's Parisian eclecticism, but it retains its effectiveness outside Paris. The first movement, Chorale, is a fine evocation of old church modes, and utilizes the organum of parallel fifths (see Ex. 178).

The second movement, a Tango, skips a near-millennium into the twentieth century (see Ex. 179). It is a nostalgic ballroom dance, stylized and contorted into a modernistic creation by changing metres and sharp rhythms. The last movement of the 'Sonata da Chiesa' is a Fugue, with a subject constructed on a series of expanding intervals; the imitation is worked out with all the strictness of academic rules.

Ex. 178

Ex. 179

Avowed romanticism is rare among American composers. Yet one of the most important figures of American music, Howard HANSON (**C**, b. 1896), admits and proclaims his faith in the primacy of romantic inspiration. As director of the Eastman School of Music in Rochester for many years, and teacher of composition, he has educated a generation of young American composers. There is little chamber music in Hanson's creative catalogue. His early String Quartet in one movement (1923) commands attention for its sincere and unassuming melodiousness. It is not devoid of modernism; for all its simple graces, the work contains twentieth-century devices—asymmetrical rhythms, progressions in fourths, a suggestion of polytonality. Similar qualities of romantic modernism distinguish Hanson's 'Fantasia on a Theme of Youth' for piano and strings (1950).

Bernard ROGERS (b. 1893), a music educator and colleague of Hanson at the Eastman School of Music, is known mostly for his symphonies and choral works, written in a tense romantic vein. In the field of chamber music he has written a string quartet and some minor pieces.

A composer who began as a romanticist and moved towards highly emotional expressionism is David DIAMOND (b. 1915). The sources of his music are in the rhapsodic inspiration of Mahler and Bloch; in his idiom, Diamond reaches remote outposts of tonality, without quite abandoning it. When his purpose lies in simple expressiveness, he adopts a correspondingly simple harmonic language, without modernistic snobbism.

Diamond's first important work of chamber music was a Quintet for flute, violin, viola, 'cello, and piano (1937). The harmonic idiom maintains a clear diatonic line in the first movement, 'Allegro deciso e molto ritmico'. The second movement (Romanza) is simple in melodic outline but increasingly discordant in harmony. The last movement, 'Allegro veloce', is a jig, with some polytonal developments in the piano part.

Diamond's 'Cello Sonata (1938) is a work of great concentration. The first movement, 'Tempo giusto e maestoso', develops forcefully; the melody soars, while the piano part supplies florid counterpoint. The second movement, 'Lento assaï', opens with a sonorous chant, which develops into a florid cantillation, followed by a rhythmic section of considerable complexity. The third movement, 'Andante con grand' espressione', is a lyric intermezzo. The epilogue is a brief rhythmic dance, in Diamond's favourite jig time (see Ex. 180).

Ex. 180

★ ♦ Strong pizzicato by lifting the string and allowing it to slap the fingerboard.

(*Copyright 1939 Theodore Presser Company, used by permission*)

In his Violin Sonata (1946) Diamond pursues the mundane object of writing a modern work in a classical manner. The music is diaphanous, the rhythm steady and uncomplicated. The predominant tonalities of each of the four movements are indicated by key signatures.

Diamond's Quintet for clarinet, two violas, and two 'cellos (1950) has a sustained mood of sombreness, even in rapid episodes, a character due perhaps to the exclusion of the violin from the scoring. The clarinet is a true soloist, introducing an angular quasi-atonal motto, unaccompanied; the first movement concludes with a retrograde form, slightly modified, of the motto. The second movement, a scherzo, is in a simple dance form, with the clarinet again in the lead. The third movement, 'Andante non troppo', includes several changes of metre and rhythm. A fragment of the motto brings the movement to a close.

The fourth and last movement, 'Allegro risoluto', is a rondo alternating between two contrasting themes and ending in a stretto.

Samuel BARBER (b. 1910) has the distinction of being the author of the most successful piece of American chamber music, known and performed frequently not only in the United States but also in Europe. It is the 'Molto adagio' from his String Quartet composed in 1936. The music is a continuous melodic chant, with some contrapuntal embroidery, finely proportioned and discreetly harmonized. Ex. 181 shows the opening bars. It is often performed by string orchestras, under the title 'Adagio for Strings'.

Ex. 181

The first movement of Barber's String Quartet, 'Molto allegro e appassionato', possesses a propulsive rhythmic energy in its main subject (see Ex. 182); its melodic material appears later in a modified rhythmic pattern; there is also an

Ex. 182

important ambling figure in even motion. After the 'Molto adagio', the Quartet concludes with a brief movement, 'Molto allegro', which virtually recapitulates the material of the opening movement.

Barber's Serenade for String Quartet, written at the age of eighteen (1928), is a slight work of youthful charm. Another youthful work is his 'Cello Sonata (1932), conceived in an expansive, quasi-Italian manner, sonorous in its instrumental writing and lyric in melodic inspiration.

Paul CRESTON (b. 1906) was born in New York of Italian parents; his real name is Joseph Guttoveggio. No adherent to any predetermined techniques, Creston writes music full of rhapsodic excitement and rhythmic energy. His harmony is modern without ostentation, and in his lyrical writing he surrenders himself to a natural flow of melodious cantilena. Of his chamber music, the most important works are the Suite for saxophone and piano (1935), String Quartet (1936), Suite for viola and piano (1937), Suite for violin and piano (1939), Suite for flute, viola, and piano (1953), and Suite for 'cello and piano (1956).

Norman DELLO JOIO (b. 1913), a New Yorker of Italian ancestry, successfully combines classical and romantic elements in his music. He composes with great facility, and his works are eminently practical in performance. His sense of tonality never falters, but his music expands freely, reaching the gates of polytonality. One of his most engaging compositions is his Trio for flute, 'cello, and piano (1947). The tonality of each movement is designated by the key signature; the modulatory plan is extensive, but the development is centripetal, so that the tonal centres are clearly established. The clarity of design and the lively sense of rhythm of Dello Joio's works are contributing factors to his success.

Among American composers whose music can be described as neo-romantic are Douglas Moore, Harold Morris, Frederick Jacobi, and Randall Thompson.

Douglas Moore (b. 1893) is distinguished as a composer of several theatre works on American subjects. Among his chamber music, the Quintet for flute, oboe, clarinet, horn, and bassoon (1942) should be noted. Here is a simple piece with a distinctly American flavour; ragtime rhythms are in evidence in the first movement; ballad-like melodies are the features of the second movement; and the last movement is a gay American march, with the piccolo leading the way to a sophisticatedly shrill ending.

A solitary figure in American music is Harold Morris (b. 1890). His sources of inspiration are post-Wagnerian; there is also a kinship with Scriabin's ecstatic muse. His Piano Trio No. 2 (1937) exemplifies these derivations. Its first movement, a passacaglia, is anything but classical; the theme is sombre, angularly constructed; it soars upward, almost escaping tonality. Contrasting dynamics lend variety to the development, and the coda is full of large pianistic sonorities. The second movement, a scherzo, is appropriately light. The third movement is a meditation, with a quasi-atonal theme; there is an excursion into a dance. The fourth and last movement is an accompanied fugue, quite orthodox as to fugal imitation, but bristling with thick polyharmonies in the piano part.

Frederick Jacobi (C, d. 1952) wrote music on Indian and on Jewish themes in his early period, but later adopted a style unconnected with any ethnic source. His String Quartet No. 2 (1933) is idiomatically written for the instruments, and orthodox as to harmony. Jacobi's String Quartet No. 3 (1945) is rhapsodic in its emotional tone; there is also a considerable rhythmic tension; the music is attractive, practical, and mildly modernistic.

One of the most successful American composers is Randall Thompson (b. 1899), whose vocal works have established themselves in the repertory of choral societies in America. In the domain of chamber music he has produced brilliant works, ingratiating to players and listeners alike. His String Quartet No. 1 (1941) hardly ever transcends the borders of nineteenth-century harmony, and is clearly a tribute to the enduring values of the past. Asymmetrical rhythms alone give a clue to its modern origin and its American provenance. Ex. 183 shows the principal theme of the first movement.

Randall Thompson's Suite for oboe, clarinet, and viola (1940) is one of the very few pieces for such a heterogeneous trio composed in America. The subject-matter in all five movements is distinctly American, redolent of the rhythms of a rustic barn dance; the main themes in the first three movements are built entirely on the pentatonic scale.

Ex. 183

The following composers adhere to the neo-classical idiom, with wide varieties of personal expression: Quincy Porter, Ross Lee Finney, Arthur Berger, Irving Fine, Vincent Persichetti, Harold Shapero, Andrew Welsh Imbrie, William Bergsma, and Peter Mennin.

Quincy PORTER (b. 1897) is one of the most prolific American composers of chamber music. Beginning with 1923, he has been writing string quartets at a steady pace. His style is eminently tonal, and invariably practical for perform-ance. His String Quartet No. 4, composed in Paris in 1931, is distinguished by a natural lyric quality in melodic writing and a vigorous rhythmic sense. The third movement is interesting in its asymmetrical patterns; here time signa-tures are dispensed with, despite, or perhaps because of, the constantly shifting rhythmic groupings.

Porter's String Quartet No. 6 (1937) is a well-balanced work, in which strong rhythmic themes alternate with lyric episodes. The first movement, 'Allegro molto', is animated by a dance-like rhythm (see Ex. 184), which is followed by

Ex. 184

(Copyright 1937 by Quincy Porter. International copyright secured.)

a second theme of lyric quality, in a rondo-like succession. The second move-ment, 'Adagio', is a songful incantation, slowly rising to an eloquent climax. The middle section of the movement contains some rapid passages, but the conclusion is serene. The third movement, 'Allegro giocoso', is a tarantella.

Porter's String Quartet No. 8 (1950) opens with a slow introduction, leading to a principal section with curiously fragmentized thematic material, while a swaying figure in the 'cello part provides unifying support. The concluding short movement, 'Adagio molto espressivo', intensifies the nervous impressionistic quality of the whole work.

In 1958 Quincy Porter completed his String Quartet No. 9, in one movement. In 1960 he composed a Divertimento for woodwind quintet (flute, oboe, clarinet, bassoon, and French horn), and in 1961 a Quintet for harpsichord and string quartet.

Ross Lee FINNEY (b. 1906) is also an industrious composer of chamber music. His String Quartet No. 6 (1950) is marked as being in E, indicating the central tonic, without specification as to major or minor. It is in fact neither, to judge by the final chords of each of the four movements. The first movement ends in a chord containing both G sharp and G natural; the second movement concludes on the unison A; the third on a chord of F minor; and the fourth on the first inversion of the tonic seventh chord, in E major. These details are significant inasmuch as they reflect the universal trend, particularly strong among American composers, towards reasserting the tonality by minimal allegiance. As for the general style of Finney's sixth string quartet, it follows a neo-classical pattern. The form is particularly strict. Despite the neoclassical appearance of Finney's String Quartet No. 6, there is present in it a seed of serialism. Themes are used as groups, and their metamorphoses follow those curious arithmetical patterns that distinguish the serial method from the classical principle of variations. The serial technique is much more strongly pronounced in Finney's String Quartets No. 7 (1955) and No. 8 (1960). Permutation, rather than inversion or retrograde motion, is Finney's chief modus operandi; also, the notes of the series are freely duplicated. And yet both quartets are tonally directed—'teleotonal', to coin a potentially useful neologism. The musical action of the String Quartet No. 7 is centripetal towards C, that of No. 8, towards D. Finney's other chamber works include three violin sonatas, two viola sonatas, two 'cello sonatas, two piano trios, a piano quartet, two piano quintets, and a string quintet.

Arthur BERGER (b. 1912) is one of the most cultured and sophisticated composers of chamber music in America. He experienced the influence of both Stravinsky and Schoenberg, but eventually established a style of his own, in which the principle of tonality is emphasized, while the melodic line is allowed to wander beyond the tonal confines. His Quartet for flute, oboe, clarinet, and bassoon (1941) is designated as being in the key of C major, the favourite key of the neo-classicists, waving the banner of tonality with a vengeance. His later work, Duo for oboe and clarinet (1955), carries a key signature; its melodic line is tangentially tonal.

Irving FINE (1914–62) handled neo-classical forms with great adroitness; he used diatonic melodic patterns in the main, but in his later works he successfully applied dodecaphonic techniques. There is considerable variety in his music; the gaiety of his fast movements, with biting asymmetric rhythms, is spontaneous and effective; his meditative episodes are subtly expressive. His Violin Sonata (1948) follows Stravinsky's neo-classical methods, particularly in stylized dance episodes. The sense of tonality is strong; even key signatures are used to mark modulatory shifts. By contrast, his String Quartet (1953) plunges into a *sui generis* dodecaphony. The serial themes are not stated explicitly at the outset, but are built up cumulatively, by sections, with a free repetition of thematic notes. The two movements of the Quartet are greatly contrasted. The first movement, 'Allegro risoluto', is built on angular intervallic patterns; tonality is neither emphasized nor shunned. The second movement, 'Lento', is a highly concentrated rhythmic improvisation; there are solo passages in the character of cadenzas; the counterpoint is saturated with dissonance. The interval of a tritone appears to be of thematic significance in the entire work.

Vincent PERSICHETTI (b. 1915) is one of the strongest exponents of chamber music in America. In a series of serenades for various instrumental groups he has evolved an individual neo-classical technique. His Pastoral for flute, oboe, clarinet, horn, and bassoon (1945) is an example of his simplest tonal style, with rapidly shifting tonics. He has further composed a String Quartet, a Piano Trio, and a Violin Sonata, all in a brilliant style, and with widely ranging idiomatic peculiarities. One of his most important works is the Quintet No. 2 for piano and strings (1954), in a protracted single movement but with frequent changes of tempo and character in its subdivisions. The remarkable feature of the work is its economy, its austere contrapuntal facture; the piano part is reduced almost to harpsichord sonorities, and chordal structures are few. None the less, the music has sustaining power throughout the long movement.

Harold SHAPERO (b. 1920) writes music of great vitality and formal logic. A modern type of classicism with a powerful lyric strain seems to be his aesthetic goal. A self-critical composer, he writes with deliberation, and his total output is relatively small. Although he has experimented with some twelve-note processes, his music is rooted in tonal relationships. The rhythmic patterns are strong and varied, but the sense of symmetry and metrical periodicity is preserved in the main outline. Among his works for chamber music are a Sonata for trumpet and piano (1939), a String Quartet (1940), and a Violin Sonata (1942).

Andrew Welsh IMBRIE (b. 1921) has written three string quartets, a Serenade for flute, viola, and piano (1952), and some other chamber music. His main concerns are expressiveness of the melodic line and clarity of contrapuntal texture. He achieves a lyric quality in slow movements by cumulative tension; in rapid passages there is a great deal of motoric energy. In his String Quartet No. 3 (1956) Imbrie introduces some dodecaphonic procedures, without sacrificing the basic classical sense of form.

William BERGSMA (b. 1921) writes successfully in many genres. From the evidence of his String Quartet No. 1 (1942), it appears that he follows a neo-classical line; the tonal foundation is strong, but in his florid melody he departs from strict tonality, so that considerable dissonance results. His Suite for brass quartet (1940) is a simple piece of utilitarian music.

One of the most consistent neo-classical American composers of instrumental music is Peter MENNIN (b. 1923). To him, the clarity of contrapuntal lines and the consequent transparency of the harmonic fabric are paramount considerations. His melodic inventiveness enables him to re-create classical forms in a modern manner. Of Mennin's chamber music, the String Quartet No. 2 (1951) is characteristic. The first movement, 'Allegro ardentemente', gives the visual impression of a classical overture, with contrasting motoric and lyric themes. The auditive results are classical, with modernistic expansions and deviations. There are vigorous accents, both coincident and non-coincident with the bar lines. This energetic section subsides into a lyric 'Andante', leading to a concluding 'Lento' in the form of a polyharmonic chorale. The second movement, 'Prestissimo', is an asymmetric scherzo, with constantly changing metres. The musical pulse never slackens, finally reaching a homorhythmic jig towards the end of the movement. The third movement, 'Adagio semplice', is a quiet peroration, ending in ethereal harmonies. After this moment of tranquillity, the final movement, 'Allegro focosamente', is launched in the softest dynamics and propulsive rhythms, without metrical changes. The music progresses cumulatively, and the alternation of pianissimo and fortissimo is continuous. The final chord is a thirdless C major.

As far as formal development is concerned, Robert PALMER (b. 1915) belongs in the neo-classical group of American composers. But he has elected to use, in many of his works, a scale that is associated with exotic music, namely, a progression of alternating tones and semitones, an old orientalistic device much in favour with Rimsky-Korsakov and his friends of the nationalist Russian school. Palmer treats this scale modally as two disjunct minor tetrachords, in order to avoid monotonous neutrality. His Piano Quartet (1947) makes use of the scale in the first movement, 'Allegro e molto energico', at the outset (see Ex. 185), but the

Ex. 185

contrasting theme is built on a pattern of wide intervals, with organ points to sustain the harmonic scheme. The second movement, 'Andante con moto e semplice', exploits the chromatic potentialities resulting from the constant alternation of major and minor triads on the same tonic. The third movement, 'Molto allegro e dinamico', veers away from Palmer's chosen scale towards open tonality, and towards pandiatonicism. The work ends with a 'Presto'.

Among Palmer's other chamber works to be mentioned are three string quartets (1939, 1947, 1954), a Sonata for viola and piano (1948), a Piano Quintet (1950), a Quintet for wind instruments (1951), and a Quintet for clarinet, piano, and strings (1952).

Benjamin LEES, born in 1924 of Russian parents in Harbin, Manchuria, was brought to the United States as an infant, and studied in California with Halsey Stevens and George Antheil. Going through a variety of influences, he eventually adopted a neoclassical style with romantic overtones. The tonal element is always strong, and the endings are explicitly triadic. For chamber music he has written two string quartets (1952, 1955), and a Violin Sonata (1954).

Easley BLACKWOOD, born in Indianapolis in 1933, is one of the youngest aspirants to fame in serious American music. Favoured by prizes and commissions, he has dedicated himself to the composition of solid instrumental works. Standing aloof from fashionable trends, he expresses himself in romantic, expansive, proclamatory music, rich in massive sonorities. In chamber-music forms, he has written a Viola Sonata (1953), two string quartets (1957 and 1959), a Concertino for Five Instruments (1959), a Violin Sonata (1960), and a Fantasy for 'cello and piano (1960).

Among younger Americans, the Texan Ramiro CORTÉS (b. 1933), of Mexican parentage, studied with Henry Cowell and others. His idiom is neoclassical, marked by quartal and quintal harmonies and sprightly counterpoint in a vivacious rhythmic manner. His Elegy for flute and piano (1952) is a poetic piece of lyric contemplation. A Divertimento for flute, clarinet, and bassoon (1953) in five movements, with antique cymbals obbligato, has a definitely Spanish-American colouring. Its fourth movement for unaccompanied flute presents an atonal pattern approximating to a serial type of melody. Among other chamber-music works by Cortés are a Piano Quintet (1954), a String Quartet (1958), and a Piano Trio (1959).

Some highly prolific American composers have written little chamber music; among these are Halsey Stevens, John Verrall, Gardner Read, George Perle, Ellis B. Kohs, and Lockrem Johnson.

Halsey STEVENS (b. 1908) has written chamber music of lucid contrapuntal quality. His Quintet for flute, violin, viola, 'cello, and piano (1945) is eminently tonal despite occasional acrid discords. He is also the composer of an ingenious set of Five Duos for two 'cellos.

John VERRALL (b. 1908) has written four string quartets, a Sonata for viola and piano, a Divertissement for clarinet, bassoon, and horn, and other chamber music. Generally speaking, his music represents an evolutionary trend, with the injection of dissonant counterpoint into an otherwise orthodox body of music.

Gardner READ (b. 1913), who has to his credit more than 100 opus numbers, did not write his first string quartet until 1957. In it he reveals his mastery of the modern style; the essence of the music is neo-romantic. In the scherzo he makes use of a dodecaphonic series, but treats it as a colouristic device rather than a doctrinal subject. A unique piece is Gardner Read's 'Sonoric Fantasia No. 1', op. 102 (1958), written for celesta, harp, and harpsichord. The three instruments naturally lend themselves to miniaturized pointillistic sonorities. The theme is hexatonic and is serially treated. There are subsequent polytonal expansions, and some ingenious fugal involvements.

George PERLE (b. 1915) combines a free dodecaphonic style with a neoclassical design. In opposition to the orthodox twelve-note idiom, he often uses symmetrical thematic figures, and even sequences, a device virtually outlawed among American modernists. Perle's String Quartet No. 3 (1947) is a representative specimen of his style.

Ellis B. KOHS (b. 1916) is the composer of several pieces of chamber music which represent a synthesis of the neo-classic, romantic, and other trends among American composers. His String Quartet (1940) is a simple but ingratiating composition. He has also written sonatas for clarinet and for bassoon.

Lockrem JOHNSON (b. 1924) diversifies his neo-classical style by percussive effects and colouristic devices that occasionally lend a touch of impressionism to his writing. His 'Sonata Breve' (1948) and 'Sonata Rinverdita' (1950) for violin and piano exemplify his style.

The chamber music of Douglas TOWNSEND (b. 1921) deserves mention. He transplants the eighteenth-century idiom into the modern world with slight atonal deviations and occasional metric alterations. The most interesting of his works in this modern *style galant* is the 'Ballet Suite' for three clarinets (1955).

Ben WEBER (b. 1916) began as an experimenter, then compromised by adopting classical form, with moderately dissonant counterpoint and atonal melodic lines. His 'Sonata da Camera' for violin and piano (1954) is a characteristic work.

A *rara avis* among American composers is Alan HOVHANESS (b. 1911). Of Armenian and Scotch descent, he has in his music re-created oriental cantillation, making effective use of melodic iteration, often confining his melodies to a few notes. Colouristic and impressionistic writing is out of fashion among American composers, but Hovhaness ignores this state of public opinion, and blithely goes on writing such cerulean-tinted pieces as *Upon Enchanted Ground*, for flute, 'cello, giant tamtam, and harp, and *October Mountain*, for marimba, glockenspiel, kettledrums, drums, and tamtam. He is very skilful in using exotic devices, and in his less flamboyant compositions, such as his *Shatakh*, for violin and piano (1953), he achieves considerable evocative power. It should be noted that after a period of almost hopeless non-recognition he became one of the most successful American composers of 'mood music'.

In a class by himself is Leonard BERNSTEIN (b. 1918), highly celebrated as symphonic conductor and composer; in addition, he is the author of several spectacularly successful musical comedies. In the field of chamber music, his Sonata for clarinet and piano (1941–2) demonstrates his versatility in handling the neo-classical idiom, with just enough spice to produce a stimulating effect.

Three American composers, George Rochberg, Leon Kirchner, and Gunther Schuller, have contributed, each in his own manner, some interesting chamber music. George ROCHBERG (b. 1918) has written music in a neo-classical vein, and later in a quasi-impressionist manner, eventually tending towards very effective colouristic twelve-note genre. His String Quartet (1952) is an excellent example of such enlightened dodecaphony. The first movement, 'Molto adagio', establishes an impressionistic mood by means of adroit application of the twelve-note technique; the rhythms oscillate between groups of three and four. The next section, 'Vivace', is a scherzo, imaginatively and airily conceived; here, too, the dodecaphonic technique is applied with great effectiveness. There follows

'Molto tranquillo', a movement of considerable subtlety; the asymmetric metres, such as 11/16, do not seem whimsical, as in so many modern works, but somehow correspond to the inner plan of the music. The 'Allegro energico' constitutes the finale. It is significant that every movement in Rochberg's String Quartet ends on a dissonant chord composed of notes of thematic importance in the dodecaphonic series.

Leon KIRCHNER (b. 1919) is one of the strongest talents among American composers of chamber music. He adopts the external characteristics of the evolutionary *style moderne*—a quasi-atonal melody, dissonant harmony mitigated by strong ground notes, percussive asymmetric rhythm, a sophisticated employment of classical forms. The resulting product is uncompromisingly intellectual, and yet curiously romantic in its projection of emotion.

Kirchner's String Quartet No. 1 (1949) is one of his best works. The first movement, 'Allegro ma non troppo', opens with a vigorous and assertive repetition of a dissonant chord (see Ex. 186). Then a melodious tune is sounded by

Ex. 186

(*Reprinted by permission of Associated Music Publishers, Inc., New York*)

the first violin, soon giving way to an asymmetric dance-like motion. The rhythmic pattern grows in complexity, and is reflected externally in a progression of changing metres, 7/16, 9/16, and 10/16. The tension subsides almost instantly with the introduction of simple rhythmic figures. There is a fading-off of general sonority, and a pause leads to an 'Andante'. Here we enter a free fantasy, with fiorituras and glissandos conjuring up a decidedly romantic mood. There are reminiscences of the opening, marked by a return of the original dissonant chord, until a recapitulation, adumbrated rather than explicitly outlined, is finally reached.

The second movement of Kirchner's quartet, 'Adagio', is a free recitative; colouristic effects, such as ponticello and glissando, are used. The employment of unusual metres (11/16, 13/16, 7/16, 5/16) seems germinal to the plan rather than a sophisticated whimsicality.

The third movement, Divertimento, is a classical dance, beginning as a waltz and ending as a gigue. The formal structure is emphasized by the use of time-honoured conventions, such as the insertion of a trio and the indicated repeat da capo.

The fourth and last movement, 'Adagio', is a summary of the previous movements. There are the asymmetrical metres (15/16, 9/16, 7/16, &c.), rhythmic ground notes, cadenza-like episodes, and quasi-atonal melodic figures, as well as repeated notes and chords. After reaching fortissimo, the solo violin brings it down to triple piano.

In his String Quartet No. 2 (1958), Kirchner adopts a style of unusual liberality in the selection and treatment of his materials. It is in three movements, which are separated by curiously evanescent cadences. The fabric remains dissonant, but these dissonances are academically arrived at, through completely unmysterious and often frankly chromatic progressions of the component voices, a procedure rather frowned upon in the inner ring of the American musical élite. The time-signatures in prime numbers in the numerator, characteristic of Kirchner's sense of asymmetrical periodicity, are very much in evidence. The formal orientation is cyclic, so that thematic materials are recurrent upon occasion.

Among Kirchner's other chamber works to be mentioned are Sonata Concertante for violin and piano (1955) and Trio for violin, 'cello, and piano (1957).

Gunther SCHULLER (b. 1925) is an experimenter by nature; he explores new possibilities through sheer curiosity, achieving signal results while adopting established modern techniques. He has written music for unusual ensembles: Fantasia Concertante for three oboes and piano (1946), Fantasia Concertante for three trombones and piano (1947), Quartet for four double basses (1947), *Perpetuum Mobile* for four muted horns and bassoon (1948), Duo Sonata for clarinet and bass clarinet (1949), and Five Pieces for five horns (1952). But perhaps his most striking work is his String Quartet No. 1 (1957), dodecaphonic in its materials. In the last movement Schuller makes an excursion into free improvisation on thematic notes selected from a prescribed twelve-note series. The first movement, 'Lento', is an essay in dissonant counterpoint marked by extreme rhythmic diversity and wide dynamic range. The twelve-note series underlying this movement is curious in that it follows the order of the chromatic scale, which is masked by scattering among successive instrumental entries. Chromatic clusters in minor seconds are in evidence in the ending of this movement. The second movement, 'Allegro', is also dodecaphonic, the elements of the basic series being composed of four mutually exclusive augmented triads. The third movement, 'Adagio', again exploits consecutive chromatic notes in the guise of a dodecaphoniç series. Before the conclusion of the movement, at a place where a classical cadenza might occur, there is a lengthy section of dodecaphonic improvisation (see Ex. 187). The quartet ends on a chromatic cluster; the final notes form a minor second, which may be regarded as thematic of the whole work.

Although Lukas FOSS (b. 1922) is not a native American composer (he was born in Berlin: his real name is Fuchs), he arrived in the United States as a boy, and has identified himself completely with the cause of American music. His gift is strong and original; his technique of composition is masterly. In his chosen idiom he has never wavered in accepting tonality as the fundamental principle

Ex. 187

of music. Stylistically, Foss is both a romanticist and a pragmatist; he writes his music for practical performance, and expresses in it his emotional attitude towards art and life. His String Quartet in G (1947) is a fairly characteristic, if early, example of his style. An introductory 'Andante' leads to the main portion of the first movement, 'Allegro', marked by a brisk rhythm; slow episodes are inserted, and the movement itself ends in an 'Andante'. The second movement is a theme with variations (see Ex. 188), in a continuous set without separations, leading to a lively finale, in fortissimo.

Ex. 188

(*Copyright 1949 by Carl Fischer, Inc., New York. International copyright secured.*)

In his Capriccio for 'cello and piano (1946) Foss appears a classicist with a vengeance; there are whole sections with figures of broken major triads; the melodic lines in this work are built by gradual and discreet movement away from the central notes. And the ending is a clear C major chord.

One of the most significant composers of modern chamber music in America is Elliott CARTER (b. 1908). His writing is terse, economical, percussively rhythmic, enormously complex without being opaque. Twelve-note configurations are in evidence, but the dodecaphonic series is not a generating factor. In the larger sense of thematic writing, virtually all of his works are based on the principle of variation. The basic idea may be a single dominating interval, for instance the minor second in the 'Eight Etudes and a Fantasy' for woodwind quartet (1950). The material of his String Quartet No. 1 (1951) is evolved from a formative four-note chord (E, F, A flat, B flat), which comprises all the intervals from a minor second to a diminished fifth, and these intervals are used thematically in contrapuntal and harmonic groups. This is essentially a serial procedure.

In quest of metric and rhythmic precision, Carter resorts to unusual time signatures, such as 21/32 in his 'Cello Sonata (1948), or 8/16 in his String Quartet No. 1. In the quartet he also applies an interesting concept of metric modulation, produced by the melodic superposition of two rhythmic groups having no common denominator. Thus a progression of four even notes against five even notes to a beat in two contiguous instrumental parts creates a combinational melody of eight uneven notes (the first notes of each group being played together), and Carter inserts an extra part spelling out the combinational melorhythm for the benefit of the players (see Ex. 189).

Ex. 189

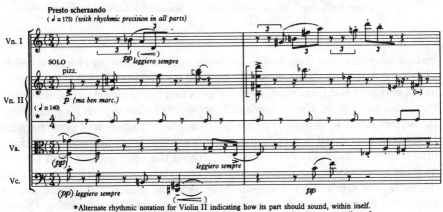

*Alternate rhythmic notation for Violin II indicating how its part should sound, within itself. This alternate notation also indicates the correct length of resonance of each note, regardless of the note-values which appear in the actual part.

Carter's String Quartet No. 2 (1959) made history, for it was awarded the Pulitzer Prize in 1960, the New York Music Critics Circle award in 1961, and was voted the best work of the 1960–1 musical season by the International Rostrum of Composers in Paris, sponsored by UNESCO. These honours are all the more extraordinary since the work is abstruse in its conception, enormously difficult to perform or to perceive intelligently by the naked ear. It is in five connected movements: 'Introduction', 'Allegro fantastico', 'Presto scherzando', 'Andante espressivo', and 'Allegro'. There are accompanied cadenzas for viola and 'cello, and an unaccompanied one for the first violin.

On general lines, Carter's String Quartet No. 2 consists of successive intensifications and rarefactions of musical materials. The climax comes in 'Tempo giusto', in which the four instruments combine in a dissonant polyrhythmic stretto. There are superpositions of rhythmic groups of seven, four, three, and five notes to a beat; on the extra stave Carter indicates the resultant intervals in the approximate vertical lines. (Example 190). Each instrument specializes in

Ex. 190

certain intervals: the first violin in thirds and its multiples (fifths, sevenths, ninths), the second violin in minor seconds and major sevenths, the viola in minor sevenths and tritones, and the 'cello in fourths in minor sixths. Because of this individualization, Carter specifically enjoins the players to sit far apart during the performance, so as to separate the instruments in space as well as in character. Every technical detail is specified in the score; various applications of pizzicato, produced with the fleshy part of the fingertip of the right hand, picked with the fingernail, or snapped against the fingerboard; slurs, accents, exact positions of the wedges of crescendo marks—all these technical indications assume importance. The errata appended to the miniature score of Carter's String Quartet No. 2 reminds one of the table of corrections in Joyce's *Finnegans Wake*—of indisputable importance to the author and the analyst, but bewildering to the uninitiated. Happily, a corrected score was issued in 1962.

In the light of such developments of melodic and rhythmic specialization, the music of Ruth CRAWFORD (1901–53) acquires, posthumously, a new significance; for she explored serial techniques long before these problems became a matter of universal concern to modern-minded composers. Her String Quartet (1931) seems to anticipate certain procedures that came into vogue, under various polysyllabic names, many years later. The first movement, 'Rubato assai', illustrates the concept of intervallic thematism, namely the prevalence of the major seventh. The second movement, 'Leggiero', is a study in contrapuntal cohesion with a predominant rhythmic theme. The third movement, 'Andante', is an essay in slow dynamic pulsations, ascending gradually to a fortissimo chord of four chromatic notes, and then descending very slowly to the lowest register, reaching quadruple pianissimo. The last movement, 'Allegro possibile', is a toccata for strings with an independent rhythmic melody in the first violin.

An interesting variant of the serial technique is employed by Henry Leland CLARKE (b. 1907) in his duet for violin and viola entitled *A Game That Two Can Play* (1959). The two instruments use two mutually exclusive groups of six notes and two mutually exclusive groups of note values, so that each instrument operates, without encroachment, in its own melodic and rhythmic domain. A type of technique that may be described as lipophonic (by analogy with lipo-grammatical verse, omitting certain letters) is applied by Clarke in his String Quartet No. 3 (1958), in which semitones are excluded from both horizontal (melodic) and vertical (harmonic) lines. His other chamber works include String Quartet No. 1 (1928), *Dialogue* for clarinet and piano (1948), String Quartet No. 2 (1953), Nocturne for viola and piano (1955), and *Saraband for the Golden Goose*, for French horn and woodwind quartet (1957).

Among native American followers of Schoenberg, Adolph WEISS (b. 1891) combines a faithful adherence to the basic tenets of dodecaphony with a genuine feeling for American folk rhythms. A professional bassoon player, he has composed much music for wind instruments; his Concerto for bassoon and string quartet (1949) is notable. In 1959 he wrote an interesting suite entitled *Vade Mecum*, consisting of 30 pieces for various combinations of five wind instruments (flute, oboe, clarinet, bassoon, and French horn), and comprising ten duos, nine trios, five quartets, and six quintets. Other chamber-music works include three String Quartets (1925, 1926, 1932), 'Sonata da Camera' for flute and viola (1929), Trio for clarinet, viola, and 'cello (1948), and Rhapsody for four French horns (1957).

Paradoxically, the trend towards total integral serial organization has generated on the outer fringe of American music its dialectical opposite, a total indeterminacy. A new term, 'Aleatory music', made its appearance in New York about 1950, to describe this indeterminate type of composition, in which notes, durations, rests, intervals, etc., are selected at random, following some numerical system, such as the calculus of probabilities. The chief prophet of aleatory music in America is John CAGE (b. 1912), who obtains basic data for his compositions by tossing coins according to the rules expounded in an ancient Chinese book of oracles. Cage's music is difficult to classify according to categories, but most of his works are for small groups, usually including a 'prepared piano', which is his own invention. The 'preparation' consists in placing miscellaneous small objects such as coins, nails, clips, etc., on the piano strings, in order to alter the timbre of each individual note. Cage's *Water Music*, scored for two prepared pianos, a radio receiver, and a container filled with water, is in a sense a quartet, or a trio with splashing water obbligato. Since the sounds emitted by the radio are unpredictable, no two performances of this work can be identical.

John Cage has already acquired a number of disciples, some of whom in turn have formed their own systems of composition. Thus Morton FELDMAN (b. 1926)

III   N

tempers aleatory indeterminacy with indications of approximate pitch (high, middle, or low) and of the total number of notes in a given fragment, leaving the realization of these partial instructions to the performer. Earle BROWN (b. 1926) experiments with recorded sounds. His 'Octet for Magnetic Tape' is the product of eight different tape recordings combined according to a numerical series. Christian WOLFF (b. 1934) extends the serial principle to embrace the eighty-eight keys of the piano, leaving the order of the note series to chance.

The ultimate aim of American composers of aleatory music is to relegate the entire process of composition to the impersonal realm of chance. It is logical therefore that attempts should be made to compose music, and specifically chamber music, with the aid of electronic computers. The first such composition was the *Illiac Suite* for string quartet, produced in 1957 by Leonard M. Isaacson and Lejaren A. Hiller, Jr., the 'Illiac' of the title being the digital computer of the University of Illinois. The so-called Monte Carlo method of multiple probabilities controls the selection of notes, rests, durations, and dynamic intensities. Since dissonances have greater frequency of incidence in random combinations, computer music, when not tampered with by the programmer, usually turns out to be modernistic-sounding.

In the wave of emigration from Europe to the United States between the two wars, several acknowledged European masters of modern music made their homes in America. The earliest settler was Ernest BLOCH (C, d. 1959). His reputation was established in Switzerland and France long before he came to New York in 1917. His style did not undergo radical changes during his American period; the haunting rhapsodic expression, the harmonious bitonality of two major keys at the distance of a tritone, the persuasive rhythmic drive, and the orientalistic melodic turn of the phrase, all these characteristics are present in Bloch's music throughout his creative career. But in the works of his later period he introduced something new—thematic dodecaphony; apparently he could not remain insensible to the tremendous influence of twelve-note composition all over the world. There are explicit twelve-note themes in his second, third, and fourth string quartets, but they are not dodecaphonic in the Schoenbergian sense; their melodic contents remain typically Blochian; Bloch's favourite interval, the tritone, is the cornerstone of most of his twelve-note themes, as it is in his bitonal harmonies. Bloch does not use the classic transformations of the basic twelve-note series, and does not introduce serial elements into the contrapuntal and harmonic fabric. In other words, he accepts the method of composition with twelve notes only in the guise of a motto, nothing more.

Bloch's *Poème mystique* for violin and piano (1925) reflects his early poetic style, with deep organ points, open fifths in parallel progressions, and quasi-ecclesiastical melodies. Toward the end of the piece the violin intones a 'Credo', and the Latin words are written out in the score (Ex. 191). There are several instances of bitonal writing, but the combination of tonalities is invariably euphonious.

Bloch's String Quartet No. 1 was written in 1916; No. 2 did not come until

1946. It is cast in four contrasting movements (Moderato, Presto, Andante, and Allegro molto). The work opens with a broad melody in the part of the first violin, suggesting a Hebraic chant. One by one the other instruments enter;

Ex. 191

oriental modes prevail; various melodic phrases combine in free counterpoint; there is an intensification of rhythmic pulse and dynamic drive; then the pace slackens gradually, and the movement ends with the same phrase with which it began. The second movement, 'Presto', is an essay in rhythmic motion, with songful episodes. The initial theme is highly syncopated; its component notes are later treated in a straightforward energetic 'allegro molto'. The next section, 'meno mosso', is an interesting example of an inverted canon, with Bloch's favourite interval, the tritone, serving as the thematic motto. The theme is actually nothing more than a sequence of tritones, comprising all twelve notes of the chromatic scale (see Ex. 192). As such it is technically dodecaphonic, in the

Ex. 192

same sense as the theme of four consecutive augmented triads, linearly spread out in the opening bars of Liszt's *Faust Symphony*. The third movement, 'Andante', is a gentle nocturne in which the original phrase from the first movement recurs as a reminiscence. The last movement, 'Allegro molto', leads to a passacaglia, the subject of which is derived from the initial notes of the first theme of the second movement; there is a canon on the dodecaphonic motto of the second movement; and finally a grand fugue, again derived from the initial notes of the first theme of the second movement. There are other intervallic references to materials previously used, so that the last movement becomes a summary of the whole work. The rhythmic energy is very high, and the climaxes powerful. The movement concludes on an Epilogue, with flowing arpeggios in the 'cello part; the thematic material is always relevant; there seems to be no fortuitous padding. The final phrase is the augmentation of the opening motto of the work.

In his String Quartet No. 3 (1951–2) Bloch is still his old self, equally capable of producing fast movements charged with motoric energy and pensive inter-ludes of poetic nostalgia. The ever-present interval of the tritone is symbolic of inner tension, and the pseudo-dodecaphonic themes serve as excellently chosen groupings of different notes lending themselves to rhythmic development with-out in the least affecting the contrapuntal and harmonic scheme. The first move-ment is an 'Allegro deciso', full of vitality and suggesting the form of a classical overture. The following 'Adagio non troppo' is a poetic air, with a simple melody projected upon a wavy line of rhythmic figuration. The third movement, 'Allegro molto', is a scherzo, with a clearly defined middle section, and an explicit recapitulation. The fourth movement, 'Allegro', is based on a twelve-note theme, which is stated at the outset in full (Ex. 193), and is then fragmented, restated

Ex. 193

in transposition, and then in a fresh rhythmic arrangement, in augmentation, and finally in inversion. There is a stretto, and after considerable agitation the twelve-note motto is presented as a fugue subject. Still, the utilization of the theme is entirely free of dodecaphonic restraints.

In 1953 Bloch wrote his String Quartet No. 4. The music presents no revela-tion; it has a familiar look and a familiar ring; yet it is no facile capitalizing on previously accumulated knowledge, imagination, and technique. The melodic writing is more angular; the harmonies more astringent. But there is no loss in the rhythmic momentum, no diminution of lyricism, no abandonment of colour-istic effects. There are twelve-note motives, utilized for thematic convenience rather than as material for dodecaphonic manipulation. The first movement, 'Tranquillo', forms a web of dissonant harmonies, with tiny motives developing slowly in a languorous introduction. Then, with complete suddenness, an 'Allegro energico' sets the mood of spirited motion; there is a brief return to initial tranquillity, whereupon the 'allegro' resumes its dash with an even greater energy. The movement ends quietly in a berceuse-like rhythm.

The second movement, 'Andante', has a folk-song quality in its simple melody (see Ex. 194). There is no immediate attempt at complication, but when the melody returns it is contorted into an atonal image. Then follows a dark agitated episode in asymmetrical rhythms; the principal theme appears in various guises, until the ending in pianissimo. The third movement, 'Presto', is melodically based

Ex. 194

on alternating tritone progressions, and the tritone also forms the foundation of bitonal harmonies in this movement. There is a middle section with a dance-like quasi-chromatic tune. The fourth and last movement opens with a meditative introduction, 'Calmo', soon leading to an 'Allegro deciso', which, after much adumbration, presents the principal dodecaphonic theme (see Ex. 195), which

Ex. 195

may be analysed as consisting of two mutually exclusive whole-tone scales (with the first and last note switching their places). The tritone is again brought to the fore; there is a lively contrapuntal accompaniment to the twelve-note theme, which appears also in canonic imitation. Finally, it is presented in slow tempo, harmonized with a descending chromatic figure in the bass. The ending is on a chord of G major in pianissimo.

Continuing to compose vigorously, Ernest Bloch completed his String Quartet No. 5 in 1956. The music of this work represents a return to the 'basic' Bloch: there is the familiar rhapsodic, emotional lyricism, and the impulsive motoric rhythm. The harmony tends toward a bitonality of two major keys at the tritone root relationship. The scale of alternating whole tones and semitones serves as the melodic foundation in some instances.

The String Quartet No. 5 opens with a long introduction, 'Grave' (Ex. 196); this

Ex. 196

leads to the main section, 'Allegro', marked by a strong rhythmic pulse (Ex. 197). After an interlude, 'più calmo', the 'Allegro' returns; there is a fugato, and a stretto in inverted imitation. The initial subject of 'Grave' reappears in a rhythmic variant, in which the thematic notes are the same, but their function is altered

Ex. 197

through changes in note values. This device of rhythmic variation appears frequently in Bloch's works of his last period. The first movement ends calmly, on a bitonal chord.

The second movement, 'Calmo', is a study in cyclic construction, not only in thematic consistency (the initial theme, quoted in Ex. 198, is obviously related to Ex. 196 from the first movement) but also in rhythm and dynamics, so that the musical architecture here appears as a sphere. The soaring melody establishes the direction at once; after an intensification of rhythm and dynamics, the music returns to its calm mood, concluding on a pure major triad.

Ex. 198

The third movement is a 'Presto'. After some preliminary passages in translucent open fifths there is a melodic episode, antiphonally distributed among the instruments. The musical motion now assumes the character of a dance, in rondo form, with duple and triple meters in alternation. A dissonant chord at the end of the movement leads to a festive finale, 'Allegro deciso'. After a solemn chordal exordium, almost rhetorical in presentation, and a pause, the 'allegro' proper begins. The rhythm is varied, composed of units of two, three, and four notes. The principal theme consists of twelve different notes (see Ex. 199), and

Ex. 199

it appears later in the form of a rhythmic variant, with the order of the twelve-note series disrupted only by the displacement of one note. Further melodic material is explicitly tonal; the rhythmic exhilaration is maintained until the coda, 'Calmo', which recapitulates the twelve-note motto. The movement concludes on the chord of C major, in widely open harmony. The tonality of

C major, which remains basic throughout the entire work, is further strengthened by the frequent use of the lowest note of the 'cello.

In 1957 Bloch composed a Piano Quintet in three movements, his second (the first, with the application of quarter-tones, was written in 1921–3). The work represents Bloch's last period, with his emotional power regulated by strong constructive thematic ideas. The leaping principal melody of the first movement, Animato, is composed of two twelve-note sections, the second of which is an exact transposition of the first, with some changes in octave position (Ex. 200). To both sections are appended two supernumerary notes, in a falling fifth, thus establishing a dominant-tonic pattern in clear tonality. The interval of the tritone is conspicuous here. By contrast, another twelve-note motive used in the first movement is built on narrow intervals (Ex. 201). It should be emphasized that Bloch uses such twelve-note themes for purely melodic purposes, without adhering to any dodecaphonic conventions.

Ex. 200

Ex. 301

The second movement, 'Andante', is in the form of an air and variations. The initial melody dominates the development, and at the climactic point is enriched by sonorous harmonies.

The third and last movement, 'Allegro', is a rollicking dance, essentially a rondo, with lyric interludes. The music is characteristically Blochian, with strongly suggested bitonal harmonies.

In the last years of his life Bloch composed a *Proclamation* for trumpet and piano (1955; also with orchestra); a 'Suite Modale' in four movements for flute and piano (1956), the essence of which is indicated by the title itself; three suites for 'cello solo (1956–7); and two suites for violin solo (1958).

Besides the major international figures, numerous other distinguished musicians have sought refuge in the United States, and have become firmly established on the American scene. Among these is Ernst TOCH (C), whose most important works of his American period include a String Trio, op. 63, Piano Quintet, op. 64, and String Quartet, op. 70. The Piano Quintet is particularly interesting because Toch gives outspoken programmatic titles to its four movements: 'The Lyrical Part', 'The Whimsical Part', 'The Contemplative Part', 'The Dramatic Part'. This shows, of course, that Toch is not afraid to admit his romantic leanings, even in this age of neo-classicism and constructivism. Toch's String Quartet, op. 70, presents a study in contrasts. The first movement is based on an involuted chromatic figure (Ex. 202), with melodic fragments pro-

Ex. 202

jected upon it. The 'più mosso' that follows is vigorous and harmonically rich. The second movement, 'Adagio', is nostalgic in its inspiration, with syncopating rhythms creating a sense of dramatic tension. The third movement bears the title 'Pensive Serenade'; the metrical and rhythmic changes are frequent, despite the professed contemplative mood. The fourth movement is extremely strong in its rhythmic and contrapuntal texture; there are some interesting technical devices in arpeggio passages (see Ex. 203). The sense of a central tonality is

Ex. 203

★ pizz. over the four strings with one finger

invariably preserved. The work ends in C major with a G flat major chord opposing it, then yielding the way. An enlightened and progressive musician, Toch does not exclude any workable technical procedure from his vocabulary. In a later String Quartet, op. 74 (1957), he applied for the first time the serial method of twelve-note composition, in a free style.

Ernst KRENEK (C) went to the U.S. in 1937 and became an American citizen. After World War II he spent much of his time in Europe. In the U.S. he composed productively, mostly in the dodecaphonic idiom; he also made use of the resources of electronic music.

Bohuslav MARTINU (C) spent the war years in America, and was active as composer of music in all genres, continuing along the stylistic lines of his works of the European period. He eventually returned to Europe and remained there until his death in 1959.

The Austrian composer Paul Amadeus PISK (C), who studied with Schoenberg but never accepted the twelve-note technique, emigrated to America in 1936, and has continued to compose prolifically without much change in his original musical style—rhythmic, strongly contrapuntal, at times atonal. His chamber music written in America includes a Suite for four clarinets (1940), Sonata for clarinet and piano (1947), a Quartet for two trumpets, horn, and trombone (1951), Sonata for horn and piano (1953), Sonata for flute and piano (1954), Suite for oboe, clarinet, and piano (1955), String Trio (1958), Woodwind Quintet (1958), and a Trio for oboe, clarinet, and bassoon (1960).

Mario CASTELNUOVO-TEDESCO (b. 1895) left Italy in 1939 and came to the United States, settling in California. His chamber-music works written in America comprise the Ballade for violin and piano (1940), Divertimento for two flutes (1943), Sonata for violin and viola (1945), Clarinet Sonata (1945), Sonata for viola and 'cello (1950), Second Piano Quintet (1951), and an interesting Quintet for guitar and strings (1950). In all these works he maintains the songful melodic line and the rich harmony characteristic of his productions during his formative years and early maturity in Italy. His mastery of instrumental writing is indisputable.

An earlier settler in America was Bernard WAGENAAR (C), who emgrated to the United States from Holland in 1920. Among his many compositions, the String Quartet No. 3 (1940) is of interest. Here he exhibits his penchant for finely woven counterpoint and opulent harmonies rooted in the ground of strong tonality. He has an aptitude for writing in an austere hymn-like style, but he is also successful in playful 'scherzando' movements. He may be generally described as a neo-romanticist.

Among Russian composers who became naturalized in America, Nicolai Berezowsky and Nikolai Lopatnikoff contributed important pieces of chamber music. BEREZOWSKY (1900–53) was active as violinist and composer in New York, where he lived from 1922 until his death. His chamber music has elements of Russian folk-song style; in several of his chamber works Berezowsky adopts impressionist devices; his two quintets for woodwind instruments (1928 and 1937) are typical of this uixed Russian-French style. He further wrote two string sextets, two string quartets, and an interesting Duo for viola and clarinet.

Nikolai LOPATNIKOFF (b. 1903), of Russian origin, acquired his early reputation in Germany. He settled in America in 1939. Of his works after that date, the Violin Sonata No. 2 is perhaps the most effective and the most characteristic of his style, neo-classical with a considerable admixture of dissonance, but firmly anchored in tonality.

Vladimir DUKELSKY (b. 1903) left Russia as a very young man, and first attracted the attention of the musical world as a ballet composer for Diaghilev in Paris. He settled in America as a writer of lucrative musical comedies, and changed his name to Vernon Duke. His most important chamber-music work is a String Quartet in three movements (1956), emphatically designated as being in the key of C. It possesses a certain ingratiatingly modernistic *élan vital*.

Nicolas NABOKOV (b. 1903) also started his career as a ballet composer for Diaghilev. From Russia, via Paris, he arrived in America in 1933. Among his works for small instrumental groups are a String Quartet (1937) and a Sonata for bassoon and piano (1941).

Alexei HAIEFF (b. 1914), a native of Siberia, received his musical education in the U.S.A. He followed the neo-classical models of Stravinsky, and from his American environment picked up elements of jazz rhythms. His Three Bagatelles for oboe and bassoon (1955) are a typical example of entertainment music, adroitly written in a sophisticated utilitarian manner.

Stefan WOLPE (b. 1902) lived in Germany and in Palestine before going to America in 1938. His music shows an extreme variety of styles, influences, and techniques; there are elements of folk-music, oriental chants, and even jazz. His melodic writing is decisively atonal, leaning towards the integral twelve-note technique. The harmonic and contrapuntal constructions are extremely discordant, and the rhythmic complications are many. His Violin Sonata (1949) is a fair example of his style. He provides special signs to indicate phrase units and focal points; the bar lines in the violin part are often non-coincident with those of the piano part.

Ingolf DAHL (b. 1912), of Swedish ancestry, was educated in Germany and arrived in the United States in 1935. His chamber music is close in style to Stravinsky's neo-classical period. The 'Concerto a tre' for clarinet, violin, and 'cello (1946) is one of his most interesting works. The impression of fine stylization persists throughout, but Dahl manages to convey a sense of persuasive power despite the artificiality of this synthetic idiom. There is some ingratiating cantilena in songful episodes, and effective rhythmic co-ordination. His 'Andante and Arioso' for flute, oboe, clarinet, bassoon, and horn (1942) also merits mention.

Carlos SURINACH (b. 1915) is a native of Barcelona, Spain. He settled in New York in 1950 and became an American citizen in 1959. His compositions written in America retain the Spanish flavour, particularly the rhythms of Flamenco dances. Among his pieces written for small instrumental ensembles are *Tres Cantos Berberes* for flute, oboe, clarinet, viola, 'cello, and harp (1952), *Ritmo Jondo* for clarinet, trumpet, xylophone, and percussion (1952), and *Tientos* for English horn, harpsichord, and timpani (1953).

A summary of the American chamber-music style may now be offered. The following qualities are characteristic of the prevalent trends:

1. Neo-classicism in the broadest sense of the term, implying strong formal structure and clear separation of consecutive movements, or parts within a movement.

2. A freely modulating or an outright atonal melody, tangential to the implied tonal centres.

3. A firm tonal substance, emphasized at times by nothing more than a focal point in the bass. In general, explicit tonal figurations are avoided, particularly arpeggios; equally avoided are sequences.

4. Economic and sometimes austere harmonies, either tonal, pandiatonic, or polytonal. Certain chords, particularly the dominant-seventh chord, the diminished-seventh chord, and the augmented triad, are shunned with remarkable unanimity. This inhibition is indicative of the reaction against the romantic type of music prevalent in the nineteenth century, but it also prevents the integration of eighteenth-century classicism, cherished by most modern American composers, with the new classicism of the twentieth century. The tonic chords in the final cadences are usually approached through secondary-seventh chords or related triadic chords.

5. Strong asymmetrical rhythms, often implied in changing metres, but the tendency is towards a reversion to non-compound metres, while producing rhythmic variety within the bar itself regardless of the time signature.

6. Free dodecaphony. Virtually every American composer of chamber music after 1940 has experimented with some type of twelve-note writing, and Stravinsky's espousal of the serial method in his late works has given an additional stimulus to this technique; several composers, notably Ernest Bloch, have made use of themes comprising twelve different notes, without further dodecaphonic transformations.

7. Practical instrumental writing, without ostentatious colouristic devices, and avoidance of impressionistic effects. Special technical devices are widely used, but they are applied for reasons of greater expressiveness, and not for the sake of colour alone.

8. Virtual abandonment of programmatic subtitles in chamber-music works, except with ironic implications, or in outspoken imitation of similar subtitles in Baroque music.

9. A recession from folk-music materials in chamber works, except for special purposes. However, jazz rhythms are adopted as logical extensions of syncopation. In such cases jazz is not regarded as folk-music, but only as a technique.

10. Time-honoured ensemble formations, such as string quartets, instrumental sonatas, piano trios, and small wind combinations, are favoured over unusual settings, but solo works for virtually every orchestral instrument with piano accompaniments are also produced, sometimes with a didactic purpose.

LATIN AMERICA

Composers of South America, Central America, and the West Indies cultivate vocal music by an innate gift and long tradition. The piano and the guitar are the preferred instruments for accompaniment and occasional solos. Chamber music occupies a very modest place in Latin America, but twentieth-century composers there are beginning to explore very seriously the potentialities of instrumental ensembles.

Whereas ostentatious Americanism is conspicuously absent from chamber music written in North America, the Latin American counterpart of the genre is full of echoes of the countryside. Latin American composers are free from compulsions and inhibitions that govern the development of modern music in the United States. The fear of being regarded as unsophisticated and old-fashioned does not haunt the creative musicians south of the border.

The most prolific, and in many ways the most remarkable, composer of South America was the Brazilian Heitor VILLA-LOBOS (C, d. 1959). In his music high sophistication, with a Parisian veneer, is combined with a most ingratiating spontaneity. His catalogue contains thousands upon thousands of works of every description. In the field of chamber music he composed fifteen string quartets, four violin sonatas, three piano trios, and numerous other works for various ensembles, of which the most striking are *Bachianas Brasileiras*. The name seeks to convey a mysterious affinity that exists, according to Villa-Lobos, between Brazilian folk-music and Bach's scientific counterpoint; even the coincidence of the initial letters is presumed to be significant. Villa-Lobos treats his Brazilian materials with Bach-like counterpoint, and the effect is impressive. The scoring of the *Bachianas Brasileiras* that fall into the category of chamber music is as follows: No. 1 (1932) for eight 'cellos, No. 2 (1933) for eight 'cellos and soprano, No. 5 (1937) also for eight 'cellos and soprano, No. 6 (1938) for flute and bassoon.

Folk-song elements in the music of Villa-Lobos are mostly re-created from the irreducible minimum of native melo-rhythms; it is but rarely that he quotes actual popular tunes. But he has said himself that he and folk-song are one. His tunes are tropically warm, and his rhythms throb with animal vitality. In consequence of the years he spent in Paris, he acquired the colouristic technique of impressionism. Bach, Brazil, and Paris all unite in his music with astonishing cohesiveness, and form a style that is both original and cosmopolitan.

Among chamber works by other Brazilian composers, 'Trio Brasileiro' by Oscar Lorenzo FERNANDEZ (1897–1948) should be mentioned. This is music charged with rhythmic verve and full of melodic invention in the native vein.

Camargo GUARNIERI (b. 1907) is a Brazilian neo-classicist, whose symphonic works are almost 'European' in their universality. In his chamber music two violin sonatas and a 'Cello Sonata are examples of a recession into a temperate zone of music.

In Argentina the strongest composer of chamber music is Alberto GINASTERA (b. 1916). His *Pampeana* for 'cello and piano (1950) conveys a distinct feeling of Argentinian folk-song, in passionate chants and whirling dance rhythms, and at the same time demonstrates an ability to handle these materials in a highly disciplined fashion, so that the music is compact and effective. Ginastera has also written a String Quartet and a Duo for flute and oboe.

Juan Carlos PAZ (b. 1897) is an Argentinian composer of the ultra-modern school. After experimenting in various styles he adopted the twelve-note technique and wrote several dodecaphonic compositions for various instruments with piano.

In Chile the most significant composer of chamber music is Domingo SANTA CRUZ (b. 1899). His '3 piezas' for violin and piano (1938) are severely contrapuntal and finely calculated; there is no denying, however, the inherent romantic quality of these pieces.

In Cuba chamber music is cultivated mainly by José ARDÉVOL (b. 1911), of Spanish birth. He settled in Havana in 1930, and developed fruitful activities as composer and conductor. A convinced neo-classicist, he writes instrumental music in which structure and texture, polyphony and variety, are paramount considerations. In his 'Música de Cámara' for six instruments (1936) he includes a movement entitled 'Quasi Habanera', but even this is not a concession to the spirit of folk-lore, but a mere substitution for a European dance form in a classical suite.

One of the most important composers of Latin America is Carlos CHÁVEZ of Mexico (C). During his travels in the United States and in Europe he came into contact with modernistic music, and his own works reflect the mechanistic and anti-romantic trends of the period. Typical of this is his *Energía* for nine instruments (1925), producing an almost brutalizing effect by the driving force of relentless rhythms and harsh sonorities. His Sonatina for violin and piano (1928) is similarly elemental in its primitivism and its absence of songfulness. His three string quartets are much more elastic in their melodic and rhythmic essence; the String Quartet No. 3 (1944) has a definite neo-classical quality, and is marked by a sense of euphony. Although Chávez never resorts to explicit quotations from Mexican songs, his music bears an unmistakable imprint of native origin; the percussive quality of his melo-rhythmic progressions definitely corresponds to popular Mexican modes.

A disciple of Chávez, Blas GALINDO (b. 1910) writes Mexican music of a neo-classical type, with strongly asymmetric rhythms. His Violin Sonata (1950) is a tour de force of diatonic (or rather pandiatonic) writing, as the score is almost totally devoid of accidentals.

Rodolfo HALFFTER (b. 1900), a Spanish composer who made his home in Mexico after the Spanish civil war, has written several pieces of chamber music of great distinction. He cultivates neo-classicism, but there is an admixture of Hispanic melodic inflexions and rhythms in his music. His Pastorale for violin and piano (1949) is a fine example of his style of composition.

As in the United States, chamber music was slow in developing in Latin America; for many decades instrumental ensembles were composed of random combinations of popular instruments. It was only in the second quarter of the twentieth century that Latin American composers began to write genuine chamber music, with a true contrapuntal and harmonic foundation, cast in a classical form. But folk-music continues to be the main source of inspiration. Latin American composers will not give up their love of colour for the sake of hemispherical respectability.

BIBLIOGRAPHY

Compiled by COLIN MASON

In preparing this selective bibliography I have, to keep it within practicable limits, confined myself, with few exceptions, to books and articles dealing exclusively with chamber music. All monographs and other similarly obvious sources of information have been excluded. Entries for which the bibliographical information is less detailed are those which I have been unable to consult, and have taken over from other bibliographies.

M. & L. = Music and Letters M.R. = Music Review
M.Q. = Musical Quarterly MbA = Musikblätter des Anbruch

BOOKS ON HISTORY AND REPERTORY

Altmann, W.	Kammermusik-Katalog, 6th edn.	Leipzig	1945
Cœuroy, A., and Rostand, C.	Les chefs-d'œuvre de la musique de chambre	Paris	1952
Heuss, A.	Kammermusikabende	Leipzig	1919
Kilburn, N.	Chamber Music and its Masters: revised edition by Gerald Abraham	London	1932
King, A. H.	Chamber Music ('World of Music' Series, No. 3)	London	1948
Lehmann, U.	Deutsches und italienisches Wesen in der Vorgeschichte des klassischen Streichquartetts	Würzburg	1939
Mersmann, H.	Die Kammermusik	Leipzig	1930
Meyer, E. H.	English Chamber Music	London	1951
Meyer, E. H.	Die mehrstimmige Spielmusik des 17. Jahrhunderts in Nord- und Mitteleuropa	Cassel	1934
Renner, H.	Reclams Kammermusikführer, 3rd edn.	Stuttgart	1959
Richter, J. F.	Kammermusik-Katalog. Verzeichnis der von 1944 bis 1958 veröffentlichten Werke für Kammermusik	Leipzig	1960
Robertson, A.	Chamber Music	London	1957
Rowen, R. H.	Early Chamber Music	New York	1949
Schumann, O.	Schumann's Kammermusikbuch	Wilhelmshaven	1951
Tovey, D. F.	Essays in Musical Analysis: Chamber Music	Oxford	1944
Ulrich, H.	Chamber Music: The Growth and Practice of an Intimate Art	New York	1948

PERFORMANCE

Aulich, B., and Heimeran, E.	The Well-tempered String Quartet (English by D. Millar Craig), 2nd edn.	London	1952
Foss, L.	A Beginning (contemporary improvised chamber music)	Juilliard Review	1958
Gertler, A.	Advice to Young Quartet Players	The Score, no. 5	Aug. 1951
Hughes, C.	Chamber Music in American Schools	New York	1933
Léner, J.	The Technique of String Quartet Playing	London	1935
Stratton, G., and Frank, A.	The Playing of Chamber Music, 2nd edn.	London	1952
Tertis, L.	The String Quartet	M. & L., vol. xxxi, no. 2	Apr. 1950

STRING QUARTET

Altmann, W.	Handbuch für Streichquartett-spieler, 4 vols.	Berlin	1928–31
Altmann, W.	Kleiner Führer durch die Streich-quartette für Haus und Schule	Berlin	1950
Aulich, B., and Hei-meran, E.	The Well-tempered String Quar-tet, 2nd edn.	London	1952
Gertler, A.	Advice to Young Quartet Players	*The Score*, no. 5	Aug. 1951
Lehmann, U.	Deutsches und italienisches Wesen in der Vorgeschichte des klas-sischen Streichquartetts	Würzburg	1939
Léner, J.	The Technique of String Quartet Playing	London	1935
Pincherle, M.	Les Instruments du Quatuor	Paris	1948
Pincherle, M.	On the Origins of the String Quartet	*M.Q.*, vol. xv, no. 1	Jan. 1929
Rothweiler, H.	Zur Entwicklung des Streich-quartetts im Rahmen der Kam-mermusik des 18. Jahrhunderts	Tübingen	1934
Tertis, L.	The String Quartet	*M. & L.*, vol. xxxi, no. 2	Apr. 1950

OTHER ENSEMBLES WITH STRINGS

Altmann, W.	Handbuch für Streichquartett-spieler, vols. iii and iv	Berlin	1928–31
Altmann, W.	Handbuch für Klavierquintett-spieler	Wolfenbüttel	1937
Altmann, W.	Handbuch für Klavierquartett-spieler	Wolfenbüttel	1937
Altmann, W.	Handbuch für Klaviertriospieler	Wolfenbüttel	1934
Altmann, W., and Borisovskij, W.	Literaturverzeichnis für Bratsche und Viola d'amore	Wolfenbüttel	1937
Planyavsky, A.	Der Kontrabass in der Kammer-musik	*Oesterreichische Musikzeitschrift*	Feb. 1958
Saam, J.	Zur Geschichte des Klavierquar-tetts bis in die Romantik	Munich	1933
Watson, J. A.	String Chamber Music	*M. & L.*, vol. x, no. 3	July 1929
Weigl, B.	Handbuch der Violoncello Litera-tur	Vienna	1929

WIND INSTRUMENTS

Altmann, W.	Handbuch für Streichquartett-spieler, vol. iv	Berlin	1928–31
Baron, S., and others	The Woodwind Quintet; a sym-posium	*Woodwind Maga-zine*	Mar.–Dec. 1954
Fitzgerald, B.	Chamber Music for Trumpet—with Strings or Woodwinds	*Instrumentalist*	Nov. 1950
Fleury, L.	Music for Two Flutes without Bass	*M. & L.*, vol. vi, no. 2	Apr. 1925
Gray, R.	The Trombone in Contemporary Chamber Music	*Brass Quarterly*, vol. i, no. 1	Sept. 1957
Helm, S. M.	Catalog of Chamber Music for Wind Instruments	Michigan	1952
Walker, B. H.	Trumpet Quartets	*The School Musi-cian*	Jan. 1950
A Bibliography of Chamber Music including parts for Horn		*Brass Quarterly*, vol. ii, no. 3 to vol. iv, no. 4	March 1959 to Summer 1961
A Bibliography of Chamber Music including parts for Trumpet or Cornetto		*Brass Quarterly*, vol. iii, no. 2	Winter 1959

| A Bibliography of Chamber Music including parts for Trombone | *Brass Quarterly*, vol. iii, no. 3 | Spring 1960 |
| A Bibliography of Chamber Music including parts for more than one different brass instrument | *Brass Quarterly*, vol. iii, no. 4 | Summer 1960 |

PIANO

Altmann, W.	Handbuch für Klavierquintett-spieler	Wolfenbüttel	1937
Altmann, W.	Handbuch für Klavierquartett-spieler	Wolfenbüttel	1937
Altmann, W.	Handbuch für Klaviertriospieler	Wolfenbüttel	1934
Holetschek, F.	Das Klavier in der klassischen Kammermusik	*Oesterreichische Musikzeitschrift*	Apr. 1958
Saam, J.	Zur Geschichte des Klavier-quartetts bis in die Romantik	Munich	1933

VOICE

| Greville, U. | The Voice in Chamber Music | *The Sackbut*, vol. vi, nos. 8 and 9 | Mar. and Apr. 1926 |

GENERAL ARTICLES

Altmann, W.	Zu unrecht vergessene Kammer-musikwerke	*Neue Musik Zeit-schrift*	1950
Antcliffe, H.	The Recent Rise of Chamber Music in England	*M.Q.*, vol. vi, no. 1	Jan. 1920
Boelza, I.	New Soviet Chamber Music	*Tempo*, no. 12	Sept. 1945
Bonavia, F.	For Lovers of Chamber Music	*M. & L.*, vol. xv, no. 2	Apr. 1934
Cadzow, D.	Contemporary American Chamber Music	*International Musician*	Apr. 1949
Donington, R.	The English Contribution to the Growth of Chamber Music	*Music Survey*, vol. iv, no. 1	Oct. 1951
Foss, L.	A Beginning (contemporary improvised chamber music)	*Juilliard Review*	1958
Genin, R.	Essai d'une définition de la musique de chambre	*Revue Musicale*, no. 232	1956
Phelps, R. P.	American Chamber Music before 1875	*Woodwind Maga-zine*	Nov. 1949
Pierce, E. H.	Certain Questionable Tendencies in Modern Chamber Music	*M.Q.*, vol. xi, no. 2	Apr. 1925
Standen, B.	Children and Chamber Music	*M. & L.*, vol. xiv, no. 1	Jan. 1933

BOOKS AND ARTICLES ON INDIVIDUAL COMPOSERS

Bartók

Abraham, G.	The Bartók of the Quartets	*M. & L.*, vol. xxvi, no. 4	Oct. 1945
Babbitt, M.	The String Quartets of Bartók	*M.Q.*, vol. xxxv, no. 3	July 1949
Chapman, R. E.	The Fifth Quartet of Béla Bartók	*M.R.*, vol. 12, no. 4	Nov. 1951
Demarquez, S.	Béla Bartók: Sonate pour deux pianos et percussion	*Art Musicale*	1939
Forte, A.	Bartók's 'Serial' Composition (refers to String Quartet No. 4)	*M.Q.*, vol. xlvi, no. 2	Apr. 1960
Gertler, A.	Souvenirs sur Béla Bartók (revised metronome markings in the String Quartet No. 2)	*Revue Musicale*, no. 224	1955
Haraszti, E.	La musique de chambre de Béla Bartók	*Revue Musicale*	1930
Jemnitz, A.	Béla Bartók: V. Streichquartett	*Musica Viva*	1936
Mason, C.	An Essay in Analysis (refers to String Quartet No. 4)	*M.R.*, vol. 18, no. 3	Aug. 1957

Perle, G.	Symmetrical Formations in the String Quartets of Béla Bartók	*M.R.*, vol. 16, no. 4	Nov. 1955
Rands, B.	The Use of Canon in Bartók's Quartets	*M.R.*, vol. 18, no. 3	Aug. 1957
Seiber, M.	Bartók's Chamber Music	*Tempo*, no. 13	Autumn 1949
Traimer, R.	Béla Bartók's Kompositionstechnik dargestellt an seinen sechs Streichquartetten	Regensburg	1956
Wellesz, E.	Die Streichquartette von Béla Bartók	*MbA*, vol. 3, no. 5	Mar. 1921
Wiesengrund-Adorno, T.	2. und 3. Streichquartette von Béla Bartók	*Auftakt*, vol. 11, no. 9/10	1931

Berg

Bouquet, Fritz	Alban Berg's Lyrische Suite	*Melos*, vol. 15, no. 8/9	Aug./Sept. 1948
Brindle, R. Smith	The Symbolism in Berg's Lyric Suite	*The Score*, no. 21	Oct. 1957
Deutsch, H.	Le Concerto de chambre d'Alban Berg	*Schweizerische Musikzeitung*	Sept. 1949

Bloch

| Chissell, J. | Style in Bloch's Chamber Music | *M. & L.*, vol. xxiv, no. 1 | Jan. 1943 |
| Rimmer, F. | Bloch's Second String Quartet | *Tempo*, no. 52 | Autumn 1959 |

Boulez

Boulez, P.	Wie arbeitet die Avantgarde? (refers to Improvisation No. 2)	*Melos*, vol. 28, no. 10	Oct. 1961
Craft, R.	Boulez and Stockhausen (refers to 'Le Marteau sans Maître')	*The Score*, no. 24	Nov. 1958
Maw, N.	Boulez and Tradition (refers to 'Le Marteau sans Maître')	*M.T.*, vol. 103, no. 1429	Mar. 1962
Saathen, F.	'Le Marteau sans Maître' von Pierre Boulez	*Schweizerische Musikzeitung*, vol. 97, no. 7/8	July 1957
Stockhausen, K.	Musik und Sprache (refers to 'Le Marteau sans Maître')	*Die Reihe*, no. 6	1960

Britten

Brown, D.	Britten's Three Canticles	*M.R.*, vol. 21, no. 1	Feb. 1960
Brown, D.	Stimulus and Form in Britten's Work (refers to String Quartet No. 2)	*M. & L.*, vol. xxxix, no. 3	July 1958
Evans, P.	Britten's Cello Sonata	*Tempo*, no. 58	Summer 1961
Keller, H.	Benjamin Britten's Second Quartet	*Tempo* (N.S.), no. 3	Mar. 1947
Mann, W. S.	Britten's 'Lachrymae'	*London Musical Events*, vol. 6, no. 12	Dec. 1951
Wood, H.	Britten's Latest Scores (refers to 'Cello Sonata)	*M.T.*, vol. 103, no. 1429	Mar. 1962

Carter

| Glock, W. | A Note on Elliott Carter (refers to 'Cello Sonata and String Quartet No. 1) | *The Score*, no. 12 | June 1955 |
| Steinberg, M. | Elliott Carter's Second String Quartet | *The Score*, no. 27 | July 1960 |

Dallapiccola

| | Facsimile, with annotations by the composer, of Improvisation (after Tartini)—later incorporated into Tartiniana Seconda | *The Score*, no. 15 | Mar. 1956 |
| Wildberger, J. | Dallapiccola's 'Cinque Canti' | *Melos*, vol. 26, no. 1 | Jan. 1959 |

Delius

| Foss, H. | The Instrumental Music of Frederick Delius | *Tempo*, no. 26 | Winter 1952–3 |

Henze

Henze, H. W.	Analysis of the subsidiary theme of the second movement of the String Quartet (1952). (Appendix to J. Rufer's 'Composition with Twelve Notes related only to one another')	London	1954
Nestler, G.	Das Bläserquintett von Hans Werner Henze	*Melos*, vol. 27, no. 5	May 1960
Stephan, R.	Hans Werner Henze (refers to String Quartet and Wind Quintet, among other works)	*Die Reihe*, no. 4	1958

Hindemith

Doflein, E.	Die sechs Streichquartette von Paul Hindemith	*Schweizerische Musikzeitung*, vol. 95, no. 11	Nov. 1955
Kehr, G.	Wir studieren eine Hindemith-Violinsonate	*Melos*, vol. 14, no. 4	Feb. 1947
Kolneder, W.	Hindemiths Streichquartett V. in Es	*Schweizerische Musikzeitung*, vol. 90, no. 3	Mar. 1950
Landau, V.	The Harmonic Theories of Paul Hindemith in relation to his Practice as a Composer of Chamber Music (Dissertation, New York University)	University Microfilms LC 58–664, Ann Arbor	1958
Pestalozza	Le Kammermusiken di Hindemith	*Rassegna Musicale*, vol. xxviii, no. 1	Mar. 1958
Strobel, H.	Neue Kammermusik von Hindemith	*Melos*, vol. 4, no. 11	July 1925
Wiesengrund-Adorno, T.	Kammermusik von Paul Hindemith	*Die Musik*, vol. xix, no. 1	Oct. 1926
Wörner, K.	Hindemiths neues Oktett	*Melos*, vol. 25, no. 11	Nov. 1958

Kodály

| Szabolcsi, B. | Die Instrumentalmusik Zoltán Kodálys | *MbA*, vol. iv, no. 17/18 | Nov. 1922 |

Koechlin

| Calvocoressi, M.-D. | Charles Koechlin's Instrumental Works | *M. & L.*, vol. v, no. 4 | Oct. 1924 |

Krenek

| Krenek, E. | Zu meinen Kammermusikwerken 1936–50 | *Schweizerische Musikzeitung*, vol. 93, no. 3 | Mar. 1953 |

Malipiero

| Alderighi, D. | La musica strumentale di Malipiero | *Rassegna Musicale*, vol. xv, no. 2 | Feb./Mar. 1942 |

Milhaud

| Helm, E. | Milhaud: XIV + XV = Oktett | *Melos*, vol. 22, no. 3 | Mar. 1955 |
| Poulenc, F. | Œuvres récentes de Darius Milhaud (refers to String Quartets Nos. 10, 11, and 12) | *Contrepoints*, no. 1 | Jan. 1946 |

Pfitzner

| Truscott, H. | The Importance of Hans Pfitzner: II. The Chamber Music | *Music Survey*, no. 2 | Winter 1948 |

Rawsthorne

Cooper, M.   Current Chronicle (refers to Clari-   *M.Q.*, vol. xxxv,   Apr. 1949
                       net Quartet and 'Cello Sonata)   no. 2

Roussel

Ferroud, P.-O.   La musique de chambre d'Albert   *Revue Musicale*   Apr. 1929
                       Roussel

Rubbra

Rubbra, E.   Edmund Rubbra's String Quartet   *M.R.*, vol. 14, no. 1   Feb. 1953
                       No. 2

Schoenberg

Boulez, P.   Trajectoires (refers to 'Pierrot   *Contrepoints*   1949
                       Lunaire')
Craft, R.   Programme notes for Schoenberg's   *Woodwind Maga-*   June 1952
                       Quintet   *zine*
Forte, A.   Contemporary Tone Structures   New York   1955
                       (refers to Fantasy, op. 47)
Godet, R.   Après une audition de 'Pierrot   *Revue Musicale*,   May 1923
                       Lunaire'   vol. 4, no. 7
Gradenwitz, P.   The Idiom and Development in   *M. & L.*, vol. xxvi,   July 1945
                       Schoenberg's Quartets   no. 3
Graf, M.   Der neueste Schoenberg (refers to   *MbA*, vol. 9, no. 10   Dec. 1927
                       String Quartet No. 3)
Greissle, F.   Die formalen Grundlagen des   *MbA*, vol. 7, no. 2   Feb. 1925
                       Bläserquintetts   von   Arnold
                       Schoenberg
Hill, R. S.   Arnold Schoenberg: Phantasy,   *Notes*, Second   Sept. 1952
                       op. 47   Series, vol. ix,
                                                            no. 4
Hill, R. S.   Arnold Schoenberg: String Trio   *Notes*, Second   Dec. 1950
                                                            Series, vol. viii,
                                                            no. 1
Hymanson, W.   Schoenberg's String Trio (1946)   *M. R.*, vol. 11, no. 3   Aug. 1950
List, K.   Ode to Napoleon   *Modern Music*   Mar./Apr.
                                                                                  1944
Mangeot, A.   Schoenberg's Fourth String Quar-   *M.R.*, vol. 3, no. 3   Feb. 1942
                       tet
Neighbour, O. W.   Dodecaphony   in   Schoenberg's   *Music Survey*, vol.   June 1952
                       String Trio   iv, no. 3
Neighbour, O. W.   A Talk on Schoenberg for Com-   *The Score*, no. 16   June 1956
                       posers' Concourse (refers to
                       String Quartet No. 4)
Newlin, D.   Schoenberg's New Fantasy   *The Canon*   Sept. 1949
Pisk, P. A.   Arnold Schoenberg's Serenade   *MbA*, vol. 6, no. 5   May 1924
Schindler, K.   Arnold Schoenberg's Quartet in   New York   1914
                       D minor, op. 7
Stein, E.   Zu Schoenbergs neuer Suite, op.   *MbA*, vol. 9, no. 7   Aug./Sept.
                       29   1927
Stein, E.   Schoenberg's new structural form   *Modern Music*   June/July
                       (refers to String Quartet No. 3)   1930
Stein, E.   The Treatment of the Speaking   London   1953
                       Voice in 'Pierrot Lunaire' (in
                       'Orpheus in New Guises')
Tenschert, R.   Eine Passacaglia   von   Arnold   *Die Musik*, vol.   May 1925
                       Schoenberg (refers to 'Pierrot   xvii, no. 8
                       Lunaire')
Wellesz, E.   Arnold Schoenberg (refers to   *Zeitschrift der*   Sept. 1911
                       String Quartets Nos. 1 and 2)   *Internationalen*
                                                             Musikgesellschaft

Seiber

Seiber, M.   Appendix to J. Rufer's 'Composi-   London   1954
                       tion with Twelve Notes related
                       only to one another' (refers to
                       String Quartet No. 2)

Seiber (cont.)

Weissmann, J. S.	Die Streichquartette von Matyas Seiber	*Melos*, vol. 22, no. 12, and 23, no. 2	Dec. 1955 and Feb. 1956

Shostakovich

Keldysh, Y.	An autobiographical Quartet (refers to String Quartet No. 8)	*M.T.*, vol. 102, no. 1418	Apr. 1961
Mason, C.	Form in Shostakovich's Quartets	*M.T.*, vol. 103, no. 1434	Aug. 1962

Stockhausen

Craft, R.	Boulez and Stockhausen (refers to 'Zeitmasse')	*The Score*, no. 24	Nov. 1958
Curjel, H.	Karlheinz Stockhausen: 'Zeitmasse'	*Melos*, vol. 27, no. 9	Sept. 1960
Scherchen, H.	Stockhausen und die Zeit: zur Geschichte (refers to 'Kontrapunkten')	*Gravesaner Blätter*, vol. 4, no. 13	1959

Stravinsky

Drew, D.	Stravinsky's Revisions (refers to Concertino)	*The Score*, no. 20	June 1957
Keller, H.	In Memorian Dylan Thomas: Strawinsky's Schoenbergian Technique	*Tempo*, no. 35	Spring 1955
Schatz, H.	Igor Strawinsky: Septett	*Melos*, vol. 25, no. 2	Feb. 1958
Schilling, H. L.	Zur Instrumentation in Igor Strawinskys Spätwerk aufgezeigt an seinem 'Septett 1953'	*Archiv für Musikwissenschaft*, vol. xiii	1956
Stein, E.	Strawinsky's Septet (1953)	*Tempo*, no. 31	Spring 1954

Van Dieren

Williams, L. Henderson	'Philandering round' Mr. Van Dieren's Quartets	*The Sackbut*, vol. xi, no. 11	July 1931

Walton

Murrill, H.	Walton's Violin Sonata	*M. & L.*, vol. xxxi, no. 3	July 1950

Webern

Leibowitz, R.	'Qu'est ce que la musique de douze sons ?' (refers to Concerto, op. 24)	Liège	1948
Newlin, D.	Webern's Quintet for String Quartet and Piano	*Notes*, Second Series, vol. x, no. 4	Sept. 1953
Stein, E.	Webern's new Quartet	*Tempo*, no. 4	July 1939
Stockhausen, K.	Analyse des ersten Satzes (refers to Concerto, op. 24)	*Melos*, vol. 20, no. 12	Dec. 1953
Die Reihe, no. 2	Webern Number (analyses by various authors of Opp. 9, 15 no. 4, 24, 28)	Vienna	1958

ADDITIONS AND CORRECTIONS TO DATES GIVEN IN THE ORIGINAL EDITION

Compiled by NICOLAS SLONIMSKY

ABBIATE, LOUIS. 1866–1933.

ABEL, KARL FRIEDRICH. Born 1723 (not 1725).

ACHRON, JOSEPH. Died 1943.

ADAIEVSKY, ELLA VON. Died 1926.

AGNIEZ, EMIL. 1856–1909.

AGOSTINI, MEZIO (not MUZIO). Died 1944.

AKIMENKO, FEODOR STEPANOVITCH. Died 1945.

ALALEONA, DOMENICO. Died 1928.

ALARY, GEORGES. 1850–1929.

ALBERT, EUGEN D'. Died 1932.

ALBERT, HEINRICH. 1870–1950.

ALBINONI, TOMMASO. 1671–1750.

ALEXANDER, FRIEDRICH. Died 1945.

ALEXANIAN, DIRAN. 1881–1954.

ALFANO, FRANCO. 1876 (not 1877)–1954.

ALFVÉN, HUGO. Died 1960.

ALLEN, CHARLES N. 1837–1903.

ALNAES, EYVIND. Died 1932.

ALOÏS, VLADISLAV. Died 1917.

ALTMANN, WILHELM. 1862–1951.

AMES, JOHN CARLOWITZ. Died 1924 (not 1925).

ANDERSEN, ANTON JÖRGEN. Died 1926.

ANDREAE, VOLKMAR. Died 1962.

ANDRÉE, ELFRIDA. 1841 (not 1844)–1929.

ANSORGE, CONRAD. Died 1930.

ANTHEIL, GEORGE. 1900–59.

ANTHIOME, EUGÈNE JEAN-BAPTISTE. Died 1911.

ANZOLETTI, MARCO. Died 1929.

ARBÓS, ENRIQUE FERNÁNDEZ. Died 1939.

ARRIAGA Y BALZOLA, JUAN. Died 1826 (not 1825).

ARTCIBOUCHEV, NICOLAI V. Died 1937.

ASHTON, A. B. L. Died 1937.

ASPLMAYR, FRANZ. Born 1728 (not 1721).

ATHERTON, PERCY LEE. Died 1944.

AUBER, D. F. E. Born 1782 (not 1792).

AUBERT, JACQUES. Born 1689 (not 1678).

AUER, LEOPOLD VON. Died 1930.

AUSTIN, ERNEST. Died 1947.

AVERKAMP, ANTON. Died 1934.

AXMAN, EMIL. Died 1949.

BACHMANN, ALBERTO. Born 1875.

BACHMETEV, NICOLAS. 1807–91.

BAINTON, EDGAR LESLIE. Died 1956.

BALAKIREV, M. A. Born 1837 (not 1836).

BALUTET, MARGUERITE. Died 1928.

BANTOCK, GRANVILLE. Died 1946.

BARBLAN, OTTO. Died 1943.

BARKWORTH, J. E. Died 1929.

BARNS, ETHEL. 1880 (not 1875)–1948.

BARTÓK, BÉLA. Died 1945.

BARTZ, J. Died 1933.

BAS, GIULIO. Died 1929.

BASTARD, WILLIAM. Died 1935.

BATON, RHENÉ. Died 1940.

BAUER, MARION. Died 1955.

BAUSSNERN, WALDEMAR VON. Died 1931.

BAX, ARNOLD E. TREVOR. Died 1953.

BAZELAIRE, PAUL. Died 1958.

BEACH, MRS. H. H. A. Died 1944.

BEACH, JOHN. 1887–1953.

BEAU, LUISE ADOLPHA LE. 1850–1927.

BECK, FRANZ. Born 1723 (not 1730).

BECKER, (2) HUGO. 1863 (not 1864)–1941.

BECKER, REINHOLD. Born 1842 (not 1843).

BECKMAN, BROR. Died 1929.

BEDFORD, HERBERT. Died 1945.

BEER-WALBRUNN, ANTON. Died 1929.

BEHM, EDUARD. Died 1946.

BELAIEV, M. P. Died 1904 (not 1903).

BELL, WILLIAM HENRY. Died 1946.

BENDIX, VICTOR EMANUEL. Died 1926.

BENESCH (or BENEŠ), JOSEPH. Died 1873.

BENJAMIN, ARTHUR. Died 1960.

BENTZON, JØRGEN (not JORGEN). 1897–1951.

BENVENUTI, GIACOMO. 1885–1943.

BERG, ALBAN. Died 1935.

BERG, NATANAEL. Died 1957.

BERNARD, ANTHONY. Born 1891.

BERNARD, ÉMILE. Born 1843 (not 1845).

BERNARD, ROBERT. Born 1900.

BERTRAND, MARCEL. 1883–1945.

BEZECNY, EMIL. Died 1930.

BITTNER, JULIUS. Died 1939.

BLOCH, ERNEST. Died 1959.

BLUMENFELD, F. M. Died 1931.

BOGHEN, FELICE. 1869 (not 1875)–1945.

BOHNKE, EMIL. Died 1928.

BÖLSCHE, FRANZ. Died 1935.

BONAVIA, FERRUCCIO. Died 1950.

BONAWITZ, JOHANN HEINRICH. Died 1917.

BONNER, EUGENE. Born 1889.

BONPORTI, FRANCESCO ANTONIO. 1672–1749.

BOORN-COCLET, HENRIETTE VAN DEN. Died 1945.

BORNE, FERNAND LE. Died 1929.
BORODIN, A. P. Born 1833 (not 1834).
BORTKIEWICZ, SERGEI EDUARDOVICH. Died 1952.
BOSSI, MARCO ENRICO. Died 1925.
BOTTESINI, GIOVANNI. Born 1821 (not 1822).
BOUCHER, M. LE. Born 1882.
BOUGHTON, RUTLAND. Died 1960.
BOULNOIS, JOSEPH. Born 1884 (not 1880).
BOUMANN, LEONARDUS CAROLUS. Died 1919.
BOWEN, YORK. Died 1961.
BRANCOUR, RENÉ. Died 1948.
BRANDTS BUYS, JAN. Died 1933.
BRÉVILLE, P. O. D'. Died 1949.
BRIDGE, FRANK. Died 1941.
BRIGHT, DORA. 1863–1951.
BROCKWAY, HOWARD A. Died 1951.
BRÜGGEMANN, ALFRED. 1873–1944.
BRÜLL, IGNAZ. Born 1846 (not 1847).
BRUN, FRITZ. Died 1959.
BRUNE, ADOLF GERHARD. Died 1935.
BRUNI, ANTONIO BARTOLOMMEO. 1751–1821 (not 1759–1823).
BRZESZINSKI, FRANCISZEK. Died 1944.
BUSCH, ADOLF. Died 1952.
BÜTTNER, PAUL. Died 1943.
BUTTYKAY, ÁKOS VON. Died 1935.

CADMAN, CHARLES WAKEFIELD. Died 1946.
CAMONDO, ISAAC DE. Died 1911.
CAMPO Y ZABALETA, CONRADO DEL. 1876 (not 1879)–1953.
CANTELOUBE DE MALARET, JOSEPH (not JEAN). 1879–1957.
CAPLET, ANDRÉ. Born 1878 (not 1879).
CARO, PAUL. Died 1914.
CARPENTER, JOHN ALDEN. Died 1951.
CARSE, ADAM. Died 1958.
CASADESUS, FRANÇOIS. Died 1954.
CASADESUS, HENRI GUSTAVE. Died 1947.
CASADESUS, MARCEL LOUIS LUCIEN. Died 1914.
CASELLA, ALFREDO. Died 1947.
CASSADÓ, GASPAR. Born 1897 (not 1898).
CASTÉRA, RENÉ D'AVEZAC DE. Died 1955.
CHADWICK, GEORGE WHITEFIELD. Died 1931.
CHAMINADE, CÉCILE. 1857 (not 1861)–1944.
CHAPUIS, AUGUSTE PAUL JEAN-BAPTISTE. Died 1933.
CHARPENTIER, RAYMOND. Died 1960.
CHÁVEZ, CARLOS. Born 1899.
CHELIUS, OSKAR VON. Died 1923.
CHEVAILLER, LUCIEN. 1883–1932.
CHRÉTIEN, MME HEDWIGE. 1859–1944.
CIMADOR, GIAMBATTISTA. 1761–1805 (not 1808).
CLAUSETTI, PIETRO. Born 1904.
CLAUSSMANN, ALOÏS. 1850–1926.
CLOUGH-LEIGHTER, HENRY. Died 1956.
COBBETT, WALTER WILLSON. Died 1937.
COERNE, LOUIS ADOLPHE. Died 1922.

COINDREAU, PIERRE. 1867–1924.
COLLET, HENRI. Died 1951.
CONVERSE, FREDERIC SHEPHERD. Died 1940.
COOLIDGE, ELIZABETH SPRAGUE. 1864–1953.
COOLS, EUGÈNE. Died 1936.
COURVOISIER, KARL. 1846 (not 1864)–1908.
CRAS, JEAN. Died 1932.
CRICKBOOM, MATHIEU. Died 1947.
CRISTIANI, GIUSEPPE. Died 1933.
CROME, FRITZ. Died 1948.
CUTTER, BENJAMIN. 1857–1910.

DAFFNER, HUGO. Died 1944.
DAHMEN, JOHAN ARNOLD. Died 1794 (not 1840).
DAHMEN, HUBERT. Died 1836 (not 1837).
DAHMEN, WILLEM HENDRIK. Born 1791 (not 1797).
DAHMEN, HERMAN JOHAN. Died 1881 (not 1875).
DALBERG, JOHANN. Born 1760 (not 1752).
DALBERG, NANCY. Died 1949.
DALCROZE, ÉMILE JACQUES. Died 1950.
DALE, BENJAMIN JAMES. Died 1943.
DALLIER, HENRI. Died 1934.
DAMROSCH, WALTER JOHANNES. Died 1950.
DANCLA, J. B. CHARLES. Born 1817 (not 1818).
DANDRIEU, JEAN-FRANÇOIS. 1682–1738 (not 1684–1740).
DANEAU, NICOLAS ADOLPHE GUSTAVE. Died 1944.
DAVID, KARL HEINRICH. Died 1951.
DAVIES, FANNY. Died 1934.
DAVIES, SIR HENRY WALFORD. Died 1941.
DAVIS, JOHN DAVID. 1867 (not 1870)–1942.
DEFESCH, WILLIAM. 1687–1761.
DELAFOSSE, LÉON. Died 1951.
DELCROIX, LÉON. Died 1938.
DELIUS, FREDERICK. 1862 (not 1863)–1934.
DELMAS, MARC. Died 1931.
DELUNE, LOUIS. Died 1940.
DELVINCOURT, CLAUDE. Died 1954.
DENÉRÉAZ, ALEXANDRE. Died 1947.
DEPAS, ERNEST. Died 1889.
DESHEVOV, VLADIMIR. 1889 (not 1902)–1955.
DESREZ, MAURICE. Born 1882.
DESTENAY, ÉDOUARD. Died 1924.
DEVANCHY, PATRICE. 1876–1942.
DIEREN, BERNARD VAN. Died 1936.
DIETRICH, OSKAR. Born 1888.
DIMITRESCO, CONSTANTIN. 1847–1920.
DOBROWEN, I. A. Died 1953.
DOHNÁNYI, ERNST VON. Died 1960.
DOIRE, RENÉ. 1879–1959.
DOLMETSCH, ARNOLD. Died 1940.
DOYEN, ALBERT. 1882–1935.
DRESDEN, SEM. Died 1957.
DROZDOV, A. N. 1883–1950.
DSÉGUÉLÉNOK, A. M. Born 1891.

Ducasse, Roger. Died 1954.
Ducoureau, Madeleine. Died 1958.
Dukas, Paul. Died 1935.
Dulaurens, André. 1872–1932.
Dumas, Louis. Died 1952.
Dunhill, Thomas Frederick. Died 1946.
Dupérier, Jean. Born 1886 (not 1896).
Dupin, Paul. Died 1949.
Dussek, Jan Ladislav. Born 1760 (not 1761).

Eberl, Anton. Born 1765 (not 1766).
Eccles, Henry. c. 1670–c. 1742.
Edmonds, Paul. 1873–1939.
Eggert, Joachim. Born 1779 (not 1780).
Eichheim, Henry. Died 1942.
Eimert, Herbert. Born 1897.
Elgar, Sir Edward. Died 1934.
Ellerton, John Lodge. Born 1801 (not 1807).
Emborg, Jens Laurson. Born 1876.
Emmanuel, Maurice. Died 1938.
Enesco, Georges. Died 1955.
Engel, Carl. Died 1944.
Engelsmann, Walter. 1881–1952.
Erb, Maria Josef. 1858 (not 1860)–1944.
Erdmann, Eduard. Died 1958.
Erhart, Dorothy. Born 1894.
Erlanger, Frédéric d'. Died 1943.
Ertel, Jean Paul. Died 1933.
Esposito, Michele. Died 1929.
Evseiev, S. V. 1893 (not 1894)–1956.
Ewald, Victor. Died 1935.
Eybler, Joseph. Born 1764 (not 1765).

Fährmann, Hans. Died 1940.
Fairchild, Blair. Died 1933.
Faisst, Clara. 1879–1948.
Falla, Manuel de. Died 1946.
Faltis, Evelyn. Died 1937.
Fanelli, Ernest. Died 1917 (not 1919).
Farjeon, Harry. Died 1948.
Farnaby, Giles. c. 1565 (not c. 1560)–1640.
Fauré, Gabriel. Died 1924 (not 1925).
Faye-Jozin, Mme Frédérique de. 1871–1942.
Ferrata, Giuseppe. 1865 (not 1866)–1928.
Février, Henri. 1875 (not 1876)–1957.
Finzi, Gerald. 1901–56.
Fiorillo, Federigo. Born 1755 (not 1753).
Fitelberg, Grigor. Died 1953.
Flament, Édouard. Died 1958.
Flégier, Ange. Died 1927.
Foerster, Adolph Martin. Died 1927.
Foerster, Josef Bohuslav. Died 1951.
Fogg, Eric. Died 1939.
Foote, Arthur William. Died 1937.
Forrester, James Cliffe. Died 1941.
Fourdrain, Félix. Died 1923.
Fowles, Ernest. Died 1932.
Franck, Richard. Died 1938.
Freitas Branco, Luiz. Died 1955.

Frey, Emil. Died 1946.
Frey, Martin. Died 1946.
Friedman, Ignaz. Died 1948.
Froberger, Johann Jakob. Born 1616.
Frugatta, Giuseppe. Died 1933.
Frühling, Karl. 1868–1937.

Gabrieli, Andrea. 1520 (not c. 1510)–1586.
Gabrieli, Giovanni. 1557–1612 (not 1613).
Gabrielski, Wilhelm. Born 1791 (not 1795).
Galliard, J. E. Born 1680 (not 1687).
Ganaye, Jean-Baptiste. 1870–1946.
Gardiner, H. Balfour. Died 1950.
Gardner, Samuel. Born 1891 (not 1892).
Gasco, Alberto. Died 1938.
Gatty, Nicholas. Died 1946.
Gaubert, Philippe. Died 1941.
Geisler, Christian. Born 1869.
German, Edward. Died 1936.
Gibbs, Cecil Armstrong. Died 1960.
Gieseking, Walter. Died 1956.
Gilles, Constantin. 1868–1934.
Gilson, Paul. Died 1942.
Giorni, Aurelio. Died 1938.
Glass, Louis. Died 1936.
Glazounov, A. C. Died 1936.
Glière, R. M. Died 1956 (not 1926).
Glinka, M. I. Born 1804 (not 1803).
Gniessin, M. F. Died 1957.
Goedicke, A. F. Died 1957.
Goeyens, Fernand. Born 1892.
Goldmark, Rubin. Died 1936.
Golestan, Stan. 1872 (not 1876)–1956.
Gompertz, Richard. Died 1921.
Goossens, Eugene. Died 1962.
Gotthelf, Felix. Died 1930.
Grabert, Martin. Died 1951.
Grädener, Hermann Theodor Otto. Died 1929.
Graener, Paul. Died 1944.
Grainger, Percy Aldridge. Died 1961.
Grasse, Edwin. 1884–1954.
Graun, Johann Gottlieb. Born 1703 (not 1698).
Gray, Alan. Died 1935.
Gretchaninov, A. T. Died 1956.
Grosz, Wilhelm. Died 1939.
Grovlez, Gabriel. Died 1944.
Gruenberg, Louis T. Born 1884 (not 1882).
Grützmacher, Friedrich. Died 1903 (not 1900).
Guilloux, Philippe. Died 1945.
Gurney, Ivor Bertie. Died 1937.

Haarklou, Johannes. Died 1925 (not 1926).
Haas, Joseph. Died 1960.
Hadley, Henry Kimball. Died 1937.
Hadow, W. H. Died 1937.

HÄGG, GUSTAF WILHELM. Died 1925.
HAHN, REYNALDO. Died 1947.
HALFFTER ESCRICHE, ERNESTO. Born 1905.
HALL, G. W. L. MARSHALL. Died 1915.
HALM, AUGUST. Died 1929.
HALVORSEN, JOHAN. Died 1935.
HANSEN, ROBERT EMIL. Died 1926.
HANSON, HOWARD. Born 1896.
HARSÁNYI, TIBOR. Died 1954.
HARTMANN, ARTHUR. 1881 (not 1882)–1956.
HARTY, SIR HAMILTON. Died 1941.
HAUER, JOSEPH MATTHIAS. Died 1959.
HAY, EDWARD NORMAN. Died 1943.
HEGNER, ANTON. Died 1915.
HEILMAN, WILLIAM CLIFFORD. Died 1946.
HELLER, STEPHEN. Born 1813 (not 1815).
HELSTED, GUSTAV CARL. Died 1924.
HENNESSY, SWAN. 1866 (not 1886)–1929.
HENRIQUES, FINI VALDEMAR. Died 1940.
HENSCHEL, SIR GEORGE. Died 1934.
HERMANN, E. HANS G. Died 1931.
HERRMANN, EDUARD. 1850–1937.
HESELTINE, PHILIP. Died 1930.
HILL, ALFRED. 1870 (not 1869)–1960.
HILL, EDWARD BURLINGAME. Died 1960.
HILLEMACHER, PAUL. Died 1933.
HINTON, ARTHUR. Died 1941.
HOBOKEN, ANTHONY VAN. Born 1887.
HÖEBERG, GEORG. Died 1950.
HOESSLIN, FRANZ VON. Died 1946.
HOLBROOKE, JOSEPH. Died 1958.
HOLLÄNDER, ALEXIS. Died 1924.
HOLLANDER, BENOÎT. Died 1942.
HOLST, GUSTAV. Died 1934.
HOLTER, IVER PAUL FREDRIK. Died 1941.
HONEGGER, ARTHUR. Died 1955.
HORN, KAMILLO. Died 1941.
HOUFFLACK, ALBERT. 1859–1935.
HOYER, KARL. Died 1936.
HUBAY, JENÖ. Died 1937.
HUGHES, HERBERT. Died 1937.
HUMISTON, WILLIAM HENRY. 1869–1923.
HUMMEL, FERDINAND. Died 1928.
HURÉ, JEAN. Died 1930.
HUSS, HENRY HOLDEN. Died 1953.
HUTSCHENRUYTER, WOUTER. 1796–1878.
HUYBRECHTS, ALBERT. Died 1938.

IARECKI (recte JARECKI), TADEUSZ (not TADDEUS). Died 1955.
IBERT, JACQUES. Died 1962.
D'INDY, VINCENT. Died 1931.
INGENHOVEN, JAN. Died 1951.
IPPISCH, FRANZ. Died 1953.
IPPOLITOV-IVANOV, M. M. Died 1935.
IRELAND, JOHN. Died 1962.
IVANOV-BORETSKY, M.V. 1874 (not 1875)–1936.

JACOBI, FREDERICK. Died 1952.

JAFFÉ, MORITZ. 1834–1925.
JEMAIN, JEAN. 1869–1954.
JENSEN, LUDVIG IRGENS. Born 1894.
JIRÁNEK, ALOIS. Died 1950.
JONGEN, JOSEPH. Died 1953.
JOTEYKO, THADDÄUS. Died 1932.
JUNCK, BENEDETTO. Died 1903 (not 1905).
JUON, PAUL. Died 1940.
JURASSOWSKY, ALEX. 1890–1922.

KAHN, ROBERT. Died 1951.
KALAFATI, VASSILY PAVLOVITCH (not B.). 1869–1942.
KALKBRENNER, FRIEDRICH WILHELM MICHAEL. Born 1785 (not 1788).
KALLENBERG, SIEGFRIED GARIBALDI. Died 1944.
KAMINSKI, HEINRICH. Died 1946.
KÄMPF, KARL. Died 1950.
KAREL, RUDOLF. Died 1945.
KARG-ELERT, SIEGFRIED. 1877 (not 1879)–1933.
KATTNIG, RUDOLF. 1895–1955.
KAUFFMANN, FRITZ. Died 1934.
KAUN, HUGO. Died 1932.
KELTERBORN, LOUIS. Died 1933.
KERSBERGEN, JAN WILLEM. Died 1937.
KES, WILLEM. Died 1934.
KIENZL, WILHELM. Died 1941.
KING, OLIVER A. Died 1923.
KLEIN, BRUNO OSKAR. Born 1858 (not 1856).
KLENGEL, PAUL. Died 1935.
KLENGEL, JULIUS. Died 1933.
KLEVEN, ARVID. 1899 (not 1900)–1929.
KLINGLER, KARL. Born 1879.
KLOSE, FRIEDRICH. Died 1942.
KNIPPER, LEV. Born 1898.
KOCH, FRIEDRICH E. Died 1927.
KOECHLIN, CHARLES. Died 1950.
KOENIG, JEAN. Died 1938.
KOESSLER, HANS. Died 1926.
KORNAUTH, EGON. Died 1959.
KORNGOLD, ERICH. Died 1957.
KOVALEV, PAVEL IVANOVITCH. Born 1890.
KOZELUH, LEOPOLD ANTON. Born 1752 (not 1748).
KRÀSA, HANS. 1899 (not 1895)–1944.
KREIN, ALEXANDER. Died 1951.
KREIN, GRIGORY. 1880 (not 1879)–1955.
KREISLER, FRITZ. Died 1962.
KREUZ, EMIL. Died 1932.
KRIENS, CHRISTIAN (not CHRISTOPH). 1881–1934.
KRISTOFFERSEN, KARL FRIDTHJOF. Born 1894.
KROEGER, ERNST RICHARD. Died 1934.
KROMMER, FRANZ. Born 1759 (not 1760).
KRONKE, EMIL. Died 1938.

KRUMPHOLTZ, JOHANN BAPTIST. Born 1742 (not *c.* 1745).
KRYJANOVSKY, I. I. Died 1924 (not 1926).
KRYZANOWSKA, HALINA. Born 1860.
KÜCKEN, FRIEDRICH WILHELM. Died 1882 (not 1872).
KUHN, SIEGFRIED. 1893–1915.
KUILER, KOR. Died 1951.
KUNC, PIERRE. Died 1942.
KUNC, AYMÉ. Died 1957.

LABOR, JOSEF. Died 1924.
LACROIX, EUGÈNE. 1858–1957.
LADMIRAULT, PAUL ÉMILE. Died 1944.
LADUKHIN, N. M. Died 1918.
LAMARTER, ERIC DE. Died 1953.
LAMBRECHTS-VOS, ANNA. Died 1932.
LAMOND, FREDERICK A. Died 1948.
LANG, HENRY ALBERT. Died 1930.
LANGE-MÜLLER, PETER ERASMUS. Died 1926.
LAPARRA, RAOUL. Died 1943.
LAQUAI, REINHOLD. Born 1894 (not 1884).
LAUBER, JOSEPH. Died 1952.
LAURENCE, FREDERICK. Born 1884 (not 1883).
LAURIDSEN, LAURIDS. 1882–1946.
LAURISCHKUS, MAX. Died 1929.
LAWES, WILLIAM. Born 1602 (not *c.* 1590).
LAZARUS, GUSTAV. Died 1920.
LAZZARI, SYLVIO. 1857 (not 1860)–1944.
LECAIL, CLOVIS. 1859–1932.
LEDUC, ALPHONSE. Born 1844 (not 1804).
LEFÉBURE, JOSEPH. 1877–1946.
LEICHTENTRITT, HUGO. Died 1951.
LENDVAI, ERWIN. Died 1949.
LENORMAND, RENÉ. Died 1932.
LERMYTE, ANDRÉ-LÉON. Born 1882.
LÉVY, HENIOT (not HENRIOT). 1879–1946.
LIEBESKIND, JOSEPH. 1866–1916.
LIEBLING, GEORG. Died 1946.
LILJEFORS, RUBEN MATTIAS. Died 1936.
LIMBERT, FRANK. Died 1938.
LIUZZI, FERNANDO. Died 1940.
LOCATELLI, PIETRO. Born 1695 (not 1693).
LOEFFLER, CHARLES MARTIN TORNOW. Died 1935.
LŒILLET, JEAN-BAPTISTE. 1680–1730 (not 1653–1728).
LONGO, ALESSANDRO. Died 1945.
LORENZ, ALFRED OTTOKAR. Died 1939.
LORENZ, JULIUS. Died 1924.
LOTH, LOUIS LESLIE. Born 1888.
LUALDI, ADRIANO. Born 1885 (not 1887).
LUCAS, BLANCHE. Died 1956.
LUDWIG, JOSEF. Died 1924.

MACCOY, WILLIAM JOHNSTON. Died 1926 (not *c.* 1927).
MCEWEN, JOHN BLACKWOOD. Died 1948.
MACKENZIE, ALEXANDER CAMPBELL. Died 1935.

MADEL-CLERC, MADELEINE, 1863–1929.
MAJOR, JULIUS JACQUES. 1858 (not 1859)–1925.
MALEINGREAU, PAUL DE. Died 1956.
MALICHEVSKY, WITOLD J. Died 1939.
MANUEL, ROLAND. Born 1891.
MARINI, BIAGIO. Died 1665 (not 1660).
MARSICK, ARMAND. 1877 (not 1878)–1959.
MARTEAU, HENRI. Died 1934.
MARTINEAU, PAUL. 1890–1915.
MARTINU, BOHUSLAV. 1890–1959.
MASON, DANIEL GREGORY. Died 1953.
MASSON, FERNAND. 1882–1942.
MATTHAY, TOBIAS AUGUSTUS. Died 1945.
MATTHISON-HANSEN, VAAGE. 1841–1911.
MEDTNER, NICOLAI KARLOVITCH (not RAZLO-VITCH). 1880 (not 1879)–1951.
MELARTIN, ERKKI. Died 1937.
MEL-BONIS (BONIS, MÉLANIE). 1858 (not 1868)–1937.
MELCER, HENRYK. Died 1928.
MELKIKH, DMITRY. Died 1943.
MENDELSSOHN, ARNOLD. Died 1933.
MEYER, ALBERT. 1847–1933.
MEYER, BERNARD. Died 1953.
MEYER-OLBERSLEBEN, MAX. Died 1927.
MIASKOVSKY, N. J. Died 1950.
MIDGLEY, SAMUEL. Died 1935.
MIERSCH, PAUL FRIEDRICH THEODOR (not THEO). Died 1956.
MIKOREY, FRANZ. Died 1947.
MOERAN, ERNEST JOHN. Died 1950.
MOFFAT, ALFRED EDWARD. Died 1950.
MOJSISOVICS, RODERICH VON. Died 1953.
MONASTERIO, JESÚS. Died 1903.
MONIUSZKO, STANISLAW (not STANISLAUS). Born 1819 (not 1820).
MOÓR, EMANUEL. 1863 (not 1862)–1931.
MOOR, KAREL. (not KARL). Died 1945.
MOREAU, LÉON EUGÈNE. Died 1946.
MORET, VICTOR. Died 1902 (not *c.* 1900).
MORRIS, REGINALD OWEN. Died 1948.
MOSER, FRANZ JOSEF. Died 1939.
MOUQUET, JULES. 1867–1946.
MRACZEK, JOSEPH GUSTAV. Died 1944.
MUFFAT, GEORG. Died 1653 (not *c.* 1645).
MÜLLER, SIGFRID WALTHER. Died 1946.
MÜLLER-HARTMANN, ROBERT. Died 1950.
MÜLLER-HERMANN, JOHANNA. Died 1941.

NACHEZ, TIVADAR. Died 1930.
NAPRAVNIK, EDUARD FRANZEVITCH. Died 1916 (not 1915).
NAVRATIL, KARL. Died 1936.
NEAL, HEINRICH. Died 1940.
NEDBAL, OSKAR. Died 1930.
NETCHAIEV, VASSILY (not NETSCHAIEV, W.). 1895–1956.
NEUMANN, FRANZ. Died 1929.
NICOLAIEV, L. V. Died 1942.

NIELSEN, CARL. Died 1931.
NIELSEN, LUDOLF. Died 1939.
NIEMANN, WALTER. Died 1953.
NIVERD, LUCIEN. Born 1879.
NOREN, HEINRICH GOTTLIEB. Died 1928.
NOVÁK, VÍTĚZSLAV. Died 1949.

OBERSTADT, CAROLUS D. Died 1940.
OHE, ADELE AUS DER. Died 1937.
OLDBERG, ARNE. Died 1962.
OLLONE, MAX D'. Died 1959.
O'NEILL, NORMAN. Died 1934.
ONSLOW, GEORGE. 1784 (not 1783) – 1853 (not 1852).
OPPEL, REINHARD. Died 1941.
ORBAN, MARCEL. Died 1958.
ORDONEZ, CARLOS. 1734–1786.
OTTERSTRÖM, THORWALD. Died 1942.
OULIBICHEV, ALEXANDER VON. Born 1794 (not 1795).

PADEREWSKI, IGNAZ JOSEPH. Died 1941.
PAGANINI, NICCOLÒ. 1782 (not 1784)–1840.
PAGELLA, GIOVANNI. Died 1944.
PÂQUE, DÉSIRÉ. Died 1939.
PARENT, ARMAND. Died 1934.
PASCAL, ANDRÉ. Born 1894.
PAUR, EMIL. Died 1932.
PEJACSEVICH, DORA VON. 1885–1923.
PERELLI, EDOARDO. Died 1885.
PÉRILHOU (not PÉRILHON), ALBERT. 1846–1936.
PERINELLO, CARLO. Died 1942.
PERLEBERG, ARTHUR. Born 1876.
PERRY, EDWARD BAXTER. Died 1924.
PESTALOZZI, HEINRICH. Died 1940.
PETERKA, RUDOLF. Died 1933.
PETERS, GUIDO. Died 1937.
PETERSON-BERGER, OLOF WILHELM. Died 1942.
PETYREK, FELIX. Died 1951.
PFITZNER, HANS. Died 1949.
PICHL, WENZEL. Died 1804 (not 1805).
PICK-MANGIAGALLI, RICCARDO. Died 1949.
PIERNÉ, (1) GABRIEL. Died 1937.
PIERNÉ, (2) PAUL. Died 1952.
PIJPER, WILLEM. Died 1947.
PIRANI, EUGENIO. Died 1939.
PLANCHET, DOMINIQUE-CHARLES. Died 1946.
POCHON, ALFRED. Died 1959.
POIRÉE, ÉLIE EMIL GABRIEL. Died 1925.
POLDOWSKI (IRENE WIENIAWSKA). 1879–1932.
POLLINI, CESARE. Died 1912.
POLSTERER, RUDOLF. Died 1945.
PONS, JUSTIN-MARIE-ANTOINE. 1866–1935.
POPPER, DAVID. Born 1843 (not 1845).
PORPORA, NICOLA (not NICCOLA). Died 1768 (not 1766).
PORTNOV, LEO. 1875–1940.
POTOLOWSKY, NICHOLAS. 1878–1927.
PRATELLA, FRANCESCO BALILLA. Died 1955.

PRESLE (not PRESLÉ), JACQUES DE LA. Born 1888.
PROKOFIEV, SERGEI. Died 1953.
PROTHEROE, DANIEL. 1866–1934.

QUEF, CHARLES. Died 1931.
QUILTER, ROGER. Died 1953.

RAASTED, NIELS OTTO. Born 1888.
RABAUD, HENRI. Died 1949.
RABL, WALTHER. Died 1940.
RACHMANINOV, SERGEI. Died 1943.
RADICATI, FELICE ALESSANDRO. 1775–1820 (not 1778–1823).
RADNAI, MIKLÓS. 1892 (not 1882)–1935.
RAHLWES, ALFRED. Died 1946.
RAMIN, GÜNTHER. Died 1956.
RANGSTRÖM, TURE. Died 1947.
RAPHAEL, GÜNTHER. Died 1960.
RASCH, HUGO. Died 1947.
RASSE, FRANÇOIS. Died 1955.
RATEZ, ÉMILE PIERRE. Died 1934.
RATHAUS, KAROL. Died 1954.
RAVEL, MAURICE JOSEPH. Died 1937.
RECHNITZER-MÖLLER, HENNING. Born 1889.
REDMAN, HARRY NEWTON. 1869–1958.
REED, WILLIAM HENRY. Died 1942.
REHBERG, WILLY. Died 1937.
REINHOLD, HUGO. Died 1935.
REISER, ALOIS. Born 1887.
REITER, JOSEPH. Died 1939.
RENDANO, ALFONSO. Died 1931.
RENIÉ, HENRIETTE. Died 1956.
RESPIGHI, OTTORINO. Died 1936.
REUSS, AUGUST. Died 1935.
REUTER, FRITZ. Born 1896.
REZNIČEK, EMIL NIKOLAUS VON. 1860 (not 1861)–1945.
RIBOLLET, ALBERT-GABRIEL. Born 1884.
RIEGGER, WALLINGFORD. 1885–1961.
RIES, (2) FRANZ. Died 1932.
RIETSCH, HEINRICH. Died 1927.
RINKENS, WILHELM. Died 1933.
RITTER, HERMANN. Died 1926.
ROGALSKI, THEODOR. Died 1954.
ROGISTER, JEAN. Born 1879.
ROGOWSKI, LUDOMIR MICHAL. Died 1954.
ROHOZINSKI, LADISLAV. 1886–1938.
RÖNTGEN, JULIUS. Died 1932.
ROOTHAM, CYRIL BRADLEY. Died 1938.
ROPARTZ, JOSEPH GUY. Died 1955.
RORICH, KARL. Died 1941.
ROSEGGER, SEPP. Died 1948.
ROSETTI, FRANZ ANTON. Born 1746 (not 1750).
ROSLAVETS, NICOLAI. Died 1944.
ROSSI, SALOMONE. c. 1570–c. 1630.
ROUMANIAN COMPOSERS. BRAILOU (not BRAILOI), CONSTANTIN. Died 1957.
ROUSSE, JOSEPH-VICTOR. 1872–1948.
ROUSSEL, ALBERT. Died 1937.

ROWLEY, ALEC. Died 1958.
ROZYCKI, LUDOMIR VON. Died 1953.
RUBINSTEIN, ANTON. Born 1829 (not 1830).
RUGGLES, CARL. Born 1876.
RUTHARDT, ADOLF. Died 1934.
RYBNER, PETER. Died 1929.

SAAR, LOUIS. Died 1937.
SABANEIEV, L. L. Born 1881 (not 1871).
SACCHINI, ANTONIO MARIA GASPERO. Born 1730 (not 1734).
SACHS, LÉO. 1856 (not 1868)–1930.
SALAZAR, ADOLFO. 1890–1958.
SALMON, JOSEPH. 1863–1943.
SALMOND, FELIX. Died 1952.
SAMINSKY, LAZARE. 1882–1959.
SAMMARTINI, GIOVANNI. Born 1698 (not c. 1700).
SAMMARTINI, GIUSEPPE. c. 1693–c. 1750.
SAMMONS, ALBERT EDWARD. 1886 (not 1889)–1957.
SANDBERGER, ADOLF. Died 1943.
SANDRÉ, GUSTAVE. 1843–1916.
SATTER, GUSTAV. Died 1879.
SAUSSINE, HENRI DE. 1859–1940.
SAUVEPLANE, HENRI. 1892–1942.
SAUVREZIS, ALICE. 1866–1946.
SAVARD, AUGUSTIN. Died 1942.
SCALERO, ROSARIO. 1870 (not 1873)–1954.
SCARLATTI, ALESSANDRO. Born 1660 (not 1659).
SCHAEFER, DIRK. Died 1931.
SCHEINPFLUG, PAUL. Died 1937.
SCHELLING, ERNEST HENRY. Died 1939.
SCHERBER, FERDINAND. Died 1944.
SCHERING, ARNOLD. Died 1941.
SCHILLINGS, MAX VON. Died 1933.
SCHLEEMÜLLER, HUGO. 1872–1918.
SCHMID, HEINRICH KASPAR. Died 1953.
SCHMIDT, FRANZ. Died 1939.
SCHMIDT, LEOPOLD. Died 1927.
SCHMITT, FLORENT. Died 1958.
SCHNABEL, ARTHUR. Died 1951.
SCHOECK, OTHMAR. Died 1957.
SCHÖNBERG, ARNOLD. Died 1951.
SCHŒNEFELD, HENRY. Died 1936.
SCHRATTENHOLZ, LEO. Died 1955.
SCHREKER, FRANZ. Died 1934.
SCHRÖDER, KARL. Died 1935.
SCHULHOFF, ERWIN. Died 1942.
SCHUMANN, GEORG ALFRED. Died 1952.
SCHÜTT, EDUARD. Died 1933.
SEITZ, FRIEDRICH. Died 1918.
SEKLES, BERNHARD. Died 1934.
SENFTER, JOHANNA. 1879–1961.
SÉRIEYX, AUGUSTE. Died 1949.
SERRANO Y RUIZ, EMILIO. Died 1939.
SETACCIOLI, GIACOMO. Died 1925.
SEVERN, EDMUND. Died 1942.
SEYFFARDT, ERNST HERMANN. Died 1942.

SGAMBATI, GIOVANNI. Born 1841 (not 1843).
SHARPE, HERBERT FRANCIS. Died 1925 (not 1926).
SHAW, MARTIN. 1875 (not 1876)–1958.
SHEBALIN, VISSARION (not VASILY). Born 1902.
SHEPHERD, ARTHUR. Died 1958.
SHERWOOD, PERCY. Died 1939.
SHOSTAKOVICH, DMITRI. Born 1906 (not 1908).
SIBELIUS, JEAN. Died 1957.
SIKLÓS, ALBERT. Died 1942.
SIMIA, G. R. 1844–1924.
SIMON, ANTHONY. 1850 (not 1851)–1916.
SIMON, MADAME C. PAUL. Born 1881.
SIMON, JAMES. Died c. 1941.
SIMONETTI, ACHILLE. Born 1857 (not 1859).
SINDING, CHRISTIAN. Died 1941.
SINGÉRY, GASTON. 1892–1942.
SINIGAGLIA, LEONE. Died 1944.
SJÖBERG, SVANTE LEONARD. Died 1935.
SKILTON, CHARLES SANFORD. Died 1941.
SLAVENSKI, JOSIP. 1896–1955.
SMITH, DAVID STANLEY. Died 1949.
SMULDERS, KARL ANTON. Died 1934.
SMYTH, ETHEL MARY. Died 1944.
SOHY, CHARLOTTE. Died 1955.
SOMERVELL, ARTHUR. Died 1937.
SORABJI, KAIKHOSRU. Born 1892 (not 1895).
SORO, ENRIQUE. Died 1954.
SOURILAS, THÉOPHILE. 1859–1907.
SPALDING, ALBERT. Died 1953.
SPANGENBERG, HEINRICH. Died 1925.
SPEAIGHT, JOSEPH. Died 1947.
SPEER, WILLIAM HENRY. Died 1937.
SPIELTER, HERMANN. Died 1925.
SPRINGER, MAX. Died 1954.
STAMITZ, CARL. Born 1745 (not 1746).
STARK, ROBERT. Died 1922.
STATKOWSKI, ROMAN. Died 1925.
STEIN, RICHARD. Died 1942.
STEINBERG, MAXIMILIAN. Died 1946.
ŠTĚPÁN, VÁCLAV. Died 1944.
STEPHENSON, MORTON. Born 1884.
STERNBERG, CONSTANTINE IVANOVITCH VON. Died 1924.
STILLMAN-KELLEY, EDGAR. Died 1944.
STOCK, FREDERICK (FRIEDRICH AUGUST). Died 1942.
STOCKHOFF, WALTER WILLIAM. Born 1876 (not 1881).
STOESSEL, ALBERT FREDERIC. Died 1943.
STOJANOVITS, PETER LAZAR. Died 1957.
STOJOWSKI, SIGISMUND. 1869 (not 1870)–1946.
STRADELLA, ALESSANDRO. Born 1642 (not c. 1645).
STRAESSER, EWALD. Died 1933.
STRAUS, OSCAR. 1870–1954.
STRAUSS, RICHARD. Died 1949.
STREICHER, THEODOR. Died 1940.

STRIEGLER, KURT. Died 1958.
STRONG, GEORGE TEMPLETON. Died 1948.
STRUBE, GUSTAV. Died 1953.
SUK, JOSEF. Died 1935.
SZÁNTÓ, THEODOR. Died 1934.
SZULC, JÓSEF ZYGMUNT. 1875–1956.
SZYMANOWSKI, KAROL. 1882 (not 1883)–1937.

TANEIEV, ALEXANDER. Died 1918.
TANSMAN, ALEXANDRE. Born 1897 (not 1900).
TAUBERT, ERNST EDUARD. Died 1934.
TCHEREPNIN, NICOLAS. Died 1945.
TETTERODE, ADRIAN VAN. Died 1931.
THIBAUD, JACQUES. Died 1953.
THIESSEN, KARL. Died 1946.
THIMAN, ERIC H. Born 1900.
THOMAS, DAVID VAUGHAN. Died 1934.
THOMASSIN, DÉSIRÉ. Died 1933.
TOMMASINI, VINCENZO. 1878 (not 1879)–1950.
TORELLI, GIUSEPPE. 1658–1709 (not 1708).
TOURNEMIRE, CHARLES. Died 1939.
TOVEY, DONALD FRANCIS. Died 1940.
TRÉPARD, ÉMILE. Died 1952.
TURINA, JOAQUÍN. Died 1949.
TURNER, ALFRED DUDLEY. 1854–88.

UHL, EDMUND. Died 1929.

VALEN, FARTEIN OLAV. Died 1952.
VASSILENKO, S. N. Died 1956.
VENTH, KARL. Died 1938.
VEPRIK, ALEXANDER. 1899–1958.
VERACINI, FRANCESCO MARIA. Born 1690 (not 1685).
VERHEY (not VERHEIY), THEODORUS HENDRICUS HUBERTUS. Died 1929.
VERNE BREDT, ALICE. 1868–1958.
VIARDOT, PAUL. Died 1941.
VIERNE, LOUIS VICTOR JULES. Died 1937.
VILLA, RICARDO. Died 1935.
VILLAIN, GEORGES (not GEORG). 1854–1930.
VILLA-LOBOS, HEITOR. 1887 (not 1890)–1959.
VINÉE, ANSELME. 1847–1921.
VINK, FRANZ. Born 1878.
VIOTTI, GIOVANNI BATTISTA. Born 1755 (not 1753).
VITALI, GIOVANNI. Born c. 1644.
VIVALDI, ANTONIO. c. 1675–1741 (not 1680–1743).
VOLBACH, FRITZ. Died 1940.
VOMÁČKA, BOLESLAV. Born 1887 (not 1886).
VRETBLAD, VIKTOR PATRIK. Died 1953.
VREULS, VICTOR. Died 1944.

WACHTMEISTER, AXEL RAOUL. Died 1947.
WAGHALTER, IGNAZ. Died 1949.
WAILLY, PAUL DE. 1854 (not 1856)–1933.

WALKER, ERNEST. Died 1949.
WALTER, BRUNO. Died 1962.
WALTHEW, RICHARD HENRY. Died 1951.
WARNER, HARRY WALDO. Died 1945.
WATERMAN, ADOLF. Born 1886.
WEBER, EDMUND VON. 1766–1828.
WEBER, LUDWIG. Died 1947.
WEBERN, ANTON. Died 1945.
WEHRLI, WERNER. Died 1944.
WEIDIG, ADOLF. Died 1931.
WEIGL, KARL. Died 1949.
WEILL, KURT. 1900–50.
WEINER, LEO. Died 1960.
WEINGARTNER, FELIX VON. Died 1942.
WEIS, KAREL. Died 1944.
WEISMANN, JULIUS. Died 1950.
WEISSE, HANS. 1892–1940.
WERNER, JOSEF. Died 1922.
WERNER, THEODOR. Died 1957.
WERTHEIM, JULIUSZ. Died 1928.
WESTERHOUT, NICCOLO VAN. Born 1857 (not 1862).
WETZ, RICHARD. Died 1935.
WETZEL, HERMANN. Died 1928.
WEYRAUCH, JOHANNES. Born 1897.
WHITE, FELIX. Died 1945.
WHITHORNE, EMERSON. Died 1958.
WHITING, GEORGE ELBRIDGE. Born 1840 (not 1842).
WHITTAKER, WILLIAM GILLIES. Died 1944.
WICHMANN, HERMANN. Died 1905.
WICKENHAUSSER, RICHARD. Died 1936.
WIDOR, CHARLES MARIE. 1844 (not 1845)–1937.
WIÉNER, JEAN. Born 1896.
WIHTOL, JOSEPH. Died 1948.
WIKLUND, ADOLF. Died 1950.
WILLIAMS, ALBERTO. Died 1952.
WILLIAMS, JOHN GERRARD. Died 1947.
WILLIAMS, RALPH VAUGHAN. Died 1958.
WILLNER, ARTHUR. Died 1959.
WILSON, MORTIMER. Died 1932.
WILTBERGER, AUGUST. Died 1928.
WINDSPERGER, LOTHAR. Died 1935.
WINGE, PER. Died 1935.
WINKLER, ALEXANDER. Died 1935.
WITKOWSKI, GEORGES MARTIN. Died 1943.
WITTE, GEORG HENDRIK. Died 1929.
WOELFL, JOSEPH. Born 1773 (not 1772).
WOLDEMAR, MICHEL. Died 1815 (not 1816).
WOLF-FERRARI, ERMANNO. Died 1948.
WOLSTENHOLME, WILLIAM. Died 1931.
WOMEN COMPOSERS (page 592, col. 2):
  DAVY, RUBY. 1883–1949.
  ELLICOTT, ROSALIND FRANCES. Died 1924.
  FOLVILLE, JULIETTE. Died 1946.
  GRANDVAL, MARIE. 1830 (not 1836)–1907.
  HOLMSEN, BORGHILD. Died 1938.
  HOOD, HELEN. 1863–1949.

LEGINSKA, ETHEL. Born 1886.
ROGERS, CLARA KATHLEEN. 1844–1931.
SCHJELDERUP, MON. Died 1934.
WURM, MARIE. Died 1938.
WOOD, HAYDN. 1882–1959.
WOOLLETT, HENRI ÉDOUARD. Died 1936.
WÖSS, JOSEF VENANTIUS VON. Died 1943.
WOUTERS, F. A. Died 1924.
WOYRSCH, FELIX VON. Died 1944.
WRANITZKY, ANTON. Died 1820 (not 1819).
WÜST, PHILIPP. Born 1894.

YOUNG, WILLIAM. Died 1671 (not 1672).
YSAŸE, EUGÈNE. Died 1931.
YSAŸE, THÉOPHILE. Died 1918 (not 1916).

ZANELLA, AMILCARE. Died 1949.
ZECKWER, CAMILLE W. 1875 (not 1850)–1924.
ZEMLINSKY, ALEXANDER VON. Died 1942.
ZILCHER, HERMANN. Died 1948.
ZOELLNER, HEINRICH. Died 1941.
ZOLOTAREV. Born 1873 (not 1879).
ZSOLT, NÁNDOR. Died 1936.

INDEX OF COMPOSERS
DISCUSSED IN VOLUME III